Supervision
THAT
Improves
Teaching AND Learning

EDITION 4

I would like to dedicate this book to my daughters,
Mara, Alene, and Elena, for their supportive love and for providing the opportunity
to try out all my interpersonal skills as they grew to young adulthood.

Susan Sullivan

I would like to dedicate this volume to my father; may peace by upon him,
because he taught me the value of education and urged me to achieve my potential.

Jeffrey Glanz

Supervision
THAT
Improves
Teaching AND Learning

EDITION

4

Strategies & Techniques

Susan Sullivan / Jeffrey Glanz
Foreword by Karen Osterman

CORWIN
A SAGE Company

CORWIN
A SAGE Company

FOR INFORMATION:

Corwin
A SAGE Company
2455 Teller Road
Thousand Oaks, California 91320
(800) 233-9936
www.corwin.com

SAGE Publications Ltd.
1 Oliver's Yard
55 City Road
London EC1Y 1SP
United Kingdom

SAGE Publications India Pvt. Ltd.
B 1/I 1 Mohan Cooperative Industrial Area
Mathura Road, New Delhi 110 044
India

SAGE Publications Asia-Pacific Pte. Ltd.
3 Church Street
#10-04 Samsung Hub
Singapore 049483

Acquisitions Editor: Arnis Burvikovs
Associate Editor: Desirée A. Bartlett
Editorial Assistant: Kimberly Greenberg
Production Editor: Cassandra Margaret Seibel
Copy Editor: Terri Lee Paulsen
Typesetter: C&M Digitals (P) Ltd.
Proofreader: Caryne Brown
Indexer: Terri Corry
Cover Designer: Rose Storey
Graphic Designer: Cristina Kubota
Permissions Editor: Karen Ehrmann

Printed in the United States of America.

Library of Congress Cataloging-in-Publication Data

Sullivan, Susan, 1943-

Supervision that improves teaching and learning: strategies and techniques / Susan Sullivan, Jeffrey Glanz.—Fourth edition.

pages cm
Includes bibliographical references and index.

ISBN 978-1-4522-5546-0 (pbk.)

1. School supervision—United States. 2. Teacher effectiveness–United States. 3. Effective teaching—United States. I. Title.

LB2806.4.S85 2013
371.2′03–dc23   2012039615

This book is printed on acid-free paper.

13 14 15 16 17 10 9 8 7 6 5 4 3 2 1

Contents

Additional materials and resources related to *Supervision That Improves Teaching and Learning: Strategies and Techniques*, Fourth Edition, can be found at www.corwin.com/supervision4e.

Foreword to the Fourth Edition

Sullivan and Glanz rightfully maintain that supervision is central to the renewal of classroom teaching and learning. This is particularly true if you believe that education, like other professions, requires continuous learning. Although needs and goals differ at different stages of career growth, everyone—whether teachers or administrators—should be engaged in a constant process of assessment and renewal. Ideally, schools should be places where professional educators, regardless of their specific roles, work as a team, sharing their expertise and contributing their efforts to continually improve student learning.

Since this book was first published in 1999, there are several things about schools that we have come to know with even greater certainty. The quality of teacher practice is most directly influenced by whether or not teachers experience schools as learning communities (Silins, Mulford, & Zarins, 2002). If the school supports collaborative work, sharing of information, and open communication among staff, it is more likely that teachers will utilize effective teaching strategies. Leaders play a direct role in determining how their schools function. Although the leadership role is complex, if leaders "encourage staff to reflect on what they are trying to achieve with students and how they are doing it" (Silins et al., 2002, p. 621), and enable them to establish and pursue their own professional goals, it is more likely that teachers will perceive their school as a learning organization.

In this text, Sullivan and Glanz provide educators with the analytic and technical tools that they need to be able to create a climate for learning. Despite our knowledge about the effectiveness of learning organizations, schools rest in the shadow of a bureaucratic and hierarchical tradition that characterizes individuals as superior and subordinate, differentially distributes power and authority, and creates artificial and often antagonistic role-based divisions. In recognizing the strength of these mindscapes that so directly shape practice, Sullivan and Glanz encourage the readers to explore and challenge their own traditional beliefs about authority and control. They then present basic but very important communication skills that facilitate reflection and dialogue and contrast these with more traditional approaches that rely on judgment, direct control, and appeasement—disempowering strategies that reinforce hierarchical barriers, preclude collaborative problem solving, and constrain personal growth and initiative (Osterman & Kottkamp, 2004).

One of the most frequent complaints from teachers is that the supervisory process is seldom useful. They sit through the preobservation, observation, and feedback cycle, but it doesn't help them improve their teaching. There are two aspects of the process that limit supervisory effectiveness (Osterman, 1994). The first is a lack of descriptive data and/or the failure to share those descriptive data directly with the teacher. There will be no change in practice if teachers are unaware of the need for change. Because our perceptions are shaped by so many factors, most of us have only an incomplete understanding of our own behavior and the effects of our actions. The new teacher, for example, may perceive only her failures. A more senior teacher, shaped by years of experience, may unknowingly adopt very different patterns of interaction with different groups of students, limiting their effectiveness with some. Data-based feedback enables teachers to "see" their practice in a new light. For that reason, clear descriptive data about practice and its effects on student learning are critical if the goal is continuous improvement.

The second problem is the tendency to use the feedback conference to offer teachers suggestions for improvement. Teachers need to have information about their work, but if the purpose of the supervisory process is to encourage learning, they also need the opportunity to assume responsibility for their own professional growth. From research and experience, we know that even when supervisors gather and share objective data with teachers, rather than encouraging dialogue about teaching and collaborative planning, they quickly shift attention to suggestions for improvement. Rather than empowering teachers to analyze and critically assess their own work, the supervisors fall into traditional patterns and provide the answers. Although well intentioned, this prescriptive approach limits teachers' potential to function as professionals.

To address these concerns, Sullivan and Glanz rightly direct the supervisor's attention to data collection and feedback. They provide a rich variety of tools for gathering data about multiple dimensions of teacher practice and its connection to student learning. Equally important, they also illustrate how supervisors—whether administrators or fellow teachers—can provide feedback and engage in reflective dialogue, optimizing professional growth and avoiding the judgmental and prescriptive approaches that limit effectiveness. In this collaborative dialogue about teaching, the responsibility for problem analysis and problem resolution shifts. Although the supervisor can still share ideas, he or she no longer assumes the *sole* responsibility for solving the teacher's problems. Basically, this approach offers educators a practical way to challenge traditional top-down models of authority and control, respect teachers' professionalism, and create positive, supportive, and collaborative relationships between teachers and their supervisors.

Even more important, this approach to supervision is one that supports deep learning. It is relatively easy to achieve some types of change. For example, a district can require teachers to use a particular curriculum. Meaningful change, however, requires change in underlying beliefs about teaching. Thus, teachers who believe that didactic methods of instruction are appropriate are unlikely to adopt constructive approaches to teaching (Torff & Warburton, 2005). Good professional development, in whatever form, encourages teachers to explore and assess their beliefs in order to facilitate change. It respects their professionalism and is based on assumptions that teachers are not only willing but anxious to improve, and that they have the expertise (at whatever level) to take an active and direct role in shaping their own development.

The strategies that Sullivan and Glanz highlight in their text are techniques that ensure that supervision really will support professional learning. Even though the techniques they describe are not unique, the authors' presentation is. Not only do they provide information about various techniques that improve the quality of feedback, but they also provide a learning framework based on principles of constructivism and reflective practice that facilitates not just understanding but application.

Reflective practice and constructivism share a common set of beliefs about learning (Osterman & Kottkamp, 2004). First is the belief that learning is an active process requiring student engagement. Learning is the ultimate responsibility of the learner, and the role of the instructor is to facilitate growth by focusing inquiry, engaging students, exploring and challenging ideas, and providing resources. The second belief is that ideas influence action. Through experience, people develop theories about how the world works, and these theories shape their behavior. Learners construct their own knowledge, building on prior experiences. Accordingly, students must have opportunities to articulate, represent, and assess as well as extend their knowledge. The third important belief is that learners construct knowledge through experience, particularly problematic experience. Pedagogically, then, it is necessary to build conceptual conflict by challenging current understanding and offering opportunities to develop and test new ways of thinking and acting.

The supervisory model Sullivan and Glanz describe is built on these pedagogical principles, and the text itself admirably incorporates these ideas. Each section poses problems to engage and challenge the learner. Realistic cases illustrate the relationship between beliefs and practice and describe the personal and organizational obstacles that perpetuate bureaucratic practices. Reflective activities in each section raise challenging questions, stimulate interest, and encourage the articulation and critical assessment of personal beliefs. The text also provides for development of skills through a series of progressively challenging activities. Initially, learners experiment with strategies in a supportive classroom environment. The second step involves testing the new strategies in the work setting. In the classroom and in the work setting, the learning process models the principles of supportive supervision. In the classroom, the students utilize a wide variety of observation strategies and practice descriptive feedback and collaborative problem solving with one another. In the work setting, they work closely with a colleague, testing the same strategies. Each of these activities develops skill, but more important, the actual experimentation establishes the validity of the specific technique and builds learner confidence in his or her ability to use these techniques effectively.

In constructivism and reflective practice, in contrast to more traditional educational models, the relationship between teacher and learners is that of a partnership based on common goals for improving practice rather than on hierarchical differences related to presumed differences in expertise. The structure of the text facilitates dialogue and creates a climate of openness. The language is accessible. The tone is personal, warm, respectful, and collegial. The authors share responsibility for learning with the readers, presuming that the readers are intelligent, informed, and capable. They invite learners to supplement the text with their own suggestions, and, in fact, use creative strategies suggested by their own students. These are empowering strategies that support the learning process and model the ideas about supervision that they espouse. In contrast with the "inspection" model that too often characterizes school supervision, the supervisory process envisioned by Sullivan and Glanz is collaborative rather than hierarchical, dialogic versus didactic, descriptive rather than judgmental, and supportive rather than punitive. This is a major shift. Although the idea is appealing and even convincing, bringing about change in the practice of supervision is no easy task. To do so, to align action more closely with theory, involves more than simply presenting a range of feasible and effective strategies. According to Argyris and Schon (1974), ideas like these will be integrated into practice only when existing theories and patterns of behavior are identified, explored, challenged, and modified. This theoretical premise has important implications for learning. If the learning process is to be effective, its learning goals must extend beyond the mere transference of knowledge to incorporating the appropriate and effective application of knowledge.

Normally, the challenge to facilitate the application of ideas rests on the shoulders of the instructor. The text provides the information, and the instructor provides the pedagogical expertise. Here, Sullivan and Glanz have developed a text that provides information but, more important, one that engages the readers in a reflective process of observation, analysis, and experimentation designed to facilitate behavioral change. By extending well beyond the normal scope of a text and exploring dimensions of belief and practice in the context of schools and leadership, the authors provide a valuable resource. The use of this text, its learning strategies and supervisory techniques, should support realization of the book's stated purpose: the development of educational leaders—whether administrators or teachers—who are able to engage in supervision designed to improve the quality of learning.

Karen Osterman
Hofstra University

Preface to the Fourth Edition

Supervision is and always will be the key to the high instructional stand-ards of America's public schools.

—Spears, 1953, p. 462

Two major foci in education dominate increasingly in the second decade of the 21st century: The high-stakes accountability of teachers and those who prepare them and the expanded use of standardized test data to monitor student achievement and the effectiveness of instruction. We believe that the goals of consistent, improved achievement for all students and a well-developed, effective teaching force to facilitate this improvement are laudable and impera-tive outcomes. Nonetheless, we are very concerned that the primacy of stan-dardized test scores as evaluation tools of students and teachers alike and the use of standardized rubrics to monitor teachers are having a detrimental effect on the collaborative environment that forms the basis of effective supervision of teaching and learning that is at the core of a culture of learning.

Therefore, in addition to continuing to focus on the issues of supervisory practice that value diverse learning styles of teachers and students alike and the technologies necessary to promote quality teaching and learning that formed the core of the third edition, we highlight an additional belief in this edition. Our declaration that instructional supervision, as best practice, is a schoolwide process in which learning and teaching are the core of the school's mission, underlies the changes in Chapter 3, the new Chapter 6, and the new case studies in Chapter 5.

The emphasis on what students are actually doing in the classroom in con-junction with what the teachers are asking the students to do lies beneath the organization of Chapter 3. We pair, wherever possible, observation instruments that permit the observer to focus on both teacher and student evidence.

The best means of instructional improvement and effectiveness is a mirror on teacher practice and student response to instruction. We firmly believe that zeroing in on a specific teacher practice and the student response to that instruc-tional strategy or vice versa provides a two-way mirror that fosters deep and long-lasting change. We prefer wherever possible the term *evidence* over the word *data.* The current use of student standardized test scores as the primary source of information for student and teacher evaluation narrows the contemporary meaning and use of the term data. Evidence retains a sense of varied ways of judging (Hazi, 2012) that can include among others, teacher and student observations, document and research review, collaborative inquiry, and myriad alternative forms of supervision.

This emphasis on the instructional core and its relation to supervision of instruction is highlighted in our new case studies on alternative approaches to supervision—Learning Walks, Lesson Study, and Book Groups—in Chapter 5. These case studies are based on work one of us did in supporting a new school leader in developing a comprehensive supervisory approach to improving teaching and learning. They focus on the professionalization of teachers within a learning community; we have eliminated less current cases. The new Chapter 6 comprises a case study that describes the journey of a leader and her school as she engages her staff in building a foundation of core beliefs and values related to the role of innovative supervision in teacher growth and student learning.

In keeping with our ongoing belief that unless attention is drawn to deep changes in instructional practice, change will remain ephemeral (e.g., Fullan, 2006), we have added observational instruments that will support the deep implementation of current practices, that is, push-in support, math common core standards, and so on.

We believe that supervision as a dynamic process that facilitates dialogue to promote instructional improvement is central to the renewal of classroom teaching and learning in the 21st century. Rather than merely describing and explaining varied models of supervision, this book presents the reader with research-based and empirically tested strategies and techniques.

By offering an overview of approaches for instructional improvement and some specific supervisory strategies, this volume encourages the reader to develop her or his own supervisory platform or personal principles of practice. The main feature of this text is the hands-on development of essential supervisory skills.

This text is meant for use in undergraduate and graduate courses on instructional improvement and by individuals in leadership positions in schools and districts, including teams of teachers and teacher leaders. It contains unique features that set it apart from similar works. The text, designed to be user friendly, provides examples of summary sheets and observation charts as well as "crib sheets" to enhance review and actual use in the classroom. Corwin provides information about web-based resources for the book and e-book purchase. Throughout each chapter are reflective microlabs and other activities designed to reinforce new material and concepts.

Why is a book of this nature important? In an era in which monitoring through brief walk-throughs, teacher accountability based primarily on standardized test scores, and the use of lengthy standardized rubrics as evaluation instruments in the guise of supervision of instruction, those individuals who argue that supervision is vital to instructional improvement must remain vigilant to preserve the best that supervision has to offer. With the continual emphasis on student outcomes and state and national standards, supervision is—more than ever—an indispensable link that inspires good teaching and promotes student learning. We believe that when teachers are encouraged to reflect on their teaching and when individuals with supervisory responsibilities engage teachers in conversations about classroom instruction, the stage for instructional improvement is set.

This book, along with other publications, such as the *Handbook of Research on School Supervision* (Firth & Pajak, 1998); *Educational Supervision: Perspectives, Issues, and Controversies* (Garman, 1997); *Handbook of Instructional Leadership: How Really Good Principals Promote Teaching and Learning* (Blase & Blase, 1998); *Mentoring and Supervision for Teacher Development* (Reiman & Thies-Sprinthall, 1998); *Differentiated Supervision* (Northern Valley Regional High School District, 1996); *SuperVision and Instructional Leadership: A Developmental Approach* (Glickman, Gordon, & Ross-Gordon, 2010); *Interpersonal and Consultant Supervision Skills: A Clinical Model* (Champagne & Hogan, 2006); *Cognitive Coaching: A Foundation for Renaissance Schools* (Costa & Garmston, 1997); *Instructional Supervision: Applying Tools and Concepts,* 3rd edition (Zepeda, 2012); *Teacher Supervision and Evaluation: Theory Into Practice,* 3rd edition (Nolan & Hoover, 2011); and *Supervising Instruction: Differentiating for Teacher Success,* 3rd edition (Pajak, 2008), indicate the resurgence and attention given to supervision. We believe that such attention is not only warranted but necessary so that the integrity of instructional improvement within classrooms across America and around the world will be maintained. Although scholars may busy themselves with philosophical intricacies or theoretical nuances about the viability and definition of supervision, practitioners know too well how important effective supervision is for maintaining and encouraging instructional excellence.

Critical assumptions about supervision underlie this work. First and foremost, we maintain that supervision of instruction as an ongoing, nonjudgmental, reflective, and collaborative process that engages teachers in dialogue for the purpose of improving teaching and student learning remains a potent force toward promoting instructional excellence in schools. Moreover, the goal of supervision is to facilitate the process of teaching and learning through a multitude of approaches that can encompass curriculum and staff development, action research, and peer, self-, and student assessment. This combination can form the basis of transformational leadership and change in a department, grade level, school, and district.

This text follows a logical and orderly progression, all the while encouraging the reader to understand the changing context of supervision and to develop requisite knowledge, skills, and dispositions about supervision. It culminates in the development of a personal supervisory platform and offers suggestions for a collaborative plan for supervision.

Chapter 1 provides a historical and theoretical framework for supervision. This foundation, along with an initial belief inventory *that should be completed before reading the chapter* and again at the end of the course, permits the reader to begin laying the groundwork for a personal supervisory platform.

Chapter 2 introduces basic interpersonal tools for initiating and providing feedback on classroom observations. The reader is introduced to "crib sheets" to practice feedback dialogue between professionals and for use on site. The theory and practice of reflection in action, a crucial tool for self-reflection and assessment, is also introduced. Chapter 3 reviews sample classroom observation tools and techniques in a way that allows readers to practice them in the college classroom or workshop and on site and to develop this essential skill. In Chapter 4, the previously learned observation tools and techniques and feedback approaches are integrated into our reflective clinical supervision cycle framework. Opportunities for practice and simulations precede recommendations for site-based initiation.

Chapter 5 presents seven alternative approaches to supervision currently in practice. Authentic case studies introduce each approach, followed by a definition and suggested steps for implementation. Chapter 6 presents a current example of how a transformational leader begins to grapple with change through a focus on instructional supervision—the beginnings, challenges, and initial successes. Chapter 7, the final chapter and the culmination of the learning process, encourages readers to create their own personal supervisory platform, that is, a personal theory or principles of practice. In addition, this chapter includes a guide to facilitating the development of a collaborative site vision and plan for supervision.

In sum, this book reviews the supervisory strategies and techniques necessary for future educational leaders so that they can promote teaching and learning—the essence of what effective supervision is really all about.

We hope you find this new edition practical and user friendly. We welcome your input for website suggestions and additional changes in future editions. Contact us at Susan.Sullivan@csi.cuny.edu and at glanz@yu.edu.

Acknowledgments

W e thank our graduate students at the College of Staten Island and at Yeshiva University for allowing us to develop various ideas in this book with them and for offering useful feedback.

Susan Sullivan would like to thank David Podell, the former provost and vice president for Academic Affairs at the College of Staten Island, for his ongoing support in all of her academic endeavors. She would also like to express appreciation to the faculty and administration of Ditmas Intermediate School, in Brooklyn, New York, and, in particular, Nancy Brogan, Lynne Pagano, Elke Savoy, Madeline Castaneda, and Nasreen Farooqui for their willingness and enthusiasm in developing a peer coaching model in the International Institute at their school. Carmen Farina and her staff were models not only in the development of alternatives to traditional supervision but also in their proactive, open sharing of their successes and challenges. Karen Osterman of Hofstra University introduced the world of reflective practice to Susan and continues to reflect with her on teaching and intellectual endeavors.

Jeffrey Glanz would like to acknowledge his colleagues in the Council of Professors of Instructional Supervision (COPIS) for stimulating, over the years, many of the ideas in this volume. Special thanks to colleagues Bert Ammerman and Jim McDonnell of Northern Valley Regional High School District for their innovative work, which formed the basis for one of the case studies in Chapter 5. Jeffrey would also like to acknowledge his marvelous doctoral students (Michael Zauderer, Adam Dobrick, Aviva Edelstein, and Shalom Rohr) who helped with elements in our revised Chapters 5 and 6. In particular, they helped create various case studies that reflected the lived realities of several schools in which we work.

About the Authors

Susan Sullivan received her BA from Elmira College, her MAT from The Johns Hopkins University, and her MEd and EdD from Teachers College, Columbia University. She served as an instructor in the Department of Romance Languages of The Johns Hopkins University for 10 years and as a teacher and administrator in Baltimore, Maryland; Rome, Italy; and the New York City area. She is currently chair of the Department of Education of the College of Staten Island, the City University of New York, and previously was coordinator of the Post Master's Program in Leadership. She continues to teach graduate courses in supervision of instruction and educational leadership. In addition to their staff development book, *Supervision in Practice,* she and Jeffrey Glanz published *Building Effective Learning Communities* for Corwin. You can reach her via Susan.Sullivan@csi.cuny.edu.

Jeffrey Glanz received his BA from the City University of New York and his MA and EdD from Teachers College, Columbia University. He currently holds the Raine and Stanley Silverstein Chair in Professional Ethics and Values in the Azrieli Graduate School of Jewish Education and Administration at Yeshiva University. He is a former chair, dean, schoolteacher, and school administrator. He is the author of 20 books, including the new second edition of *Teaching 101,* the *Assistant Principal's Handbook,* and the seven-volume set of *What Every Principal Should Know About Leadership,* all with Corwin. You can reach him via glanz@yu.edu and visit his web page at www.yu.edu/faculty/glanz.

A Brief Note to Instructors

We are certain that this text can be used in many effective ways in your classroom or in your school. We would like to highlight some of the strategies that we have found most successful in developing supervisory and interpersonal skills. Detailed instructions for several of these strategies are provided in the text. We know that you will think of additional suggestions and hope that you will share your ideas with us.

1. *Journal writing.* Encourage students to reflect on their and others' class and site supervisory experiences in a personal journal. Reflections on supervisory practices that the students observe in their buildings and in other schools are invaluable in forming their own beliefs. The suggested *reflections* in the text also can be thought out in the journal. Students can choose to share journal entries online to solicit feedback on their ideas.

2. *Microlabs.* As explained in the Microlab Guidelines in Resource A, the microlab permits individualized collegial sharing, while at the same time developing reflective and nonjudgmental listening skills. Groups of three to five people address two to four questions suggested in the text or inspired by students or the instructor. Small-group and whole-class debriefing ties thoughts together, promotes more ideas, and brings closure to the process. Again, microlabs are effective online on a Blackboard site or as wikis, and can also be set up interactively.

3. *The fishbowl.* This process can be used to discuss the ideas generated in small groups within a large-group setting. Representatives from each small group form a circle in the middle of the room and share the ideas generated in the small groups while the rest of the class listens and observes. We also use the fishbowl to allow volunteers to model feedback approaches for the rest of the class. The class learns the approach and at the same time serves as observers of the process. Directions for this approach are provided in Resource B.

4. *Videotaping.* We strongly encourage the use of videos of classroom and site practices, particularly of the planning and feedback conversations. The videos can be used in two ways: They can be part of the actual assignment and graded, or they can be used for the students' own learning; the

knowledge that the videos will not be shared with instructors or colleagues may increase their authenticity and acceptance. Many students tape themselves several times for scaffolded learning from their own practice.

5. *Intervisitation.* In all of our work with teachers, aspiring administrators, and practicing leaders, we have found that intervisitation within schools, between schools, and between districts plays a crucial role in creating a climate for growth. The opportunity to see the practices and models explained in a text is "worth a thousand words." Professionals see the ideas in practice ("it works") and can ask questions and debrief after the visit, reflecting on what they think might or might not work for them. The "learning walks" we describe in Chapter 5 are one of the many variations of the intervisitation.

6. *E-mail, the Internet, and social networks.* One of the most effective ways to involve all students in dialogue and reflection is through e-mail, Internet discussion boards, wikis, and blogs. These electronic sites can increase participation of some students who are more comfortable with the written than the spoken word. You can assign pairs of students to discuss reflections on e-mail, and you can set up a discussion board, wikis, or blogs through school or college media centers. Microlabs can be assigned on the discussion board, and students can share experiences and challenges with their colleagues. The whole realm of the Internet is also available to enrich discussion and knowledge. School colleagues, cohorts, or class colleagues are encouraged to take advantage of social networks for a more personal type of dialogue that promotes personal and professional networking.

7. *Distance learning and the virtual classroom.* The precise descriptions and directions for site practice and the classroom segments on the website facilitate the use of this book for distance learning and the virtual classroom. In the distance learning classroom, students can practice the role plays and receive feedback from their colleagues and professors. The use of videos for site assignments can provide the instructor with direct knowledge of the students' practice and progress. In the virtual classroom, videos replace the university classroom experience. In addition, all the other technological resources—that is, e-mail, discussion boards, wikis, blogs, and the Internet, among others—enrich learning and discussion in the virtual classroom. New and innovative interactive programs are continually introduced in the market. See our companion website at www.corwin.com/supervision4e to download observation instruments. See Resource C for further information.

1

The Changing Context of Supervision

Democracy can provide the direction, goals, purposes, and standards of conduct that our profession and society desperately need. Clinical supervision can provide the means of translating democratic values into action, while strengthening teachers' teaching skills, conceptual understanding and moral commitment.

—Pajak, 2000, p. 292

Note: Before you begin reading this chapter, please complete the questionnaire in Figure 1.2 on pages 33–34.

CHAPTER OVERVIEW

1. Supervision Defined

2. The Influence of History
   a. Vignettes Within a Historical Context
   b. The History

3. Understanding the History of Supervision
   a. The Dilemma of Supervision vs. Evaluation

4. Assessing Belief Systems

WHAT IS SUPERVISION?

Defining supervision has been a source of much debate for years (Bolin, 1987). Is supervision a function of administration, curriculum, staff development, action research, or a combination of these and other activities? Alfonso and Firth (1990) noted that the study of supervision lacks focus largely due to the "lack of research and continuing disagreement on the definition and purposes of supervision" (p. 188). In this volume, we view supervision as the center for the improvement of instruction. Supervision is the process of engaging teachers in instructional dialogue for the purpose of improving teaching and increasing student achievement. We believe that supervision for the improvement of instruction will continue to be the foremost concern of supervisors and other educational leaders well into the 21st century.

The Evolution of Supervision

Supervisory practice has evolved since its origins in colonial times, and its effectiveness as a means of improving instruction depends on the ability of educational leaders to remain responsive to the needs of teachers and students. An educational leader's resolve to remain adaptable also depends on an appreciation of the changing and evolving nature of supervision, especially in the new millennium. An educational leader who understands the history of supervision and how current demands are influenced by that history will be better able to confront the technological, social, political, and moral issues of the day. Educational leaders also will have to develop the requisite knowledge, skills, and dispositions that are the foundation of effective supervisory practice. This chapter explicates how supervision has evolved to its current state, how you might respond to ever-increasing supervisory needs and demands, and how your beliefs and attitudes affect how you react to daily challenges.

Vignette

Arlene Spiotta was recently appointed vice principal of Regional Valley High School, where she has worked as a teacher for three years. An affable, popular teacher, Arlene had been a teacher at Westfield High School, located in a neighboring township, for eight years. Prior to that, she was a teacher for five years in two schools in another state. She recently earned her supervisory certification and master's degree in administration and supervision at a local college.

Although Arlene received a warm welcome on the opening day of school in September, she noticed that teachers on the grade levels she supervises react much differently to her now. In one instance, she was passing the room of a former teacher-colleague, Linda Evans, who at the time was at her desk, assisting a student. When Linda noticed Arlene looking into the classroom, she stiffened in her chair and abruptly sent the pupil back to his desk. After receiving a stern and cold stare, Arlene proceeded down the hallway to her office. Arlene wondered why her colleague Linda acted so differently when she saw her now.

Arlene Spiotta took for granted the fact that she was now in a position very different from that of Linda Evans. Although they were former colleagues and friends, Arlene was now a supervisor. As a supervisor, she was expected to assist and evaluate her former colleagues.

Linda, on seeing Arlene apparently staring into the classroom (an assumption, we might add, that may or may not have been accurate), reacted as she had previously to other supervisors for whom she had worked. Her former supervisors were overbearing bureaucrats who looked for evidence of teacher incompetence at every turn.

Arlene, too, may have been influenced by what she considered to be behavior "expected" of a supervisor, that is, daily patrol or inspection of the hallways. After all, not only had Arlene been certified and trained as a supervisor in a state that mandates that all teachers be formally observed at least twice a year (eight times for nontenured teachers), but as an experienced teacher (of how many years? Right—16), she had been exposed to many supervisors who had conducted themselves in very autocratic and bureaucratic ways.

Had Arlene been cognizant of how past practices of supervision can affect current relationships between teachers and supervisors, she might have tried more earnestly to establish a spirit of mutual understanding and cooperation.

> **Reflection**
>
> *Why do you think Linda reacted to Arlene the way she did? What factor(s) may have contributed to this situation? What dilemma is she facing in her new role?*

> **Reflection**
>
> *How might Arlene establish this "spirit of mutual understanding and cooperation"?*

One of the authors recalls a time when he confronted a similar situation and the difficulty he had in circumventing expected supervisory roles. An excerpt from Jeffrey's diary is instructive:

My first appointment as an assistant principal was at P.S. "Anywhere, USA." I arrived at the school in September. My predecessor's reputation was there to greet me.

Mr. Stuart Oswald Blenheim was known as a stickler for every jot, tittle, and iota inscribed in the Board of Ed's rules and regulations. He carried a tape measure, a portable tape recorder, and a stethoscope, and considered teachers to be one of the lower forms of sapient life. The others were nonprofessional staff members and students—in "descending" order.

This supervisor made his opinions abundantly clear by word and deed. Woe to the pupil caught wandering the halls without appropriate documentation. No excuses accepted. Period. End of message.

Furthermore, the offending miscreant's pedagogue was called on the carpet, raked over the coals, strung up by the thumbs, and subjected to a wide variety of other abusive clichés.

Stuart Oswald Blenheim was short; so short that it was difficult to see him among a group of eighth or ninth graders. He took full advantage of his camouflage, so that he could spy on his charges. He was known to walk up quietly to a room, place his stethoscope to the door, and gradually straighten his knees and stand on his toes so as to see through the small glass window. Teachers were constantly on the lookout for a bald head rising in their doors' windows.

Any teacher who observed this latter-day Napoleon lurking in the halls was honor bound to pass the information on to his or her neighbors. A note referring to "Pearl Harbor," "Incoming Scud Missiles," "Sneak Attack," or "Raid's Here" was enough to raise blood pressure and churn digestive juices.

Last spring, he was appointed as principal in a school on the other side of the city.

Such was Blenheim's repute that all the teachers whom I supervised avoided my presence like the very plague. On one occasion, I passed by a room and noticed a teacher caringly assisting a pupil at her desk. Suddenly, the teacher "felt" my presence, quickly straightened her posture, and proceeded nervously to the front of the room to resume writing on the board. I walked away bewildered. However, after ascertaining that I did not suffer from halitosis, dandruff, or terminal body odor, I realized the problem. Honestly, I couldn't blame them. After all, Blenheim's initials suited him perfectly.

Thus, I was forced to overcome these habits of fear and distrust and, somehow, to win my teachers' and students' trust.

During my first meeting with my teachers, I asked rather than told them not to think of me as their supervisor. I hoped that they would consider me a colleague with perhaps more experience and responsibility in certain areas. I wanted to work with them and learn about their own expertise, knowledge, interests, and ideas. . . . I was not going to spy on them. I was not going to humiliate them. I was a real human being, just like they were, just like the children were.

They had a difficult time accepting this. They had been abused for seven years by a petty tyrant and did not believe that any AP could think differently. After all, Blenheim had been rewarded for his fine methods. This had to be the AP road to promotion.

I promised that there would be no sneak attacks. We would do our best to cooperate and learn together. I would share my experiences and readily seek their expertise and ideas so that they could be effective teachers.

It took three to six months of hard work on my part and caution on theirs, but we've finally reached the point where we smile at each other when we meet in the hall. Several of them have come to me with professional and personal problems. They were a bit surprised at some of my proposed solutions. The word got around that Blenheim was really gone.

Stuart Oswald Blenheim is, of course, a caricature of an autocratic supervisor who occupied the position Jeffrey Glanz assumed many years ago. Yet the essential message is clear: Autocratic methods in supervision still prevail, and if changes are to be made, then understanding the antecedents for such practices is necessary. To understand the changing context of supervision, a brief excursion into the history of supervision is necessary.

THE INFLUENCE OF HISTORY

History can be understood as an attempt to study the events and ideas of the past that have shaped human experience over time; doing so informs current practice and helps us make more intelligent decisions for the future. How are prevailing practices and advocated theories connected to the past? How is what you currently do influenced, in any way, by previous practices and theories of supervision? How can an understanding of the past help us practice supervision today?

Our intention in this chapter is to indicate that past supervisory theory and practice influence what we believe about supervision and how we carry out our work with teachers and others. This chapter will help you identify your belief systems related to supervisory practice and how these beliefs are connected to history and the history of supervision. This identification will lay the initial foundation for the construction of a supervisory platform.

As we indicate, what you believe about teaching and learning, for example, inevitably affects how you approach the practice of supervision. Subsequent chapters will encourage you to develop a "personal supervisory platform" that builds upon your personal vision statement.

> ### Reflection/Microlab*
>
> *Who or what in your personal or professional background influenced your present supervisory beliefs? What are some positive supervisory experiences you have encountered? What are some negative supervisory experiences you recall? Why did you feel that way? What does supervision look like in your school?*
>
> *See Resource A for microlab guidelines. Set up an Internet discussion board or wiki through your school or university media center to exchange reflections and hold electronic microlabs. Also, choose an e-mail partner and share reflections via e-mail between classes.

Site Practice

1. Prepare five questions to ask two school supervisors about their beliefs and practices in relation to improvement of classroom instruction:
   - Record the questions and responses.
   - Reflect on each supervisor's answers. Describe consistencies and inconsistencies in the responses and compare the supervisors' actual practices to the responses given. Do they "walk the talk" (practice what they preach)?
   - What surprised you in their responses (positively or negatively)? Why?
   - Compare the two supervisors' responses and reflect on the similarities and differences between their answers.

or

2. Ask two supervisors and two teachers what they consider to be the five most important tasks of instructional supervision.
   - Include a script of their responses.
   - What were the differences and similarities in the teachers' answers and in the supervisors' responses?
   - Compare the teachers' responses with those of the supervisors. Explain the differences and similarities. What surprised you in their responses (positively or negatively)?

(Continued)

(Continued)

Shadowing Assignment: Shadow a supervisor of instruction for one day or on a few days when the supervisor is observing classes.

1. Provide a detailed log of the supervision of instruction that you observed. You may include *any* activities that you feel were related to supervision of instruction.

2. Describe the interpersonal approaches and the process that the supervisor used.

3. What was effective in what you observed? Why? How will these effective practices improve classroom instruction? What did the teacher(s) learn?

4. Did the supervisor do anything that you would have done yourself? What and why or why not?

5. Were there supervisory practices that need improvement? Why? Did the supervisor do anything that you would *not* do? Were you surprised by anything the supervisor did? Why or why not? What would you do differently?

6. How did you feel about the "activities" before shadowing? After?

Source: The first and second sections of this site practice were adapted from Glickman, Gordon, and Ross-Gordon (2010).

The History

Supervision has medieval Latin origins and was defined originally as "a process of perusing or scanning a text for errors or deviations from the original text" (Smyth, 1991, p. 30). Later recorded instances of the word *supervision* established the process as entailing "general management, direction, control, and oversight" (see, e.g., Grumet, 1979). An examination of early records during the colonial period indicates that the term *inspector* is referenced frequently. Note the definition of supervision in Boston in 1709:

> Be there hereby established a committee of inspectors to visit ye School from time to time, when and as oft as they shall think fit, to Enform themselves of the methodes used in teaching of ye Schollars and to Inquire of their proficiency, and be present at the performance of some of their Exercises, the Master being before Notified of their Coming, And with him to consult and Advise of further Methods for ye Advancement of Learning and the Good Government of the Schoole.
>
> —*Reports of the Record Commissions of the City of Boston,* 1709

The inspectors were often ministers, selectmen, schoolmasters, and other distinguished citizens. Their methods of supervision stressed strict control and close inspection of school facilities. As Spears (1953) explained, "The early period of school supervision, from the colonization of America on down through at least the first half of the nineteenth century, was based on the idea of maintaining the existing standards of instruction, rather than on the idea of improving them" (p. 14).

American schooling, in general, during the better part of the 19th century was rural, unbureaucratic, and in the hands of local authorities. The prototypical 19th century school was a small, one-room schoolhouse. Teachers were "young, poorly paid, and rarely educated beyond the elementary subjects"; teachers were "hired and supervised largely by local lay trustees, they were not members of a self-regulating profession" (Tyack & Hansot, 1982, p. 17). These local lay trustees (called ward boards) who supervised schools were not professionally trained or very much interested in the improvement of instruction (Button, 1961).

The tradition of lay supervision continued from the American Revolution through the middle of the 19th century. Despite the emergence during this period of a new "American system of educational thought and practice . . . the quality of supervision would not improve appreciably" (Tanner & Tanner, 1987, p. 10). With the advent of a district system of supervision and then state-controlled supervision beginning in the late 19th century, however, the character of supervision did, in fact, change dramatically.

> ### Reflection
>
> *School supervision originally referred to a procedure in which someone would "examine" a teacher's classroom "looking for errors." What impact or significance, if any, does this original meaning or intention of supervision have for you as a supervisor today? How does the current climate of accountability influence supervisory practices?*

SUPERVISION IN THE LATE 19TH CENTURY

In general, unprecedented growth precipitated by the Industrial Revolution characterized the second half of the 19th century. The expansion of American education, which had started in the days of Horace Mann, whom Tanner and Tanner (1987) characterized as the "first professional supervisor," continued and assumed a new dimension in the latter decades of the 19th century. The schoolmen, specifically superintendents, began shaping schools in large cities into organized networks. Organization was the rallying cry nationally and locally. There was a firm belief that highly organized and efficient schools would meet the demands of a newly born industrialized age. That hierarchically organized public schools, as social institutions, would meet the crises and challenges that lay ahead was beyond doubt (Bullough, 1974; Cronin, 1973; Hammock, 1969; Kaestle, 1973; Lazerson, 1971).

The reform movement in education in the late 19th century was reflective of the larger, more encompassing changes that were occurring in society. Although rapid economic growth characterized the 19th century, reformers realized that there were serious problems in the nation's schools. In the battle that ensued to reorganize the nation's schools, sources of authority and responsibility in education were permanently transformed (Tyack, 1974). By the end of the 19th century, reformers concerned with undermining inefficiency and corruption transformed schools into streamlined, central administrative bureaucracies with superintendents as supervisors in charge. Supervision, during this struggle, became an important tool by which the superintendent legitimized his existence in the school system (Glanz, 1991).

Supervision, therefore, was a function that superintendents performed to oversee schools more efficiently.

Supervision as inspection was the dominant method for administering schools. Payne (1875), author of the first published textbook on supervision, stated emphatically that teachers must be "held responsible" for work performed in the classroom and that the supervisor, as expert inspector, would "oversee" and ensure "harmony and efficiency" (p. 521). A prominent superintendent, James M. Greenwood (1888), stated emphatically that "very much of my time is devoted to visiting schools and inspecting the work." Three years later, Greenwood (1891) again illustrated his idea of how supervision should be performed: The skilled superintendent, he said, should simply walk into the classroom and "judge from a compound sensation of the disease at work among the inmates" (p. 227). A review of the literature of the period indicates that Greenwood's supervisory methods, which relied on inspection based on intuition rather than technical or scientific knowledge, were practiced widely.

Supervisors using inspectional practices did not view favorably the competency of most teachers. For instance, Balliet (1894), a superintendent from Massachusetts, insisted that there were only two types of teachers: the efficient and the inefficient. The only way to reform the schools, thought Balliet, was to "secure a competent superintendent; second, to let him 'reform' all the teachers who are incompetent and can be 'reformed'; thirdly, to bury the dead" (pp. 437–438). Characteristic of the remedies applied to improve teaching was this suggestion: "Weak teachers should place themselves in such a position in the room that every pupil's face may be seen without turning the head" (Fitzpatrick, 1893, p. 76). Teachers, for the most part, were seen by 19th century supervisors as inept. As Bolin and Panaritis (1992) explained, "Teachers (mostly female and disenfranchised) were seen as a bedraggled troop—incompetent and backward in outlook" (p. 33).

The practice of supervision by inspection was indeed compatible with the emerging bureaucratic school system, with its assumption that expertise was concentrated in the upper echelons of the hierarchy. Many teachers perceived supervision as inspectional, rather than as a helping function.

Because supervision as inspection through visitation gained wide application in schools, it is the first model that characterizes early methods in supervision (see Table 1.1, Model 1).

Our brief examination of early methods of supervision indicates that (1) amid the upheavals of late 19th century America, supervision emerged as an important function performed by superintendents, and (2) inspectional practices dominated supervision.

> **Reflection/Microlab**
>
> *What vestiges of inspectional supervisory practices remain today? To what extent do you or others you know function as "inspectors"? How do you feel about that? Would you feel comfortable "inspecting" classrooms? Why or why not? Do certain conditions in your school/district/ state exist that involve an "inspectional mind-set"? Explain.*

The Emergence of the Distinct Position of Supervisor

In the first two decades of the 20th century, schooling grew dramatically. As the size and complexity of schools increased, greater administrative specialization was readily apparent. Supervisors gained in stature and authority in the early 20th century. In addition to the building principal, a new cadre of administrative officers emerged to assume major responsibility for day-to-day classroom supervision. Two specific groups of supervisors were commonly found in schools in the early 20th century (see Table 1.1).

First, a *special supervisor*, most often female, was chosen by the building principal to help assist less experienced teachers in subject matter mastery. Special supervisors were relieved of some teaching responsibilities to allow time for these tasks, but no formal training was required. Larger schools, for example, had a number of special supervisors in each major subject area.

Second, a *general supervisor*, usually male, was selected not only to deal with more general subjects such as mathematics and science but also to "assist" the principal in the more administrative, logistical operations of a school. The general supervisor, subsequently called *vice principal* or *assistant principal*, prepared attendance reports, collected data for evaluation purposes, and coordinated special school programs, among other administrative duties.

Differences in functions between special and general supervisors were reflective of prevalent 19th century notions of male-female role relationships. William E. Chancellor (1904), a prominent 19th century superintendent, remarked, "That men make better administrators I have already said. As a general proposition, women make the better special supervisors. They are more interested in details. They do not make as good general supervisors or assistant superintendents, however" (p. 210). Representative of the bias against women in the educational workplace were notions espoused by William H. Payne (1875): "Women cannot do man's work in the schools" (p. 49). Payne, like many of his contemporaries, believed that men were better suited to the more prestigious and lucrative job opportunities in education.

It is also interesting to note that teachers readily accepted the special supervisors. Special supervisors played a very useful and helpful role by assisting teachers in practical areas of spelling, penmanship, and art, for example. In addition, these special supervisors did not have any independent authority and did not serve in an evaluative capacity, as did, for example, the general supervisor, who was given authority, albeit limited, to evaluate instruction in the classroom. Therefore, teachers were not likely to be threatened by the appearance of a special supervisor in the classroom. General supervisors, on the other hand, were concerned with more administrative and evaluative matters and, consequently, were viewed by the classroom teachers as more menacing. Special supervisors also probably gained more acceptance by teachers, most of whom were female, because they too were female. General supervisors were almost exclusively male and perhaps were perceived differently as a result. Frank Spaulding (1955), in his analysis of this period of time, concurred and stated that general supervisors "were quite generally looked upon, not as helpers, but as critics bent on the discovery and revelation of teachers' weaknesses and failures . . . they were dubbed Snoopervisors" (p. 130).

The position of the special supervisor did not, however, endure for a very long period in schools. General supervisors gradually usurped their duties and responsibilities. The relative obscurity of special supervisors after the early 1920s can be attributed to discrimination based on gender. As a group comprising an overwhelming number of females, special supervisors were not

Reflection

How does gender affect your role and function as a supervisor today? Explain and provide an example.

perceived in the same light as were general supervisors, principals, assistant superintendents, and superintendents, who were, of course, mostly male. Gender bias and the sexual division of labor in schools go far toward explaining the disappearance of the special supervisor as such.[1] In short, general supervisors gained wider acceptance simply because they were men.

Bureaucratic Methods in Supervision as Social Efficiency

Numerous technological advances greatly influenced American education after 1900. As a result of the work of Frederick Winslow Taylor (1911), who published a book titled *The Principles of Scientific Management*, "efficiency" became the watchword of the day. Taylor's book stressed scientific management and efficiency in the workplace. The worker, according to Taylor, was merely a cog in the business machinery, and the main purpose of management was to promote the efficiency of the worker. Within a relatively short period of time, *Taylorism* and *efficiency* became household words and ultimately had a profound impact on administrative and supervisory practices in schools.

Franklin Bobbitt (1913), a professor at the University of Chicago, tried to apply the ideas that Taylor espoused to the "problems of educational management and supervision" (p. 8). Bobbitt's work, particularly his discussion of supervision, is significant because his ideas shaped the character and nature of supervision for many years. On the surface, these ideas appeared to advance professional supervision, but in reality they were the antithesis of professionalism. What Bobbitt called "scientific and professional supervisory methods" (p. 9) were, in fact, *scientistic* and bureaucratic methods of supervision aimed not at professionalizing but at finding a legitimate and secure niche for control-oriented supervision within the school bureaucracy.

In 1913, Bobbitt published an article titled "Some General Principles of Management Applied to the Problems of City-School Systems," which presented 11 major principles of scientific management as applied to education. Bobbitt firmly held that management, direction, and supervision of schools were necessary to achieve "organizational goals." Bobbitt maintained that supervision was an essential function "to coordinate school affairs. . . . Supervisory members must co-ordinate the labors of all . . . find the best methods of work, and enforce the use of these methods on the part of the workers" (Bobbitt, 1913, pp. 76, 78). The employment of scientific principles in supervision, said Bobbitt, is a necessity for the continued progress of the school system.

Many supervisors were eager to adopt Bobbitt's ideas of scientific management for use in schools. However, a few did not readily accept his views. One of the more vociferous opponents of Bobbitt's ideas was James Hosic (1924), a professor of education at Teachers College, Columbia University. Hosic contended that Bobbitt's analogy was largely false:

Teaching cannot be "directed" in the same way as bricklaying. . . . In education, the supervisor's function is not to devise all plans and work out all standards and merely inform his co-workers as to what they are. . . . [The supervisor] should not so much give orders as hold conferences. . . . His prototype is not a captain, lieutenant, or officer of the guard in industry, but chairman of committee or consulting expert. (pp. 82–84)

Despite Hosic's criticism, schoolmen of the day readily adopted the business model, as evidenced by William McAndrew (1922), who said about his role as supervisor in the school, "I am the captain of big business" (p. 91).

The criticisms against Bobbitt's methods, nonetheless, accurately stressed a number of disturbing ideas. First and foremost was the ill-conceived notion that "education in a school" is analogous to "production in a factory." Bobbitt claimed that "education is a shaping process as much as the manufacture of steel rails." Supervisors in the early 20th century were becoming aware of the fallacy of this logic as well as realizing the negative effects of bureaucracy in education. Bobbitt's "scientific management and supervision" found justification within a school organization that was bureaucratically organized.

Still, it remains clear that the significance of Bobbitt's work was in his advocacy of scientific and professional supervisory methods. Supervisors thought that their work in schools would be more clearly defined and accepted by adopting Bobbitt's principles of scientific management. Supervisors believed, as did Bobbitt, that "the way to eliminate the personal element from administration and supervision is to introduce impersonal methods of scientific administration and supervision" (p. 7). This was often translated into rating schemes. In a short time, supervision became synonymous with teacher rating.

In sum, just as "supervision as inspection" reflected the emergence of bureaucracy in education, so too "supervision as social efficiency" was largely influenced by scientific management in education (see Table 1.1, Model 2). Supervision as social efficiency was compatible with and a natural consequence of bureaucracy in education.

Democratic Methods in Supervision

Bureaucratic supervision, relying on inspectional methods and seeking efficiency above all else, dominated discourse in the field from 1870–1920. This sort of supervision attracted much criticism from teachers and others (Rousmaniere, 1992). Representative of the nature of this opposition were the comments of Sallie Hill (1918), a teacher speaking before the Department of Classroom Teachers, decrying supervisory methods of rating. Hill charged:

There is no democracy in our schools. . . . Here let me say that I do not want to give the impression that we are sensitive. No person who has remained a teacher for ten years can be sensitive. She is either dead or has gone into some other business. . . . There are too many supervisors with big salaries and undue rating powers. (p. 506)

The movement to alter supervisory theory and practice to more democratic and improvement foci, while at the same time minimizing the evaluative function, occurred in the 1920s as a direct result of growing opposition to autocratic supervisory methods (see Table 1.1, Model 3). Consequently, supervisors tried to change their image as "snoopervisors" by adopting alternate methods of supervision. The following poem, quoted in part, indicates the desired change of focus to more democratic methods in supervision:

With keenly peering eyes and snooping nose,

From room to room the Snoopervisor goes.

He notes each slip, each fault with lofty frown,

And on his rating card he writes it down;

His duty done, when he has brought to light,

The things the teachers do that are not right . . .

The supervisor enters quietly, "What do you need? How can I help today?

John, let me show you. Mary, try this way."

He aims to help, encourage and suggest,

That teachers, pupils all may do their best.

—Anonymous, 1929

Influenced in large measure by Dewey's (1929) theories of democratic and scientific thinking as well as by Hosic's (1920) ideas of democratic supervision, supervisors attempted to apply scientific methods and cooperative problem-solving approaches to educational problems (Pajak, 2000). Hosic cautioned the supervisor to eschew his "autocratic past": "The fact that he is invested for the time being with a good deal of delegated authority does not justify him in playing the autocrat. . . . To do so is neither humane, wise, nor expedient" (1920, pp. 331, 332). Continuing to build a philosophic rationale for the supervisor's involvement in "democratic pursuits," Hosic explained that it was no longer viable to apply techniques of the past. Hosic believed, as did Dewey, that it was possible to reshape a school system that had originated with the idea of bureaucratic maintenance so that it would comply with the principles of democracy.

Democratic supervision, in particular, implied that educators, including teachers, curriculum specialists, and supervisors, would cooperate to improve instruction. Efforts by prominent superintendent Jesse Newlon reinforced democracy in supervision. In an article titled "Attitude of the Teacher Toward Supervision," Newlon (1923) asked, "How can the ends of supervision best be achieved?" He maintained that the school organization must be set up to "invite the participation of the teacher in the development of courses." The ends of supervision could be realized when teacher and supervisor worked in a coordinated fashion. Newlon developed the idea of setting up "supervisory councils" to offer "genuine assistance" to teachers. In this way, he continued, "the teacher will be regarded as a fellow-worker rather than a mere cog in a big machine" (pp. 547–549). Participatory school management and supervision had their origins in the work of Newlon.

Scientific Supervision

In the 1930s and 1940s, educators believed that autocratic supervisory practices were no longer viable. They urged more scientific approaches to supervisory practice in schools. The early attempts to apply science via rating cards were now losing favor. Burton (1930), a prolific writer in supervision, explained that the use of "rating schemes from our prescientific days . . . would be wholly inadequate today." Although Burton recognized the usefulness of rating in some instances, he believed that "it is desirable and rapidly becoming possible to have more objectively determined items by means of which to evaluate the teacher's procedure" (p. 405).

One of the foremost proponents of science in education and supervision was A. S. Barr (1931). He stated emphatically that the application of scientific principles "is a part of a general movement to place supervision on a professional basis." Barr stated in precise terms what the supervisor needed to know:

> Supervisors must have the ability to analyze teaching situations and to locate the probable causes for poor work with a certain degree of expertness; they must have the ability to use an array of data-gathering devices peculiar to the field of supervision itself; they must possess certain constructive skills for the development of new means, methods, and materials of instruction; they must know how teachers learn to teach; they must have the ability to teach teachers how to teach; and they must be able to evaluate. In short, they must possess training in both the science of instructing pupils and the science of instructing teachers. Both are included in the science of supervision. (pp. x, xi)

Barr (1931) said the supervisor should first formulate objectives, followed by measurement surveys to determine the instructional status of schools. Then, probable causes of poor work should be explored through the use of tests, rating scales, and observational instruments. The results of supervision, continued Barr, must be measured. Most important, according to Barr, the methods of science should be applied to the study and practice of supervision. More concretely, Barr (1925) asserted that a scientific analysis of teaching is a necessary part of the training of a supervisor: "How can the scientific knowledge of the teaching process be brought to bear upon the study and improvement of teaching?" Barr contended that teaching could be broken down into its component parts and that each part had to be studied scientifically. If good teaching procedures could be isolated, thought Barr, then specific standards could be established to guide the supervisor in judging the quality of instruction. He based his scientific approach to supervision "upon the success of the professional student of education in breaking up this complex mass into its innumerable elements and to study each objectively" (pp. 360, 363).

Throughout the 1930s, 1940s, and 1950s, the idea that supervision involves improving instruction based on classroom observation gained momentum. Supervision as a means of improving instruction through observation was reinforced by the use of "stenographic reports," which were the brainchild of Romiett Stevens, a professor at Teachers College, Columbia University.

Stevens thought that the best way to improve instruction was to record verbatim accounts of actual lessons "without criticism or comment." Stevens's stenographic accounts were "the first major systematic study of classroom behavior" (Hoetker & Ahlbrand, 1969).

Supervisors during this era advocated a scientific approach toward their work in schools (see Table 1.1, Model 4). Scientific supervision was considered to be distinct from social efficiency and entirely compatible with democratic practices (Dewey, 1929). Burton and Brueckner (1955) claimed that "a few individuals still speak, write, and supervise as if science and democracy were antagonistic, or at least not easily combined. The truth is that each is necessary in an integrated theory and practice" (p. 82).

Supervision as Leadership

Democratic and scientific supervision continued well into the 1950s. Democratic methods in supervision, however, clearly were expanded and clarified in the 1960s in the form of supervision as leadership (see Table 1.1, Model 5).

The political and social upheavals resulting from the urban plight, concerns for justice and equality, and antiwar sentiments dramatically affected education—and supervision, in particular. Virulent criticisms of educational practice and school bureaucracy were pervasive (e.g., Silberman's *Crisis in the Classroom*, 1970). Educators also took a serious look at supervisory practices in schools. The legacy of supervision as inspection that found justification in the production-oriented, social efficiency era was no longer viable. Bureaucratic supervision was not viable either. A new vision for the function of supervision was framed.

The work most representative of the 1960s was undoubtedly the anthology of articles that originally appeared in *Educational Leadership*, compiled by then-editor and associate director of the Association for Supervision and Curriculum Development, Robert R. Leeper (1969). Leeper and the authors of this anthology maintained that supervisors must extend "democracy in their relationships with teachers" (p. 69). The way to accomplish this was to promulgate supervision as a leadership function.

Harris (1969) expressed the ideals of supervisory leadership this way:

The word *leadership* refers to showing the way and guiding the organization in definitive directions. New leadership is needed in this sense of the word. Two kinds are required:

1. Those in status positions must lead out with new boldness and find better ways of influencing the schools toward rationally planned, timed change.

2. New leadership positions must be created, and coordinated to facilitate the enormously complex job of leading instructional change. (p. 36)

Although issues of instructional leadership would not gain popularity for another 15 years, supervision as leadership essentially emerged in the 1960s.

The principal focus of supervision during this time was a concerted effort by those engaged in supervision to provide leadership in five ways: (1) developing mutually acceptable goals, (2) extending cooperative and democratic methods of supervision, (3) improving classroom instruction, (4) promoting research into educational problems, and (5) promoting professional leadership.

Reflection/Microlab

What does instructional leadership mean to you?

Clinical Supervision

Uncertainty plagued the field of supervision by the 1970s. Markowitz (1976) stated,

> The supervisor in the educational system is plagued by ambiguities. His or her position in the authority structure is ill-defined and quite often vulnerable. There is a lack of clarity in the definition of his or her role and a lack of agreement on the functions associated with supervision. (p. 367)

Alfonso, Firth, and Neville (1975) described this role ambiguity in terms of a "power limbo;" that is, supervisors are "neither line nor staff, neither administration nor faculty, but somewhere in between" (p. 342). Wilhelms (1969) concurred that supervision had witnessed tremendous change: "Roles are changing; staff organization is swirling; titles and functions are shifting," said Wilhelms, "but whether his [sic] title is 'principal,' 'supervisor,' 'curriculum coordinator,' or what not, the person in a position of supervisory leadership is caught in the middle" (p. x).

Lacking focus, a sound conceptual base, and purpose, supervision explored alternative notions to guide theory and practice in the field. Efforts to reform supervision were reflective of a broader attempt to seek alternatives to traditional educational practice. Clinical supervision grew out of this dissatisfaction with traditional educational practice and supervisory methods. Goldhammer (1969), one of the early proponents of clinical supervision, stated that the model for clinical supervision was "motivated, primarily, by contemporary views of weaknesses that commonly exist in educational practice" (p. 1).

The premise of clinical supervision was that teaching could be improved by a prescribed, formal process of collaboration between teacher and supervisor. The literature of clinical supervision has been replete with concepts of collegiality, collaboration, assistance, and improvement of instruction. Bolin and Panaritis (1992) explained that clinical supervision "appealed to many educators" because of its "emphasis on 'collegiality.'" The rhetoric of clinical supervision favored collaborative practice over inspectional, fault-finding supervision.

Most researchers identify Morris Cogan (1973) as the progenitor of clinical supervision (Anderson, 1993), although Pajak (1989) credits William M. Hill (1968) with incorporating a "lesser known version of the preconference, observation, postconference cycle" of supervision. Tanner and Tanner (1987), acknowledging Cogan's influence in developing the theory of clinical supervision, attributed the idea to Conant in 1936.

Reflection

What are the chief characteristics of clinical supervision that distinguish it from other models of supervision? Have you ever used or been involved with clinical supervision? What obstacles might impede successful implementation of a clinical model in your school or district?

Clinical supervision, although advocated by professors and authors of textbooks, did not by any means gain wide acceptance in schools (see, e.g., Garman, 1997). Although clinical supervision received its share of criticism (e.g., Bolin & Panaritis, 1992; Tanner & Tanner, 1987), educators throughout the 1970s continued to argue that democratic methods of supervision should be extended and that vestiges of bureaucratic supervision should be excised. Supervision to improve instruction and promote pupil learning, instructional leadership, and democratic practices remained as prominent goals throughout the 1970s (see Table 1.1, Model 6).

DEMOCRATIC METHODS AND SUPERVISION

During the early 1980s, public education continued to receive voluminous criticism for being bureaucratic and unresponsive to the needs of teachers, parents, and children (see, e.g., S. M. Johnson, 1990). One of the prominent proposals for disenfranchising bureaucracy was the dissolution of autocratic administrative practices where overbearing supervisors ruled by fiat. Favored was greater and more meaningful decision making at the grassroots level (Dunlap & Goldman, 1991). This idea translated into giving teachers more formal responsibility for setting school policies, thus enhancing democratic governance in schools (Glanz, 1992; Kirby, 1991). S. M. Johnson (1990) observed that "although schools have long been under the control of administrators, local districts are increasingly granting teachers more formal responsibility for setting school policies" (p. 337).

Criticism leveled at the educational bureaucracy has had consequences for school supervision (Firth & Eiken, 1982). Throughout this period, educators continued to consider alternative methods of supervision. In the early 1980s, developmental supervision, in which varied levels of teaching abilities were acknowledged, gained attention (Glickman, 1981). By the end of the decade, transformational leadership, which advocated that supervisors serve as change agents, became popular (e.g., Leithwood & Jantzi, 1990). Other writers advanced their notions of supervision as well (e.g., Bowers & Flinders, 1991).

Teacher empowerment (e.g., Darling-Hammond & Goodwin, 1993) gained attention as teachers became active participants in decision-making processes in schools. Pajak (2000) reviewed the literature on the "teacher as leader" during the previous five years. Peer supervision (e.g., Willerman, McNeely, & Koffman Cooper, 1991) appeared in the literature as an alternative to traditional supervision by "professionally trained supervisors," as did cognitive coaching (Costa & Garmston, 1997). Other collegial and democratic supervisory methods continued to receive notice (e.g., Smyth, 1991).

The publication of *Supervision in Transition* (Glickman, 1992) by the Association for Supervision and Curriculum Development marked a refinement in the changing conception of supervision as a democratic enterprise. Glickman, editor of the yearbook, clearly set the tone by stating emphatically that the very term *supervision* connoted a distasteful, even "disgusting" metaphor for school improvement. Instead of using the words *supervision* or *supervisor*, educators, or what Glickman called "risk-taking practitioners," were more comfortable with terms such as *instructional leadership* and *instructional leader*. The transition that Glickman and the authors of this comprehensive account of supervision envisioned was one that valued collegiality. Supervision, in the words of Sergiovanni (1992), was viewed as "professional and moral."

Other models and conceptions of supervision emerged in an attempt to extend democratic methods and to dissociate from bureaucratic and inspectional supervision. Clinical, developmental, and transformational supervision, among other models, had a common bond in that they emerged to counter the ill effects of supervision's bureaucratic legacy (see Table 1.1, Model 7).

> **Reflection/Microlab**
>
> *From your experience, are collegiality and democratic supervision viable options for your school, district, or state? Explain. Are you familiar with the implementation of any existing collegial or democratic processes? If so, which ones? How have staff and administration responded to them?*

STANDARDS-BASED SUPERVISION

Although the democratic methods "changing concepts" model had an impact on supervision in the 1990s, over the past several years, especially since the turn of the new century, supervisory practice has been shaped and influenced by the general movement toward standards-based reform. Standards-based reform has affected supervision so greatly that we have identified a new and current model of supervision that has impacted and will in all likelihood continue to impact supervision as a field of study and practice. We call that model "Standards-Based Supervision" (see Table 1.1).

Although they are not new, standards-based teaching and learning have influenced curriculum, supervision, and teacher education in significant ways.

Supervisors and those concerned with supervision have been particularly challenged in the past several years to implement supervisory practices that ensure the technical competence of teachers. Receiving strong political backing from both state and national agencies, standards-based supervision has, in some quarters, relegated supervisors to relying on checklists to ascertain the extent to which teachers are meeting various curricular and instructional objectives embedded in core curriculum standards at various grade levels. Such supervisory practices thwart meaningful supervision aimed at fostering closer collaboration and instructional dialogue to improve teaching and learning. Pajak (2000) points to the compatibility problem of trying to use standards-based supervision with clinical supervision. He warns, "If we fail to provide empathy-based supervision, the current standards-based environment will ultimately prove stultifying for both teachers and their students" (p. 241).

To best understand standards-based supervision, some background knowledge on standards-based reform is necessary. The national movement toward standards-based education, including high-stakes testing, has served to legitimize and bolster local reform proposals that have influenced supervisory practices. Raising standards and promoting uniformity of curricular offerings to raise academic achievement has been an established reform proposal since the 1890s (Seguel, 1966).

During the first half of the 20th century, the College Entrance Examination Board (formed in the 1890s), the Scholastic Aptitude Test (the first SAT was administered in 1926), and the American College Testing Program (established in 1959) were the guardians of standards, as applied to the academic curriculum. As a result of the Russian launch of the first artificial satellite (Sputnik) in 1957, American education was attacked vociferously. Only months after the Sputnik launching, Congress passed the National Defense Education Act (NDEA), which poured millions of dollars into mathematics, sciences, and engineering. For several years following Sputnik, the postwar baby boom increased enrollments dramatically in high schools, and achievement scores in many academic areas also improved. Academic standards, up until this time, continued to be driven by levels of student achievement and assessed by national standardized tests (Ravitch, 1995).

After a lull in the tumultuous mid-1960s, the publication of the National Commission on Excellence in Education's 1983 report, *A Nation at Risk: The Imperative for Educational Reform*, drew attention to the assertion that schools had lowered their standards too much and that American students were not competitive with their international counterparts. The authors of this 1983 report were perturbed by the fact that American schoolchildren lagged behind students in other industrialized nations. The National Commission on Excellence in Education reported that among students from various industrialized nations, U.S. students scored lowest on 7 of 19 academic tests and failed to score first or second on any test. Similar results were reported by the Educational Testing Service (1992). Moreover, the study found that nearly 40% of U.S. 17-year-olds couldn't perform tasks requiring higher-order thinking skills.

Pressure to improve the quality of American education by articulating concrete standards for performance increased. Consequently, a spate of national and state reports continued through the 1980s, each advocating fundamental educational change. Commitment to democratic ideals and the influence of public education was reinforced once again in 1986 with the publication of the report, sponsored by the Carnegie Foundation, *A Nation Prepared: Teachers for the 21st Century* (Carnegie Forum on Education and the Economy, 1986), and the Holmes Group (1986) report. The national curriculum reform movement was catapulted into prominence and action with the Education Summit held in 1989 by then-President George Bush and state governors. A year later, in his State of the Union Address, President Bush affirmed his commitment to excellence in education by establishing six national education goals to be achieved by the year 2000. Signed into law by Congress during the Clinton Administration on March 31, 1994, *Goals 2000* proclaimed, in part, that by the year 2000 "U.S. students will be first in the world in science and mathematics achievement" and "Every school will be free of drugs and violence and will offer a disciplined environment conducive to learning" (http://www.nd.edu/~rbarger/and www7/goals200.html).

The adoption of national goals has been a major impetus for the increased attention to standards at the state level. More than 40 states have revised their curricula to reflect the standards they established.

Continuing in the tradition of standards-based education, President George W. Bush signed into law the No Child Left Behind Act of 2001, a reauthorization of the Elementary and Secondary Education Act Legislation of 1965. The purpose of the new legislation was to redefine the federal role in K–12 education and to help raise student achievement, especially for disadvantaged and minority students. Four basic principles were evident: (1) stronger accountability for results, (2) increased flexibility and local control, (3) expanded options for parents, and (4) an emphasis on teaching methods that presumably have been proven to work.

What can the history of standards-based education teach us about the practice of supervision? Pajak (2000) maintains that the "use of clinical supervision in standards-based environments is so recent that no clear consensus has yet emerged about whether this marriage is either desirable or successful" (p. 238). Our experiences and view of what is happening in the field tell us that a clear consensus is indeed apparent. The movement of standards-based education is indeed shaping supervisory practice by frequently compelling supervisors to incorporate a checklist approach to supervision. The pressure practitioners face to raise student achievement as measured on high-stakes tests is enormous. Principals and assistant principals are more accountable than ever for addressing prescribed core curriculum standards, promoting teaching to the standards, and ensuring higher student academic performance on standardized tests. Consequently, those concerned with supervision have been more inclined to incorporate supervisory practices that are a throwback to the 1930s, 1940s, and 1950s (Table 1.1, Model 4). Directive approaches of supervision find justification within a standards-based educational milieu.

The Persistence of Standards-Based Supervision or the New Accountability Era

As we are writing, we are approaching the national elections. Still, bipartisan support for heightened accountabilities in education exists. Since the last edition of this book, the following accountability measures have swept the nation and are dramatically affecting "life" in the classroom for both teachers and children, as well as having implications for the practice of supervision of instruction that we and others advocate.

1. The persistence of testing for accountability via high-stakes testing.

2. Even with the reauthorization of NCLB, a significant number of schools are no longer standing (hence, the sarcastic comment made by many that NCLB is really No School Left Standing).

3. The use of standardized test scores in some cases as the primary means to assess (i.e., evaluate) teachers in terms of their reappointment and tenure. In New York City, for instance, where we the authors live and

work, despite legal action, newspapers have published the names of teachers and their students' standardized test scores without any context.

4. The persistence of meaningless walk-throughs (also called sarcastically by many teachers "drive-bys") to inspect rather than engage in serious conversations about pedagogical practices.

5. The persistence of hiring administrators (e.g., principals, heads of schools) even in university schools of education who lack education credentials but are rather psychologists, sociologists, political scientists, MBAs, and even former attorneys, to manage and lead schools. Noreen Garmen, a scholar of supervision and curriculum, once quipped that as time goes on it appears more and more frequent that we appoint "outsiders" because of the false premise that teaching, in fact education, is too important to be left in the hands of educators.

6. Finally, but certainly not least, an onerous, top-down evaluative mechanism or system to rate teacher performance.

These more recent measures have strained already frayed relationships between teachers and school administrators, unions and departments of education, parents and teachers, and so on. Students too are experiencing greater levels of stress requiring, at times, medical treatment to deal with the ever-increasing pressures of testing. Supervisory practices are more constrained and inspectional than ever, at least since the early 20th century. Efforts to reform supervision of instruction along the lines we advocate in *Supervision That Improves Teaching and Learning* appear more tenuous and arduous than in the past. The directive and inspectional practices in supervising instruction once again find likely justification within this neo-liberal movement to disenfranchise education from educators and institute a rigid system of accountability that stifles teacher creativity and student learning that is enjoyable and meaningful.

UNDERSTANDING THE HISTORY OF SUPERVISION

Historically, the function and conception of supervision have changed. The earliest notions of supervision addressed the need for selectmen, committees, or clergymen to inspect the physical plant of schools and to ensure that children were receiving instruction as required by law. The legacy of inspectional supervision from the colonial period continued into the late 19th century as supervision became little more than an inspectional function local and city superintendents performed attempting to bureaucratize urban education. In the early 1900s, supervision as bureaucratic inspection was reinforced and strengthened as "social efficiency" became the watchword. Influenced by social and economic forces as well as by opposition to inspectional bureaucratic methods, supervision in the 1920s and 1930s embraced democratic theory; this trend would continue throughout the century, albeit in different forms.

What can we learn from this excursion into history? For some theorists and practitioners, a lesson learned is that authoritarian supervision aimed at fault-finding and suspecting the competence of teachers should not be compatible with the modern practice of supervision. Some view the evolution of the practice of supervision as a progression from crude, unsophisticated *bureaucratic inspectional* approaches to more refined democratic participatory techniques and methodologies.

For some theorists and practitioners, the legacy of inspectional supervision lives on in the form of evaluation. Democratic supervision is viewed as helping teachers improve instruction, whereas bureaucratic supervision is associated with accountability and judgments about teachers' efficiency. This conflict between the helping and evaluative functions of supervision is long standing. Tanner and Tanner (1987) asserted that this dilemma presents an almost insurmountable problem for supervisors: "The basic conflict between these functions is probably the most serious and, up until now, unresolved problem in the field of supervision" (p. 106).

Historically, the *evaluative* function of supervision is rooted in bureaucratic inspectional-type supervision. Maintaining an efficient and effective school organization as well as a sound instructional program mandates that teacher competency be evaluated. In other words, the evaluative aspect of the supervisory function emanates from organizational requirements to measure and assess teaching effectiveness. The origins of the *helping* or *improvement* function of supervision date back to democratic practices in the early 20th century. That is, helping teachers improve instruction and promote pupil achievement grew out of the democratic theory of supervision.

Supervisors or people concerned with supervision, however, have faced a basic role conflict, namely, the unresolved dilemma between the necessity to evaluate (a bureaucratic function) and the desire to genuinely assist teachers in the instructional process (a democratic and professional goal).

Catherine Marshall (1992), in a comprehensive study of assistant principals, described such role conflicts:

> An assistant principal might be required to help teachers develop coordinated curricula—a "teacher support" function. But this function conflicts with the monitoring, supervising, and evaluating functions. . . . The assistant may be working with a teacher as a colleague in one meeting and, perhaps one hour later, the same assistant may be meeting to chastise the same teacher for noncompliance with the district's new homework policy. . . . When they must monitor teachers' compliance, assistants have difficulty maintaining equal collegial and professional relationships with them. (pp. 6–7)

The field of supervision has attempted to resolve this basic conflict between evaluation and improvement (e.g., Hazi, 1994; Poole, 1994; Tsui, 1995). It clearly is evident throughout the history of supervision that efforts have been made to extricate supervision from its bureaucratic heritage. Nonetheless,

Table 1.1 Timeline

	Social/Cultural Markers of the Times	Models of Supervision
Pre-1900		
1893–1897 Grover Cleveland 1897–1901 William McKinley	• Debates about the Spanish–American War, territorial acquisitions, and the economy dominated thought and literature. • Thorstein Veblen's *Theory of the Leisure Class* (1899) attacked predatory wealth and conspicuous consumption of the new rich. • Jacob Riis in *How the Other Half Lives* (1890) documented gnawing poverty, illness, crime, and despair of New York's slums. • Frank Norris's *The Octopus* (1901) condemned monopoly. **From REA U.S. History Review Book:** Teachers as the factory workers and the students as the raw material to be turned into the product that was to meet the specifications of the needs of the 20th century. (http://www.ux1.eiu.edu/~cfrnb/ impbusin.html) Education was conducted with military-like schedules and discipline, and emphasized farming and other manual skills. The daily schedule was split between academics and vocational training. (lcweb2.loc.gov/learn/community/NA_toolkit/overview.pdf)	**Model 1: Supervision as Inspection, Payne-Greenwood** Payne (1875), author of the first published textbook on supervision. Greenwood's supervisory methods (1891), which relied on inspection based on intuition rather than technical or scientific knowledge. Balliet (1894), a superintendent from Massachusetts, insisted that there were only two types of teachers: the efficient and the inefficient.
1900–1919		
1901–1909 Theodore Roosevelt 1909–1913 William H. Taft	• 1906: Upton Sinclair writes *The Jungle*, which depicts the poverty, absence of social programs, unpleasant living and working conditions, and hopelessness prevalent among have-nots in contrast with the corruption on the part of the haves. (wiki) • 1906: Pres. Roosevelt wins Nobel Peace Prize for mediating the Russo–Japanese War. • 1909: NAACP formed. • 1914: World War I begins. • 1917: United States declares war on Germany. • 1917: Russian Revolution. • 1919: Over 20% of U.S. labor force goes on strike. Purpose of education was to prepare youth for jobs in factories. (http://tiger.towson.edu/users/rturnb1/ Education%20Presentation_files/frame.htm)	**Model 2: Supervision as Social Efficiency, Taylor-Bobbitt** Taylor—author of *The Principles of Scientific Management* (1911). Main point of management was to promote the efficiency of the worker. Bobbitt—professor, University of Chicago, control-oriented supervision (1913).

	Social/Cultural Markers of the Times	Models of Supervision
1920s		
1913–1921 Woodrow Wilson	• 1920: 19th Amendment—Women's Suffrage ratified. • Literary Trends—reflected disgust with hypocrisy and materialism of American society: ○ Hemingway's *The Sun Also Rises*; F. Scott Fitzgerald's *The Great Gatsby*; John Dos Passos's *Three Soldiers*. • Popular Culture—Movies—Introduction of Sound—*The Jazz Singer*; Major League Baseball—Babe Ruth; Boxing—Jack Dempsey.	**Model 3: Democracy in Supervision, Dewey–Hosic–Newlon** Teachers, curriculum specialists, and supervisors would cooperate to improve instruction.
1921–1923 Warren G. Harding		
1923–1929 Calvin Coolidge	• Social Conflicts—the automobile, the revolution in morals, rapid urbanization with immigrants, and blacks inhabiting the cities. • 1920–1929: Roaring Twenties. • 1929: Stock market crashes in October. During the 1920s, when education turned increasingly to "scientific" techniques such as intelligence testing and cost-benefit management, progressive educators insisted on the importance of the emotional, artistic, and creative aspects of human development. (http://www.uvm.edu/~dewey/articles/proged.html)	
1930–1950s		
1929–1933 Herbert C. Hoover	• 1929–1933: Depression. Literary trends depicted the crushing poverty in America: James T. Farrell's trilogy, *Studs Lonigan*, about the struggles of lower-middle-class Irish Catholics in Chicago; Erskine Caldwell's *Tobacco Road*, about impoverished Georgia sharecroppers; John Steinbeck's *The Grapes of Wrath* depicting the "Okies" migrating to California in the midst of the Depression. • 1939–1945: World War II.	**Model 4: Scientific Supervision Burton—writer.** Barr—proponent of science in education—supervisors must possess expertise in instructing pupils and teachers.
1933–1945 Franklin D. Roosevelt	• 1949: NATO formed.	Stevens—professor, Teachers College, Columbia University—
1945–1953 Harry S. Truman	• 1954: *Brown vs. Board of Education* challenged the doctrine of separate but equal. • 1957: The launching of Soviet space satellite Sputnik created fear that America was falling behind technologically. • 1957: National Defense Education Act—millions of dollars allocated to education for math, sciences, and engineering. Dramatic enrollments in high school.	classroom observation through recording verbatim accounts of lessons was the first systematic study of classroom behavior.
1953–1961 Dwight D. Eisenhower	• 1959: James Conant, in *The American High School Today*, questioned the adequacy of American education. 1930s: Child-centered (progressive) education. (http://www.brillion.k12.wi.us/hswebpage/Schools%20of%20the%201930's%20Lesson/index.htm) 1940s: Progressive educational philosophy; influenced by John Dewey and New Deal liberalism, predominant among educators. 1950s: New emphasis on science and technology emerges after 1957. (http://www.archives.nysed.gov/edpolicy/research/res_chronology1944.shtml)	

(Continued)

(Continued)

	Social/Cultural Markers of the Times	Models of Supervision
1960s		
1961–1963 John F. Kennedy

1963–1969 Lyndon B. Johnson | • Political and social upheavals resulting from urban blight, concerns for justice and equality, and antiwar sentiments.
• American school curriculum shifted from academic to nonacademic.
• 1964–1975: Vietnam War.
• 1964: President Johnson announces war on poverty.
• 1965: The Elementary and Secondary Education Act provided $1.5 billion to school districts to improve the education of the poor.

1960s: "Activity learning" (versus passive students and active teachers). Led to Jerome Bruner's *Man: A Course of Study (MACOS)* in 1962, calling for research-based curriculum stressing critical thinking, collaboration, and questioning of traditional thought and values. Met strong resistance and was never implemented. (http://www.archives.nysed.gov/edpolicy/research/res_chronology1960.shtml) | **Model 5: Supervision as Leadership**

Leeper—Associate director of Association for Supervision and Curriculum Development (1969). Supervisors must extend democracy in their relationships with teachers. |
| **1970–1980s** | | |
| 1969–1974 Richard M. Nixon

1974–1977 Gerald Ford

1977–1981 Jimmy Carter

1981–1989 Ronald Reagan | • 1964–1975: Vietnam War.
• 1979–1983: New York Regents Action Plan for Improvement of Elementary and Secondary Education developed and approved. The nation's first comprehensive reform plan based on standards for student achievement and school and teacher accountability.
• Political corruption: Watergate.
• Feminism.
• Environmentalism.
• 1983: *A Nation at Risk: The Report of the National Commission on Excellence in Education.*

President Reagan's Department of Education report finds inadequate or declining achievement scores, graduation rates, expectations of students, and focus on academics. Criticizes absence of standards and calls for major reforms. | **Model 6: Clinical Supervision, Goldhammer–Cogan**

Formal process of collaboration between teacher and supervisor. |
| 1981–1989 Ronald Reagan | • 1986: *A Nation Prepared: Teachers for the 21st Century*, sponsored by the Carnegie Corporation, calls for national teacher standards, restructuring of schools, increased teacher salaries, and aid for minorities becoming teachers.
• 1989: National Education Summit convened by President Bush and the National Governors' Association at Charlottesville, VA. First statement of National Goals for Education approved. (http://www.archives.nysed.gov/edpolicy/research/res_chronology2000.shtml) Publication of Nat Hentoff's *Our Children Are Dying*, Jonathan Kozol's *Death at an Early Age*, Herbert Kohl's *36 Children*, and Charles Silberman's *Crisis in the Classroom*. | |

	Social/Cultural Markers of the Times	Models of Supervision
1990s		
1989–1993 George H. W. Bush 1993–2001 Bill Clinton	• Clinton administration signed President Bush's *Goals 2000*—students will be first in world in math and science and every school will be drug and violence free. • U.S. Congress. National Council of Educational Standards—converted vague goals into curriculum standards. • 1994: Educate America Act: Goals 2000. Clinton administration adds two goals to the National Educational Goals: increased parental involvement and professional development for teachers. Provides support to states to develop standards and assessments. (http://www.archives.nysed.gov/edpolicy/research/res_chronology2000.shtml)	**Model 7: Changing Concepts Model of Supervision** Glickman's (1992) *Supervision in Transition*—set the tone by changing the word *supervision* to *instructional leadership* and *supervisor to instructional leader* Sergiovanni (1992) viewed supervision as professional and moral.
2000–Present		
2001–2009 George W. Bush 2009– Barack Obama	• President George W. Bush—No Child Left Behind—2001; a reauthorization of the Elementary and Secondary Education Act of 1965. Stronger accountability for results, increased flexibility and local control. expanded options for parents, emphasis on teaching methods that have been proven to work. • 2001: Requires all students to be "proficient" in reading, mathematics, and science by 2014, with Adequate Yearly Progress measures to determine school success: annual standardized tests (developed by the states) in grades 3–8 in reading and mathematics. (http://www.archives.nysed.gov/edpolicy/research/res_chronology2000.shtml) • 2003–2010: War in Iraq. • 2001–: War in Afghanistan • 2008: The Great Recession • 2009: Barack Obama appoints Arne Duncan, CEO of Chicago schools, to lead U.S. schools as Secretary of Education during troubled economic times. • 2011: Japanese Tohoku earthquake and tsunami. • 2012: Osama Bin Laden killed. • Supreme Court validates Obamacare. • Mayoral control and charter schools proliferate in urban centers. • Creation of state systems of evaluation to categorize teachers as competent or incompetent • Use of standardized test scores to rank teacher competence and used in reappointments and tenure considerations • Increased use by states of performance-based teacher certification exams	**Model 8: Standards-Based Supervision** Includes high-stakes testing. Accountability based on high-stakes testing and quantitative data thrives and influences supervision.

advances in theory are not necessarily reflected in practice. Many, if not most, studies still conclude that teachers do not find supervision helpful (Zepeda & Ponticell, 1998).

We present, in brief, the rationales of the two camps and challenge you to take a stance. We definitely have an opinion on this issue, as you might discover with a careful read of this book. Still, we prefer not to indicate our view, but rather encourage you, especially in developing your vision, to address the issue in ways that make sense to you. Please e-mail us with your view, and we'd be happy, if asked, to indicate our own conception of the relationship between supervision and evaluation.

Camp 1 views supervision as a process that engages teachers as professional colleagues for the purpose of encouraging instructional dialogue so as to improve teaching practices. Judgments as to the competence of the teacher are eschewed during the supervision process. Supervisors serve, among other ways, as another set of eyes to help the teacher reflect on her teaching behaviors, for instance, in the classroom during instruction. Supervisors provide teachers with descriptions of what occurred during a lesson and then encourage teachers to make some observations and draw conclusions from the evidence presented. Supervisors function as a mirror for teachers. Through instructional dialogue, teachers decide a course of action on their own, with facilitation by the supervisor. Maria, a fourth-grade teacher, for instance, might realize that she is asking questions that may be too complicated for her students. After examining Bloom's Taxonomy, she, in working with her supervisor, develops more appropriate lower-level questions for implementation next time. Evaluation, as opposed to supervision, is the process in which decisions are made about the competencies of a teacher and functions as an accountability measure. It is usually performed, in formal observation fashion, several times a year, with a summative evaluation report for the teacher's file at the end of the school year. Reappointment and tenure decisions are made as a result of such evaluations. Camp 1 adherents believe that the two processes are distinct and serve different purposes and should be kept separate for a variety of reasons. One such reason, according to adherents, is that teachers are unlikely to indicate any willingness to change teaching behaviors in a supervisory process when they know that disclosures may influence negatively on their formative or summative evaluative reports. "Supervision and evaluation are like oil and water; they don't mix," stated a supervisor who adheres to such a division between the processes.

Camp 2, on the other hand, maintains that the two processes, if implemented properly, are compatible and that a distinction or separation is artificial and impractical. Adherents maintain that trust is a necessary condition that must be established if supervision and evaluation are to work properly. Once established (that is, supervisors establish legitimacy in the eyes of teachers), a supervisor can easily work with teachers, wearing one hat, so to speak, in terms of working with them as colleagues to examine teaching in the classroom, and then, at some other point in time, serve as evaluator, when specified by legal mandates. Teachers are professionals who understand their role and importance in schools and should readily accept and expect that supervision and evaluation are employed to improve teacher performance so as to promote student learning and achievement.

We presented both views in caricature form for purposes of analysis. Finer distinctions exist as well as other rationales for their use and function. In addition, a good number of evaluation systems or approaches have been advocated in the literature that support each camp (Danielson & McGreal, 2000; Goldstein, 2007; Marzano, Frontier, & Livingston, 2011). We encourage you to consider this issue by reading some sources on the subject.

IMPLICATIONS FOR THE PRACTICE OF SUPERVISION

Present Context and Future Necessities

For most of the 20th century, schools retained features of the factory organizational model, a legacy of 19th century industrial society. Schools relied on hierarchical supervisory control and representative democracy. We are now, however, undergoing major societal transformations into a postindustrial era (Ambrose & Cohen, 1997) characterized "by exponential information growth, fast-paced innovation, organizational change, and participatory democracy" (p. 20). As a result of these technological, political, economic, and social changes, schools (teachers and supervisors) are "being called on today to rethink and restructure how schools operate and how teachers relate to students. . . . We sorely need new ways of thinking about educational supervision and leadership" (Pajak, 1993, p. 159).

Attempts to restructure schools, classrooms, and practices (both teaching and supervisory) abound (see, e.g., Murphy & Hallinger, 1993). Over the past several years, alternative models or approaches to school and instructional improvement and teacher evaluation have gained prominence. Among these innovative ideas are site-based management, union-sponsored peer coaching, professional partnerships, reflective practice, professional learning communities (PLCs), and teacher self-evaluation. Based on our brief discussion of the history of supervision in this chapter,[2] we believe these innovations can be seen as ways to extend participatory democracy in supervision.

The changing context of supervision necessitates that both prospective and practicing supervisors remain responsive to unprecedented demands and opportunities. Supervisors need specialized knowledge and skills to meet organizational challenges in the 21st century. They need to base their practice of supervision on a foundation of dispositions and beliefs. Supervisors have to place a premium on initiative, flexibility, tolerance for ambiguity, collaboration, and an ethical mind-set. In the future, supervisors will need to be more and more collaborative and assist teachers in reflecting about classroom instruction in meaningful ways despite the bureaucratic environment of accountability. We believe that reflective clinical supervision can exist within the current climate. The vignettes and case studies in the text bear witness to this feasibility.

As we saw earlier in this chapter, with a firmly entrenched bureaucratic heritage, people have tried to reshape the image of supervision into a democratic enterprise aimed at instructional improvement. We maintain that your ability to facilitate teaching and learning depends on your belief system, because it requires knowledge and skills about instructional improvement. Much of this book is devoted to knowledge and skill development. The remainder of this chapter, however, is aimed at indicating how your beliefs might affect your response to daily instructional challenges. Are you more inclined to conceive of supervision as an inspectional, bureaucratic process, are you genuinely more concerned with developing collaborative relationships with teachers in an effort to improve instruction, or are you inclined to follow a path somewhere in the middle?

We make a bold assertion in this chapter: Bureaucratic inspectional supervision should have no place in schools in the 21st century. We must prepare supervisors who truly espouse participatory democratic values. We have found that some supervisors espouse collaboration when, in practice, they operate in rather autocratic ways. These supervisors are probably influenced very much by the traditional conceptions of supervision described earlier and the current climate of accountability.

Case Study

Dr. William Jones believes that teachers need close scrutiny. "Many of the new teachers," explains Dr. Jones, "are generally weak. They have just been certified and need close supervision." He continues, "In fact, even experienced teachers continually need the guidance of an expert who can provide the needed instructional and managerial assistance."

Other supervisors are genuinely interested in working with teachers collaboratively, as evidenced by Elizabeth Gonzalez, a vice principal in Elmsville Elementary School, a suburban district in the Midwest. Elizabeth believes in forging collaborative relationships with teacher professionals. "I think that every teacher should develop a unique style of teaching that is right for her or him," she explains. "As a supervisor, I am really most effective as facilitator and guide, rather than an overseer."

Why does Dr. Jones rely only on inspectional practices, yet Elizabeth acts in a much more collaborative way? We believe that each of these supervisors operates from a different belief system that inevitably affects how he or she approaches supervisory responsibilities.

ASSESSING BELIEF SYSTEMS[3]

The bureaucratic model of schooling is based on what we believe are erroneous assumptions about how people work together most efficiently in schools. There is a growing awareness that the key to successfully shifting to a collaborative educational paradigm is dependent on the degree to which we alter our thinking patterns, belief systems, and mind-sets, or as Sergiovanni calls them, "mindscapes" (Sergiovanni, 1992, p. 41). Our belief systems are intimately connected to the language we use to articulate and communicate meanings. The needed transformation in education requires a realignment of educational phraseology with an entirely different set of definitions, meanings, and purposes. For example, a reexamination of the metaphors we use is essential. Using supervision or reflective coaching not only clearly indicates "where we're coming from" but also defines human interactions in the workplace.

Yet a caveat about beliefs and actions or behaviors is in order. Reflective practice (see Osterman & Kottkamp, 2004) posits that our actions often are inconsistent with our intentions (or beliefs) and that new ideas do not necessarily lead to new behaviors. *Espoused theories* represent our conscious ideas, intentions, and beliefs. Following exposure to new ideas in graduate courses and workshops, we often believe that this information and the beliefs acquired through experience and formal education will guide our actions. Espoused theories, however, do not influence behavior directly. How many times have you thought after a leader's speech, "Why doesn't he or she practice what he or she preaches?" How many impressive workshops have we all attended with the best of intentions to implement our new knowledge, only to return to our old practices? How many supervisors preach active learning for all students and then conduct a feedback conference where they tell the teacher everything he or she must do without even thinking of asking for the teacher's input?

Although we may consciously adopt new ideas, these action theories are ingrained so deeply in our consciousness that we cannot change them easily. *Theories-in-use* build and crystallize over a long period of time and become such an integral part of our beings that we are unaware of the discrepancies between our beliefs and actions or between our actions and intended outcomes. Actual change in our behaviors will take place only when we become aware of the discrepancy between a predominant theory-in-use and an unacceptable practice or outcome. Figure 1.1 shows how theories-in-use directly impact behavior. Espoused theories do not directly influence behavior and may or may not be consistent with theories-in-use.

Nonetheless, we believe that it is essential to articulate our espoused theories in the form of vision statements. It is, however, through the use of reflective practice (which is presented in more detail in Chapter 2) that the new ideas we will be learning in this book and the beliefs we will develop will become theories-in-use. In Chapter 6, you will develop your personal supervisory platforms based on the espoused theories and the theories-in-use that you will have developed.

Figure 1.1   A Conceptual Framework Underlying Reflective Practice

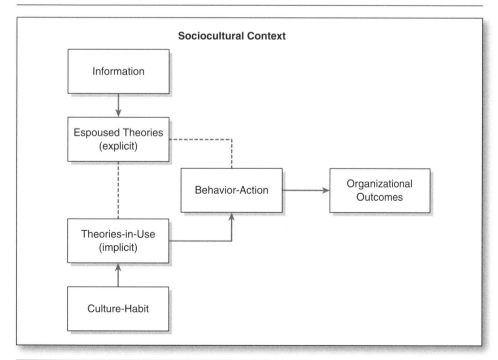

Source: K. F. Osterman and R. B. Kottkamp. (2004). *Reflective Practice for Educators: Professional Development to Improve Student Learning* (2nd ed.), p. 11 (Figure 1.1 Reflective Practice: A Conceptual Framework). Thousand Oaks, CA: Corwin. Reprinted with permission.

Philosophy, at least indirectly, influences actions, which in turn affect behavior. How we think shapes the world in which we live. For example, our values and beliefs shape the kinds of experiences we want young children to have in classrooms. They also influence what adults do in schools and define role relationships among members of a school system. If our attitudes about how best to organize large groups of people focus on hierarchical notions of differentiation and classification, then we will tend to conceptualize supervision as, for example, didactic and evaluative. Conversely, if our view of school management stresses collaboration and shared leadership, we will not be willing to construct an educational environment where disempowered individuals become spectators of, rather than participants in, their own work. This worldview will define supervision as collegial and interactive.

> **Reflection**
>
> *Compose a list of your beliefs about teaching and learning, about teachers, about supervision, and about yourself.*

What are the qualities or dispositions we want future supervisors to possess? Are you willing and able to meet new supervisory challenges in the 21st century? The questionnaire in Figure 1.2 is designed to help you sort out your beliefs. More specifically, the survey is designed to assess your preference to function along the bureaucratic, inspectional, democratic, collegial continuum. You should have completed this questionnaire before you read this chapter. Make sure you retake the questionnaire when you have completed reading the book to assess whether any of your beliefs have changed.

Interpreting Answers to the Questionnaire

The following responses to each statement indicate that your supervisory preferences or inclinations operate along bureaucratic, authoritarian lines:

1. T	6. T	11. F	16. T	21. T	26. F	31. F	36. F
2. T	7. T	12. T	17. F	22. F	27. T	32. F	37. T
3. F	8. T	13. F	18. T	23. T	28. F	33. T	38. F
4. F	9. T	14. T	19. F	24. F	29. T	34. F	39. F
5. T	10. F	15. T	20. F	25. F	30. F	35. T	40. T

The following responses to each statement indicate that your supervisory preferences or inclinations operate along democratic, collaborative lines:

1. F	6. F	11. T	16. F	21. F	26. T	31. T	36. T
2. F	7. F	12. F	17. T	22. T	27. F	32. T	37. F
3. T	8. F	13. T	18. F	23. F	28. T	33. F	38. T
4. T	9. F	14. F	19. T	24. T	29. F	34. T	39. T
5. F	10. T	15. F	20. T	25. T	30. T	35. F	40. F

Figure 1.2 Questionnaire: Beliefs About Supervision

Please answer true (T) or false (F) to each of the following statements. Be honest: Answer true if the statement generally describes a belief you once held or currently hold. If a statement represents a belief that holds true in most situations, although not in all, answer true. Answer false if the statement in no way describes a belief you once held or currently hold. If a statement represents a belief that is false in most situations, although not in all, answer false. There is no need to share your responses with anyone.

T	F	1.	When it comes down to it, supervision, as I conceive of it, is essentially about looking for errors.
T	F	2.	Guided directed approaches to supervision are most appropriate for teachers at low levels of personal and professional development.
T	F	3.	Teaching is a highly complex, context-specific, interactive activity.
T	F	4.	Organizational concerns are almost always secondary to individual needs.
T	F	5.	The supervisor's position in the hierarchy, as compared to the teacher's, is unproblematic.
T	F	6.	Hierarchy of offices is necessary for organizational efficiency.
T	F	7.	I am not comfortable participating with teachers as partners.
T	F	8.	Supervision is about offering teachers specialized help in improving instruction.
T	F	9.	Supervision is about examining and analyzing classroom teaching behaviors so that recommendations can be made with regard to the course of action teachers should take instructionally.
T	F	10.	Teachers can help supervisors improve their performance.
T	F	11.	Most teachers are self-directed.
T	F	12.	Supervisors should be expert diagnosticians.
T	F	13.	Supervision is primarily a collaborative process in which teachers and supervisors talk about ways to improve instruction.
T	F	14.	Supervision is about looking for errors and then engaging teachers in dialogue so that they realize these deficiencies on their own.
T	F	15.	The focus of supervision should be about helping teachers change and improve instruction.
T	F	16.	Without assistance, teachers generally will not make changes.
T	F	17.	Reality in classrooms is essentially subjective, not objective, and teaching is a complex endeavor that requires continual study.

(Continued)

33

T	F	18.	Although supervisor-teacher collaboration is important, a supervisor's judgment must ultimately hold sway.
T	F	19.	Schools are centers of inquiry in which teachers themselves must assume responsibility for instructional excellence.
T	F	20.	Teacher self-evaluation plays a prominent role in instructional improvement.
T	F	21.	The supervisor is the agent of improved instruction.
T	F	22.	Qualitative approaches to instructional improvement are just as valid as quantitative approaches.
T	F	23.	Supervisors help teachers change.
T	F	24.	Reflective dialogue is an integral component of supervision.
T	F	25.	Instructional improvement activities include peer coaching, action research projects, and problem-solving groups, as well as more traditional development activities.
T	F	26.	Supervision is primarily about asking questions that facilitate the examination of teacher practice in the classroom.
T	F	27.	When I offer teachers constructive criticisms, I expect they will consider them carefully.
T	F	28.	Experienced, high-functioning teachers should have complete control over their professional development.
T	F	29.	The supervisor ultimately should determine what and how a teacher should teach.
T	F	30.	Teachers should be encouraged to carry out their own educational goals and curricular decisions.
T	F	31.	Teachers should be given options on how they want to teach.
T	F	32.	Teachers should disobey official regulations if they feel that they interfere with the welfare of students.
T	F	33.	Teachers don't spend enough time thinking about ways to improve instruction.
T	F	34.	Supervisors should create opportunities for teachers to make professional and personal choices, not shape their behavior.
T	F	35.	Supervisors should attentively listen to the teachers' concerns and offer critical assessment and constructive ideas for change.
T	F	36.	Schools will improve primarily when a norm of collegiality exists in which shared discussion and shared work among all staff members exist.
T	F	37.	The knowledge base of a supervisor is generally superior to that of a teacher.
T	F	38.	Supervisors should actively seek input from teachers, parents, and students about ways to improve instruction.
T	F	39.	Most teachers don't need specific instructions on what to teach and how to teach.
T	F	40.	Supervisors should have more expertise than teachers with respect to teaching and learning.

As we stated earlier, we believe that bureaucratic inspectional supervision should have no place in schools in the 21st century. For the future, we must prepare supervisors who truly espouse and practice participatory democratic values. Supervision that assumes that supervisors are experts and superior to teachers represents vestiges of control-oriented, inspectional practices. Although these kinds of practices were prevalent in early supervision, we argue that they should no longer be accorded attention.

(*Note:* In the ensuing discussion, statement numbers refer to the questionnaire in Figure 1.2.)

Bureaucratic thought essentially suggests that

- Supervision is inspectional (Statements 1 and 14).
- Hierarchy is necessary for organizational efficiency (Statements 5 and 6).
- Supervisors are experts and teachers are not (Statements 12, 18, 27, 29, 37, and 40).
- Teachers and supervisors are not equal partners (Statement 7).
- Teachers will not improve instruction on their own (Statements 16 and 33).

That hierarchy equals expertise and supervisors know more than teachers is axiomatic according to the bureaucratic belief system.

Furthermore, the following assumptions that, at first glance, might appear unproblematic also represent bureaucratic conceptions of supervision:

- Supervision is primarily about helping teachers improve instruction (Statements 8 and 9). This belief subtly implies that teachers are deficient, need help, and could not or would not seek improvement on their own.
- Supervisors help teachers change, as if teachers are deficient and necessarily need to change (Statements 15, 23, and 35). This belief implies that something is wrong with a teacher's teaching.
- Teachers at low levels need assistance (Statement 2). This belief implies that supervisors can identify with certainty that a teacher is deficient. It also implies that supervisors should *help* teachers because they cannot improve through collaboration or self-reflection.
- Supervisors are agents of improved instruction (Statement 21). This belief implies that supervisors, not teachers, are agents of improved instruction.

The aforementioned conceptions of supervision underscore the superordinate–subordinate relationship between teachers and supervisors. Bureaucratic conceptions of supervision imply that teachers don't know as much about teaching as do supervisors and, conversely, that supervisors possess greater teaching expertise than do teachers.

Democratic thought essentially suggests that

- Teaching is complex and not easily defined or understood (Statements 3 and 17).
- Individuals are more important than the organizations (Statements 4 and 32).

- Most teachers are self-directed, responsible, and competent (Statements 10, 11, 19, 20, 28, 30, 31, and 39).
- Supervision is a truly collaborative process (Statements 13, 34, 36, and 38).
- Qualitative approaches to classroom improvement are just as valid as quantitative ones (Statements 22 and 24).
- Alternative approaches to traditional supervision are viable (Statement 25).
- Supervisors function at their best when they pose questions for critical analysis by teachers (Statement 26).

The aforementioned conceptions of supervision underscore the empowering nature of supervisor–teacher relationships. Teachers and supervisors work as collaborative inquirers for the benefit of students. The telling-and-prescribing nature of traditional supervision has no place in such a paradigm for school improvement.

CONCLUSION

The supervisory landscape has evolved since the early inspectional practices of supervisors in the 19th and early 20th centuries. Supervision in a postindustrial society requires a new breed of supervisor, one who advocates and affirms participatory democratic practices. Who are these supervisors? What kind of supervisors do we want to attract into the field? Are you more inclined to encourage teachers in ongoing, meaningful dialogue about instructional improvement, or do you feel more comfortable suggesting to teachers ways to improve their teaching?

We have suggested in this chapter that supervision in postindustrial times requires that supervisors develop a personal vision statement so that they begin to consciously affirm their beliefs about teaching and supervision. Such reflective practice is a powerful way to enhance professional development.

Confronted by complex and seemingly perplexing social, political, technological, and moral issues, educational supervisors, perhaps more than ever before, play a crucial role in developing sound educational programming that is both educative and meaningfully relevant. Considering these awesome and challenging responsibilities, we believe educational supervision can play a vital role in promoting excellent instruction.

NOTES

1. Although the special supervisor as a specific title disappeared, a host of other supervisors later emerged, such as supervisors of curriculum, instruction, and reading, among others.
2. For a more in-depth historical analysis, see Glanz (1998).
3. This section is informed by the work of Reitzug (1997).

Three Interpersonal Approaches to Supervision

A barrier to communication is something that keeps meanings from meeting. . . . Because so much of our education misleads people into thinking that communication is easier than it is, they become discouraged and give up when they run into difficulty. Because they do not understand the nature of the problem, they do not know what to do. The wonder is not that communicating is as difficult as it is, but that it occurs as much as it does.

—Howe, 1963, pp. 23–24

CHAPTER OVERVIEW

1. Interpersonal Skills
   a. Listening, Reflecting, and Clarifying Techniques
   b. Barriers to Communication

2. Approaches to Providing Feedback
   a. Directive Informational Approach
   b. Collaborative Approach
   c. Self-Directed Approach

3. Guidelines for Reflective Practice
   a. Reflective Practice Process
   b. Reflector's Feedback Guidelines

In the previous chapter, you became acquainted with the historical frame-work of supervision and began to examine your present personal beliefs within the current context of supervision. This chapter explores and develops the interpersonal skills that we believe are a prerequisite to all effective supervisory practice. After a brief introduction to the philosophical principles underlying the supervisory beliefs and methods presented in this book, we briefly discuss the various communication techniques that are essential for all effective interpersonal relationships: listening, nonverbal clues, and reflecting, clarifying statements. We then offer exercises that hone these techniques. A description of the three interpersonal approaches that we believe are most effective in working with teachers follows. Before practicing each of the three interpersonal approaches in a group, we introduce a reflective practice model and provide guidelines for reflective practice that are used throughout this book to build and reinforce skills. This chapter concludes with two exercises that permit you to begin to internalize these approaches prior to implementing them on site.

HOW WE LEARN

> *People learn best through active involvement and through thinking about and becoming articulate about what they have learned. Processes, practices, and policies built on this view of learning are at the heart of a more expanded view of teacher development that encourages teachers to involve themselves as learners—in much the same way as they wish their students would.*
>
> —Lieberman, 1995, p. 592

How many lectures have we all sat through during which the speaker expounded at great length about the importance of student-centered learning in the classroom? How many workshops have we attended where the presenter talked on and on about student-centered practices? A district superintendent recently hired one of us to facilitate a teacher-centered retreat, which he began with a two-hour speech. Ann Lieberman (1995) pointed out that "what everyone appears to want for students—a wide array of learning opportunities that engage students in experiencing, creating, and solving real problems, using their own experiences, and working with others—is for some reason denied to teachers when they are learners." The main goal of this book is to "walk the talk": to enable students of supervision not only to learn teacher-centered supervisory methods but also to have the opportunity to practice the skills and experience the perspectives as they are exposed to them.

The approaches to providing feedback outlined in this chapter and the methods presented for becoming proficient in their use are based on constructivist principles. In the Preface to *In Search of Understanding: The Case for Constructivist Classrooms*, Catherine Twomey Fosnot (1993) draws on a synthesis of work in cognitive psychology, philosophy, and anthropology to define constructivism as a theory not about teaching but about knowledge and learning. Knowledge is defined as temporary, developmental, socially and culturally mediated, and nonobjective. Learning is "a self-regulated process of resolving inner cognitive conflicts that often become apparent through concrete experience, collaborative discourse, and reflection" (Fosnot, 1993, p. 2). In other words, meaningful knowledge and learning are centered around the learner and are best constructed through collaboration and reflection around personal experience. Deborah Walker, drawing from Fosnot's and Dewey's antecedents, describes constructive leadership as the "reciprocal processes that enable participants in a community to construct meanings that lead toward a shared purpose of schooling" (Lambert et al., 2002, p. 1).

These beliefs have ramifications for the two principal focuses of this chapter: interpersonal approaches for providing feedback and the use of reflective practice in working with teachers and in learning supervisory skills. With respect to working with teachers, no matter what the developmental level of the staff member or the interpersonal orientation of the supervisor, the person receiving feedback should be involved in generating ideas and solutions for the situation under discussion. With regard to learning how to provide feedback, it is only through practicing the skills and reflecting on their development that students of supervision will internalize and personalize what they have learned.

LISTENING, REFLECTING, AND CLARIFYING TECHNIQUES

Before we begin learning and practicing the three different approaches to providing feedback, it is important to incorporate skills that promote communication as well as to become aware of those that create barriers. Table 2.1 provides three types of skills that foster bridging the interpersonal gap. Each category can be integrated into any of the feedback approaches. In each approach, we want to encourage the teacher to provide as complete a picture of his or her perspective as possible. The listening techniques and the nonverbal clues are key means to promote open responses. The reflecting and clarifying techniques are also crucial to all the approaches because they facilitate avoiding or clearing up potential misunderstandings and miscommunications. They provide verbal techniques for separating the supervisor's understandings and perceptions from the teacher's without accusing or putting the other person on the defensive. To remind you of appropriate responses, we recommend that you use the crib sheets that summarize the key techniques and steps for practice and actual implementation. Detachable cards for these techniques are provided on a perforated page at the back of the book.

Table 2.2 contains a summary of common communication spoilers and high-risk responses culled from the interpersonal skills literature. We refer to them as "high-risk" responses because their impact is frequently negative, and as a general rule, they should be avoided. Nonetheless, a few of them can be effective in special circumstances.[1]

The communication techniques and barriers to avoid are critical components of feedback. Effective and appropriate responses are difficult to develop because the barriers to communication are ingrained in our language and habits. For these reasons, it is important to practice the communication

Table 2.1   Communication Techniques

Listening	Nonverbal Clues	Reflecting and Clarifying
"Uh-huh." "OK." "I'm following you." "For instance," "And?" "Mmm." "I understand." "This is great information for me." "Really?" "Then?" "So?" "Tell me more." "Go on." "I see." "Right."	Affirmative nods and smiles Open body language, e.g., arms open Appropriate distance from speaker—not too close or too far Eye contact Nondistracting environment Face speaker and lean forward Barrier-free space, e.g., desk not used as blocker	"You're angry because . . ." "You feel . . . because . . ." "You seem quite upset." "So, you would like . . ." "I understand that you see the problem as . . ." "I'm not sure, but I think you mean . . ." "I think you're saying . . ."

Table 2.2   Barriers to Communication

Barrier Type	Examples

1. Judging
  • Criticizing
  • Name calling and labeling
  • Diagnosing—analyzing motives instead of listening
  • Praising evaluatively
	1. Judging
	  • "You are lazy; your lesson plan is poor."
	  • "You are inexperienced, an intellectual."
	  • "You're taking out your anger on her."
	  • "I know what you need."
	  • "You're terrific!"

2. Solutions
  • Ordering
  • Threatening
  • Moralizing or preaching
  • Inappropriate questioning or prying
  • Advising
  • Lecturing
	2. Solutions
	  • "You must . . ." "You have to . . ." "You will . . ."
	  • "If you don't . . ." "You had better or else."
	  • "It is your duty/responsibility; you should."
	  • "Why?" "What?" "How?" "When?"
	
	  • "What I would do is . . ." "It would be best for you."
	  • "Here is why you are wrong . . ." "Do you realize . . . ?"

3. Avoiding the other's concerns
  • Diverting
 	
  • Reassuring
  • Withdrawing
 	
  • Sarcasm
	3. Avoiding the other's concerns
	  • "Speaking of . . ." "Apropos . . ." "You know what happened to . . ."
	  • "It's not so bad . . ." "You're lucky . . ." "You'll feel better."
	  • "I'm very busy . . ." "I can't talk right now . . ." "I'll get back to you . . ."
	  • "I really feel sorry for you."

techniques in class and in your professional and personal lives as much as possible before proceeding to the feedback approaches. As the communication techniques begin to be a part of your repertoire, they will enhance the feedback approaches. The following exercises are an introduction to the type of reflective practice role plays that you will find throughout the book.

Communication in the Age of the Internet and Social Media

In this era of social media and accountability, e-mail and Twitter are often the most expedient methods of communication for leaders and faculty on overload. We recommend that all important and substantial conversations take place in person. Use of communication techniques and avoidance of barriers to communication are most effective face-to-face. In-person conversations also permit immediate clarification of misunderstandings and clear expression of feelings. Skype and other media such as FaceTime and Google Talk can eliminate many of the dangers of written communication and increase contact between supervisors and teachers. We suggest that e-mail and Twitter be used primarily for setting up meetings and appointments and for the sharing and dissemination of information as well as asking for noncontroversial feedback. Media such as Doodle and SurveyMonkey are time-savers and can be used to reduce time spent on organizing meetings and surveys. That time can be devoted to quality interactions among staff and with leaders.

Reflective Practice

Class Practice

Everyone in the class should find a partner and face that person. Each student will take a turn listening and responding to his or her partner. The goal is to use the communication techniques to foster an effective interchange and to avoid falling into any of the barrier traps. Keep Tables 2.1 and 2.2 handy to facilitate the learning process.

Step 1. Each partner should take a minute to think of a current personal or professional dilemma.

Step 2. Partner No. 1 will recount his or her dilemma.

Step 3. Partner No. 2 will show interest in the speaker's situation by using the listening and nonverbal techniques and avoiding the barriers (Tables 2.1 and 2.2).

Step 4. Partner No. 2 will choose reflecting and clarifying techniques to verify what he or she heard and show understanding of the feelings expressed.

Step 5. Partner No. 1 will give feedback on how well partner No. 2 used the techniques.

Change partners and repeat the cycle. Each cycle should take no more than 5 minutes.

Site Practice

During the next week, target someone who is going to share an experience, problem, or dilemma with you. It can be a spouse, a child, a colleague, or a student. Have your cards with Tables 2.1 and 2.2 on hand, and practice your listening and communication techniques. When the interchange is completed, reflect on what worked well and what areas need improvement. Jot down notes so that you can share your reflections on the experience with your colleagues, first in an e-mail, a discussion board, a wiki, or a blog, and then in class. You may feel a little uncomfortable at first using these techniques. Remember that because the listeners are involved in their virtually uninterrupted sharing, they won't be aware of your novice status as active listeners.

APPROACHES TO PROVIDING FEEDBACK

With communication techniques now in hand, we can introduce and discuss approaches that are fundamental to providing effective feedback.[2] Some textbooks suggest that individual behavior can be divided into four major groups that require four styles of responses (Glickman, Gordon, & Ross-Gordon, 2010). For example, in his developmental model, Glickman et al. recommend four approaches to working with individuals:

1. Directive control

2. Directive informational

3. Collaborative

4. Self-directed

These approaches range from almost total supervisor control to primarily teacher control. The approach the supervisor chooses is supposed to match the specific teacher's level of development. In reality, many of us tend to favor one approach in our interactions with others. In the directive control approach, the supervisor makes the decision and tells the individual or group how to proceed. The supervisor who uses the directive informational approach frames the choices for the group or individual and then asks for input. In the collaborative approach, the supervisor and the individual or group share information and possible solutions as equals to arrive at a mutual plan. In the fourth approach, the supervisor facilitates the individual or group in developing a self-plan or in making its own decision. Glickman et al. (2010) believe that the teacher's level of development, expertise, and commitment and the nature of the situation determine the choice of approach. We agree that "different folks need different strokes" and that varying school circumstances call for a range of approaches; however, *we believe that meaningful learning is dependent on the learner's involvement in constructing that knowledge and so there is no need for the directive control approach.* Many supervisors over the years have used this approach, many continue to follow it, and you may favor it yourself. Nonetheless, we think that the collaborative and self-directed models are the most effective, with the occasional application of a modified directive informational approach.

Elena's Dilemma

To illustrate the use of the three approaches, we will present three variations of the same dilemma and offer suggestions on how the different models could be applied to the scenarios (see Table 2.3 for a summary and comparison of the three approaches).

Elena Santiago was appointed principal of New Hope Middle School in September. New Hope Middle School is a large, urban school that has a reputation for lax discipline and an unruly atmosphere and has recently seen significant population changes. Over the past 10 years, an increasing number of English-language learners (ELLs) have been entering the school. The range of their language and academic skills is vast. This new group of students has created new challenges for the faculty and staff and a very recent district "needs improvement" citation. In Elena's previous position as an assistant principal, also in a demanding environment with a large ELL student body, she had gained the confidence of the staff through her high expectations, blended with excellent interpersonal skills and a collaborative manner. She had also effectively addressed the ELL needs through teamwork. The school district's awareness of her effectiveness led to her appointment as principal of New Hope Middle School. In her first weeks at the school, she has been working closely with all constituencies to address the ELL challenge.

In her daily classroom visits, Elena has noticed some consistent ELL issues. Elena has decided to discuss one issue individually with three teachers she has observed who have struggling ELL students.

Scenario I

Elena approaches Martha before school one morning. Martha also joined the New Hope faculty in September as a seventh-grade language arts teacher. New Hope is her first teaching job, and despite a solid academic background and an assigned mentor, she seems somewhat overwhelmed.

Elena: Good morning, Martha. How are you doing?

Martha: OK, I guess.

Elena: As I've been visiting classes, I've noticed some newer ELL students who seem to be struggling. A couple of them, Jorge and Carlos, are in your third period language arts class. How do you feel they are progressing?

Martha: I honestly haven't had time to focus on them. It takes all my energy to plan and deliver my lessons and, of course, to keep the class's attention. I have noticed that Jorge and Carlos don't participate in class and haven't been handing in their assignments.

Elena: I remember those first days of teaching. It took me quite a while until I could begin to see the forest for the trees. I think there are a few initial steps you can take to help Jorge and Carlos that will not add to your classroom stress. First, it is important to call their homes to determine what kind of family support they have. Second, you can meet with the ESL teacher to find out their language skills and knowledge levels. With this information, you can then meet with your mentor and grade colleagues to discuss strategies for Jorge and Carlos. Could these suggestions work for you?

Martha: I appreciate your bringing Carlos and Jorge to my attention, and I will focus on them, especially with so many people to turn to for support. Is it OK if I ask Ana to assist in the phone calls in case no one speaks English in their homes?

Elena: Of course. It could be very helpful. Since you see Jorge and Carlos every day, do any other ideas come to mind that you could implement while you are obtaining more information?

Martha: There are two Spanish-speaking girls in the class whose English is quite good. What if I seat one next to each boy and put them in the same cooperative groups for now? I can ask the girls before class if it's OK with them.

Elena: That sounds like a good idea. Let's go over your plan. First, you will contact Jorge's and Carlos's homes to ascertain what kind of family support they have. Second, you'll meet with the ESL teacher to find out their language and knowledge levels. With this information in hand, you will meet with your mentor and your grade-level teachers to discuss strategies. In the meantime, you will seat the two Spanish-speaking girls in the class with Jorge and Carlos and put each pair in the same group. Do you want to restate the plan to make sure we're on the same page?

Martha: Sure. I'll call Jorge's and Carlos's homes today and set up a meeting with the ESL teacher. As soon as I have family and ESL information, I'll meet with my mentor and the grade teachers to brainstorm strategies to assist Jorge and Carlos. I'll also seat Jorge and Carlos with the Spanish-speaking girls, at least until I have other strategies.

Reflection

How does Elena approach Martha? How does she foster Elena's "buy-in" of her suggestions? What does she do to ensure that the suggestions don't just remain suggestions?

Elena: Sounds like a plan. How about setting up a time for us to meet and see what transpires over the next couple of weeks with Jorge and Carlos and determine how these strategies are working? I can meet with you at the same time in two weeks so we can catch any glitches that may have surfaced.

Martha: OK. I'll see you before school on Thursday, September 23, after I have attended my Wednesday grade-level meeting.

I. The Directive Informational Approach

This approach is used primarily for new teachers or those who are experiencing difficulties that they don't have the knowledge, expertise, or confidence to resolve on their own or collaboratively. These teachers are seeking or need direction and guidance from a supervisor who can provide expert information and experienced guidance. Nonetheless, the supervisor wants the teacher to seek solutions and generate ideas so as to feel at least some ownership of the final choices. Therefore, the supervisor is the initiator of suggestions and alternatives, which the teacher can then revise and refine and to which he or she can add ideas.

N.B. We discourage you from using this approach with "burned out" teachers. It is highly unlikely that they will respond to this approach.

Key Steps: Directive Informational Approach

1. Identify the problem or goal and solicit clarifying information.

2. Offer solutions. Ask for the teacher's input into the alternatives offered and request additional ideas.

3. Summarize chosen alternatives, ask for confirmation, and request that the teacher restate final choices.

4. Set a follow-up plan and meeting.

---

1. *Identify the problem or goal and solicit clarifying information.* Avoid small talk and focus immediately on the problem or goal in question. Ask the teacher for clarification of the situation so that you are both sure that you are addressing the same problem or goal.

2. *Offer solutions.* Ask for the teacher's input into the alternatives offered and request additional ideas. Even though the new teacher might feel overwhelmed, the supervisor's ideas will probably stimulate his or her thinking. Offering input and requesting additional ideas will give the teacher a feeling of ownership and allow him or her to begin constructing a personal perspective. Separating the alternatives from the request for additional ideas allows the teacher to think through the suggestions and then come up with modifications or new possibilities.

3. *Summarize chosen alternatives, ask for confirmation, and request that the teacher restate final choices.* Verification that both supervisor and teacher have the same understanding of the final choices is crucial. Two people can easily interpret the same words differently or hear different words. Therefore, if each party repeats his or her understanding, any misunderstandings or differences in perceptions can be cleared up before action is taken.

4. *Set up a follow-up plan and meeting.* A concrete plan (written is preferable) and a scheduled meeting are the only ways that two very busy professionals can be sure of the follow-through that is crucial to the success of any plan.

Scenario 2

Ann has been teaching at New Hope for 10 years. Her reputation is that of a cooperative, collaborative, and effective teacher. Elena is therefore surprised to notice in her daily walk-around that Jorge and Carlos, two new ELL arrivals, don't seem involved in the class. Elena decides to stop by during Ann's free period to find out what has been preventing her from providing support to Jorge and Carlos.

Elena: Hi, Ann. How's it going? I know that you are already aware of our need to focus on our ELL students. I've been discussing with faculty how they are doing with their new arrivals. I noticed that Jorge and Carlos are in your math class. How are they doing?

Ann: I'm happy you stopped by. With the start of classes, I haven't been able to focus on Carlos and Jorge as much as I would like to. Since Carlos has stronger English skills, I thought he might be able to assist Jorge, whose English knowledge is very limited. Carlos seems to be more interested in socializing than in math, and rather than helping Jorge, he seems to be distracting him. Given that it is a very social class, I have been looking mostly at whole-class strategies.

Elena: So what you're saying is that the combination of new scholastic-year adjustments and monitoring the whole class's socializing has limited your individual involvement with Carlos and Jorge. Is this accurate?

Ann: Sounds right to me.

Elena: Well, I'm pleased that you have been addressing the "lively" socializing of this class. Tell me more about Carlos and Jorge. Maybe we can figure out something together.

Ann: Jorge is lost, and now Carlos is making the situation worse. I called their homes—to no avail. No one speaks English. I spoke to the ESL teacher, who confirmed what I already knew. He also mentioned that their actual math skills are pretty good. There are two Spanish-speaking girls in the class whose English skills are stronger, but whose math skills are not at grade level. Maybe if I seat them together, the girls can assist the boys with their English skills and the boys can help with the girls' math. Mercedes is very quiet and probably wouldn't respond to Carlos's antics. Alma's English is solid, so she can work with Jorge.

Elena: Those ideas seem like an effective first step. Since Alma and Mercedes need math support, I can place all four of them together in the extended-day program. That way we can also make sure that their homework gets completed. Let's ask Ana if she can call their home. The family may be able to support more if they can communicate with a Spanish-speaking person.

Ann: I'm sure that both of those strategies will help. I also think that if I am having difficulty with Carlos and Jorge, the less experienced teachers in our grade also need ideas. I can ask if we can devote a part of our next grade-level meeting to discussing our ELL students.

Elena: Your suggestion is very important. If you address your ELL students at the grade level, I will tackle the problem at the school level. Would you like me to attend your next meeting?

Ann: I'd prefer meeting with them on my own the first time. Two of our grade-level teachers are new and might feel intimidated if you're there. I'd like to get as much honest information as possible.

Elena: Fine. Just provide me with written or verbal feedback following the meeting to help me address the problem schoolwide. So, let's see what we've agreed on. First, you'll pair up Carlos with Mercedes and Jorge with Alma. They will all go to the extended-day program to work on math and English skills. Ana will call Carlos's and Jorge's families to seek support in Spanish. You will also request that at least part of the next grade-level meeting be devoted to ELL students. And, you'll provide me feedback so that I can incorporate your results into a school plan.

Ann: Sounds like a go for me. Our grade-level meeting is next Wednesday.

Elena: I'll set up the afterschool program today and ask Ana to get in contact with you. Could we meet here during your prep on Thursday so that you can give me feedback on your grade-level meeting?

Ann: Sure. My prep is third period on Thursday. See you then.

> ### Reflection
>
> *How does Elena make sure she understands what Ann explains? Does Elena approach Ann differently than she approaches Martha? If so, how? How do Ann and Elena deal with their differences?*

II. The Collaborative Approach

In the collaborative approach, the goal is to resolve a problem or reach a goal through shared decision making. The supervisor encourages the teacher to develop his or her ideas first to allow maximum ownership. Nonetheless, the brainstorming and problem solving are shared, and disagreement is encouraged, with assurances that a mutual solution will be reached. The conference always ends with a restatement of agreed-on plans and the setting up of a follow-up meeting. Unresolved issues can be included in the planning process and revisited at the follow-up session.

1. *Identify the problem from the teacher's perspective, soliciting as much clarifying information as possible.* With the exception of some new teachers and those with problematic practices, the supervisor wants the teacher to initiate the discussion from his or her perspective. The more information provided, the clearer the situation for both parties. Therefore, a more complete description can be drawn out with prompts, that is, eye contact and encouraging open body language and nonverbal cues, paraphrasing, probing questions, and phrases such as "Tell me more," "Uh-huh," "I see," and "I understand."

2. *Reflect back on what you've heard for accuracy.* It is crucial that you verify that you've heard accurately the content and perspective of the teacher.

A summary of what you understood, with the teacher's verification of what you heard, can avoid many misunderstandings and problems down the road. You may feel that you sound silly repeating; rest assured that the teacher is hanging on your every word to be sure that you heard and understood.

3. *Begin collaborative brainstorming, asking the teacher for his or her ideas first.* If the supervisor proposes options first, the teacher might not try to develop his or her own ideas and might just follow what the supervisor suggests. Because the teacher is the one most familiar with the situation, it is important to allow him or her to build on that knowledge or to decide to construct a different or new resolution.

4. *Problem solve through a sharing and discussion of options.* One of the greatest challenges to a supervisor in a collaborative approach is to encourage disagreement convincingly. Few teachers are accustomed to administrators fostering challenges and encouraging risk taking. Asking for the teacher's suggestions is a first step. Promoting an open dialogue about the options is the second step.

5. *Agree on a plan and follow-up meeting.* In the complex lives of teachers and administrators, a written plan on agreed-on solutions and those yet to be resolved will save a lot of time in the long run. What often seems time-consuming can be cost-effective in the final analysis. Taking the time to write out a plan and set up the next appointment is the essential concluding step.

Scenario 3

Will has been teaching for many years. He has his routines down to a science. He teaches in a traditional manner, peppering his well-organized lectures with amusing anecdotes. He tends to avoid new initiatives and believes that if "it ain't broke, don't fix it." As the new kid on the block, Elena wants to solicit cooperation from this veteran teacher without his feeling imposed upon. For this reason, she chooses the self-directed approach to try to encourage him to become involved with the ELL challenge.

Elena: How's it going so far, Will?

Will: It's always fine behind my closed door. It's what goes on outside my room that can infiltrate my classroom.

Elena: So, you feel that your classroom is under control, but outside events are having an effect on your teaching. Do you want to explain that a little further for me?

Will: As you know, we've had an influx of non-English-speaking students. I believe in maintaining the same high standards for all students, but if these new arrivals aren't learning English fast enough in their ESL classes, I'm left in the lurch.

Elena: I understand what a challenge it is to maintain your standards with such a varied student body. As I've been visiting the seventh-grade classes, I've been particularly concerned with the difficulties that Jorge and Carlos seem to be having.

Will: I'm ready to give up on them. I've told them to come after school for extra help, but they don't come. I even called their homes, but either no one answered or no one spoke English. Their ESL teacher must not be doing much with them. You should speak to him.

Elena: I hear your frustration with their lack of response and your inability to communicate with their families. I commend you for extending yourself. Since you are an experienced, effective teacher, do you have any other suggestions that might work for you and perhaps for all the teachers?

Will: Since it has become a schoolwide problem, I think that the initiative has to come from you, our new leader. We have so many new teachers in the seventh grade, I don't think they could be much help. The only thing that I can think of is that I could meet with Ann and we might be able to lead a discussion at our grade-level meeting.

Elena: Great minds think alike! That is exactly what Ann suggested. Could you talk to her about planning for the meeting? I could release both of you for an hour prior to the grade-level meeting so that you could create an agenda.

Will: I guess we could. What are *you* going to do about the influx of ELL students?

Elena: I'm hoping to get feedback from grade-level meetings like yours and devote our next faculty meetings to professional development on ELL learners. I also think that sharing the strategies the different grade teams come up with will be another initial step. Addressing our new arrivals will be a long-term goal. I look forward to the support of experienced teachers like yourself to help get this initiative off the ground.

Will: Just don't make me the head of any committee. I'm not really into this collaborative stuff. I just want to keep getting the results I am used to getting.

Elena: I hear you. Can you, Ann, and I meet after your grade-level meeting next week to see what you come up with that I can incorporate into the faculty meeting?

Will: I think that Ann and I have a common prep on Thursday. We could meet then.

Elena: Thanks so much for your assistance. I really look forward to hearing the ideas that emerge from the grade-level meeting.

> **Reflection**
>
> *Why doesn't Elena start out mentioning to Will the problems with ELL students? What does Elena do to avoid negativity? What specific words and phrases does she use to encourage Will's participation?*

III. The Self-Directed Approach

Key Steps: Self-Directed Approach

1. Listen carefully to the teacher's initial statement.

2. Reflect back on your understanding of the problem.

3. Constantly clarify and reflect until the real problem is identified.

4. Have the teacher problem solve and explore the consequences of various actions.

5. The teacher commits to a decision and firms up a plan.

6. The supervisor restates the teacher's plan and sets up a follow-up meeting.

The goal of the self-directed approach is to enable the teacher to reflect on the problem, draw conclusions, and construct his or her own alternatives. The supervisor serves more as a coach who does not express his or her point of view or ideas unless the teacher specifically requests them. The supervisor functions as the facilitator of the teacher's development of his or her own ideas. The outcome should always be the teacher's autonomous decision. This approach is appropriate for a very knowledgeable and often experienced teacher. It also can be successful in providing a sense of ownership when the teacher is the primary person responsible for carrying out a decision or when the decision or problem at hand has limited ramifications. A less experienced, but creative, promising teacher can also benefit from the guided ownership that this approach affords.

1. *Listen carefully to the teacher's initial statement.* As in the collaborative approach, the starting point is the teacher's perspective of the situation. The techniques and prompts are the same as in the collaborative approach: eye contact, body language, paraphrasing, verbal cues, and probing questions.

2. *Reflect back on your understanding of the problem.* Again, as in the collaborative approach, verification that you have clearly and accurately understood the teacher's perspective is essential. Reflecting back on what has been heard begins to accomplish this task. In addition, paraphrasing can clarify any uncertainty the supervisor may have about what has been expressed and can even allow the teacher to distance himself or herself from what was said and reflect on it from the outside.

3. *Constantly clarify and reflect until the real problem is identified.* The crucial prerequisite to solving a problem is to conceptualize accurately what the problem is. Solutions often are hidden in the identification of the problem, thereby limiting the range of resolutions. Thus, the real need must be ascertained. For example, your husband says he's taking the car, and you have a meeting. Your need is not necessarily to take the car but to find a way to get to the meeting. The facilitator's role is to use the reflecting/ prompting/questioning process judiciously to permit the teacher to arrive at a crystallization of the need.

4. *Have the teacher problem solve and explore the consequences of various actions.* Once the need has been identified, simply ask the teacher to think of possible alternatives. Assist the teacher in walking through the steps, process, and consequences of each action. Ask questions such as "What would happen if . . . ?" or "How would you . . . ?" Then ask the teacher to explore the advantages and disadvantages of the alternatives. At this point, the teacher may be ready to respond to concluding questions, that is, "Which do you think will work best? Why? In what ways would it be better?" If the teacher declares that he or she is at a loss, you can ask what he or she has done in the past that has worked.

5. *The teacher commits to a decision and firms up a plan.* Once the teacher makes a choice, you can request a plan and encourage a walk-through of the next steps. "What, who, when, how, where" may be part of the plan, or the provision of simple planning forms that the teacher can complete.

6. *The supervisor restates the teacher's plan and sets up a follow-up meeting.* It is important for the supervisor to restate the teacher's plan before ending the meeting. This verification will avoid future misunderstandings. In addition, even though the teacher owns the plan, the scheduling of a follow-up meeting to see how it's working should always conclude the session.

Table 2.3 includes a summary of each of the three interpersonal approaches to supervision.

Table 2.3 Approach Comparison

Direct Informational	Collaborative	Self-Directed
1. Supervisor identifies problem, then solicits clarifying information.	1. Supervisor seeks to identify problem from teacher's perspective.	1. Supervisor asks teacher to identify problem.
2. Supervisor offers solutions and then requests input.	2. Collaborative brainstorming for solutions.	2. Clarification and reflection until teacher identifies problem.
3. Supervisor summarizes and then asks for confirmation.	3. Problem solve through sharing and discussion.	3. Teacher problem solves and explores consequences.
4. Teacher restates final choices.	4. Joint agreement on plan.	4. Teacher commits to decision.

GUIDELINES FOR REFLECTIVE PRACTICE

We believe that learning is most effective when the learner is actively involved in the learning process, when it takes place as a collaborative activity (Bridges, 1992), and when reflection is the means of observing, analyzing, considering, and reconceptualizing the experience. As we mentioned in Chapter 1, the process used in reflective practice can guide our development of new skills and change ingrained behaviors that may be inconsistent with internalization of the new skills. We first look at the stages of reflective practice and then discuss how they guide our development of supervisory skills.

Reflective practice is based primarily on two learning theories:

- Experiential learning theory, popularly associated with Dewey and Piaget, maintains that learning is most effective and likely to lead to behavior change when it begins with experience, especially problematic experience (Osterman & Kottkamp, 2004).
- The situated cognition perspective that Bridges (1992) popularized in problem-based learning argues that learning is most effective when the learner is actively involved in the learning process, when it takes place as a collaborative rather than an isolated activity, and when it is in a context relevant to the learner. This dialectic and cyclical process consists of four stages: experience, observation and reflection, abstract reconceptualization, and experimentation (Kolb, 1984).

In reflective practice, the first stage is to identify a problematic situation; the second is to reflect on the problem or experience—preferably in a collaborative, cooperative environment; the third is to consider alternate ways of thinking and acting; and the fourth is to test the reconceptualized behavior and assumptions. The cycle can begin again with the new concrete experience (see Figure 2.1).

Reflective practice serves two principal purposes in this book:

1. Every idea, tool, and technique that fosters internalization of the new learning is accompanied by directions for reflective practice in the course classroom and on site.

Figure 2.1   Experiential Learning Cycle

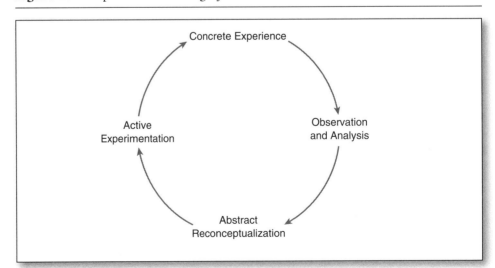

Source: K. F. Osterman and R. B. Kottkamp. (2004). *Reflective Practice for Educators: Professional Development to Improve Student Learning* (2nd ed.). Thousand Oaks, CA: Corwin. Reprinted with permission.

2. We hope to instill the ongoing experience of reflecting individually and collaboratively on developing skills as a habit that you carry with you in your personal and professional lives and that you model as an educational leader.

Before you try out your new skills in a classroom or with another teacher, it is important that you have the opportunity to experience and reflect on them in a safe environment. We have developed a method for you to role-play all the interpersonal skills in this book. This method can also serve as a model for experiencing and reflecting on any communication skills or problematic situations you might want to rehearse. The only tools you need are two people who interact and a reflector with a watch or timer. We recommend that you use the "Fishbowl" method outlined in Resource B to model each role play. This method involves student volunteers who model each approach before the whole class attempts each role play. View the accompanying video that models the role plays before practicing.

For the purposes of developing supervisory skills, the model presented is limited to the roles of observer, observee, and reflector. We first outline the roles and responsibilities in the process (see Table 2.4) and then provide specific feedback guidelines for the reflector (see Table 2.5).

Table 2.4   Reflective Practice Process—Three Steps, Three Responsibilities

Steps	Observer* (Person Practicing)	Observee*	Reflector
1. Setting the scene (5 min.)	• Describes situation • Describes other person and possible reactions • Reviews steps on card and mentally rehearses	• Listens carefully • Asks clarifying questions • Mentally rehearses responses	• Starts monitoring time • Takes notes on key points • Reviews steps on card
2. Practice (10 min.)	• Practices each step	• Responds based on the description of the other person	• Observes practice • Takes notes • Keeps practice on track • Monitors time
3. Feedback and reflections (10 min.)	• Provides personal reflections first • Follows reflection guidelines	• Expresses personal feedback and reflections second • Follows reflection guidelines	• Facilitates reflections and feedback • Provides personal feedback and reflections last • Gives notes to person practicing

* Either the observer or the observee can present the situation for the role play.

Source: Copyright 1999 AchieveGlobal, Inc. Used with permission. All rights reserved.

Table 2.5 Reflector's Feedback Guidelines

1. Ask:
   • The supervisor/observer: What do you think went well in each of the steps?
   • The teacher: What do you feel the supervisor/observer did effectively?
   • The reflector: Offer your reflections on what went well.

2. Ask:
   • The supervisor/observer: What do you think needs improvement?
   • The teacher: What areas do you feel need improvement?
   • The reflector: Provide your feedback.

3. Ask:
   • The supervisor/observer: How would you implement these changes?
   • The teacher: What suggestions do you have for future interactions?
   • The reflector:
     o Provide suggestions.
     o Ask the supervisor/observer for questions or comments.
     o Give your written reflections to supervisor.

Note: To promote self-reflection, make sure that the reflector asks the person role-playing the supervisor/observer for input first. Also, separate carefully the response to "What needs improvement?" from suggestions. The problematic areas need to be thought out before solutions are addressed.

Reflective Practice

Class Practice

During the next three weeks, each of you is going to create three scenarios. If possible, model the scenarios on existing challenges or dilemmas currently occurring in your school or on real-life situations with which you are familiar.

- The first scenario involves a supervisor and either a new teacher or a teacher in difficulty for whom the directive informational approach is appropriate.
- The second scenario takes place between you and a colleague who is an experienced and/or effective teacher with whom you feel comfortable using the collaborative approach.
- The third scenario involves an interaction with a teacher who is so knowledgeable that he or she just needs prompting to come up with solutions or when you feel it would be beneficial for the teacher to solve the problem on his or her own using the self-directed approach.

Each week, you should practice a different approach in the course. Observe the appropriate role play on the video. Then, three volunteers will model the approach in front of the class before breaking into groups of three. Videotaping at least the three volunteers is recommended. It is very useful for other groups to volunteer to be videotaped so they can observe themselves on tape in the privacy of their homes. All students will have the opportunity to role-play the observer for each approach.

Site Practice

Each week, after you have practiced an approach, try it out by solving a site-based challenge. Where feasible, look for classroom-based problems as the basis of communication. Keep your detachable cards from the back of the book available so that you can refer to them when the occasion arises. Be certain to reflect on how the interchange worked. What went well? What could be improved? What would you do differently next time? Take notes to facilitate class discussion of your experiences.

SUMMARY

In this chapter, we began to lay the groundwork for developing the interpersonal skills that are a prerequisite for all effective supervisory practice. Case studies introduced the three interpersonal approaches we recommend for providing feedback: the directive informational approach, the collaborative approach, and the self-directed approach. Before actually learning and practicing these approaches, the listening skills integral to the three approaches were outlined: phrases that show attentive listening, nonverbal cues, and reflecting and clarifying techniques. Class- and site-based exercises for practicing the listening and feedback approaches were accompanied by the introduction of the reflective practice process and guidelines that will be used throughout the book. With these skills and techniques under our belts, we can now tackle the observational tools and techniques for observing classroom teaching and learning that will be presented in Chapter 3.

NOTES

1. *People Skills* by Robert Bolton (1979) is an excellent source of many communication skills.

2. The approaches in this section are adapted from Glickman, Gordon, and Ross-Gordon (2010).

3

Observation Tools and Techniques

You can observe a lot by watching.

—Yogi Berra

CHAPTER OVERVIEW

1. Supervision Case Study

2. Ten Guidelines of Observation

3. Summary of Tools and Techniques
   a. By Approach
   b. By Content

4. Thirty-two Quantitative Observation Tools

5. Ten Qualitative Observation Tools

6. Summary
   a. Reflective Clinical Supervision in a Standards-Based Environment

7. Conclusion

A major assumption of the authors is that judicious use of reliable and easy-to-use observation techniques can increase a teacher's awareness of classroom behavior and therefore become instrumental in improving the teaching and learning process. To this end, a variety of teaching tools and techniques for use in the classroom are included in this chapter. These tools are by no means a complete compilation; rather, they are a sampling. The authors encourage you to begin thinking about your individual needs in the classroom and creating your own tools. This chapter will help you begin the process.

Teaching is a challenging art and science. Complicating matters are the incredibly fast-paced interactions between teachers and students and between students and students. Given the complex nature of classroom life (Jackson, 1990), tools for systematically recording classroom interactions are especially useful in assisting teachers in understanding classroom behavior more fully and becoming aware of it (Good & Brophy, 2002). The use of observation instruments, however, has been criticized because of its presumed directive, behaviorist, and positivist orientation (e.g., Eisner, 1994). We heartily agree that use of observation instruments can be problematic when directly connected to evaluation. We believe that "life in classrooms" is context bound, situationally determined, and complex. The supervisor is not and should not be the overseer or prescriber but rather the guide, facilitator, or collaborator. Relying on enhanced communication and shared understandings, the supervisor can effectively use observation instruments to encourage interpersonal and collegial relationships.

A major assumption of this chapter is that judicious use of reliable and easy-to-use observation techniques can increase a teacher's awareness of classroom behavior. Moreover, we would be negligent if we didn't include observation instrumentation in a volume devoted to instructional improvement. Through the use of these observation tools and techniques, supervisors and others involved with the supervision process will work more ably with teachers to improve instruction and, hence, promote student achievement.

Another major assumption in this chapter is that instructional improvement is best encouraged through instructional dialogue. Supervision, as a reflective process, is essentially concerned with enhancing teacher thought and commitment to improving instruction. Through the use of observation instruments, supervisors or those concerned with supervision are able to promote such improvement.

An additional assumption of this chapter is that instructional improvement is most effective when the observational process includes both observation of the focus that the teacher is implementing and the student response to that instructional approach. We have therefore paired together, wherever appropriate, a tool for observing the teacher and another with the same focus to observe the student(s).

Many books or parts of books are devoted to describing various observation instruments, strategies, and techniques (e.g., Acheson & Gall, 1997; Boehm & Weinberg, 1997; Borich, 2002; Pajak, 2000; Willerman et al., 1991). From our experience, we have found that some of these systems are difficult to implement. We have selected for this chapter only those observation tools and techniques that we have personally experienced as easy to implement and

Microlab

Think of different kinds of observation instruments or strategies you have personally experienced. Which seemed most effective? Which seemed least effective? What did you learn from these experiences? What was the impact on students?

effective toward promoting that all-important instructional conversation between supervisors and teachers.[1]

We should note again that many observation instruments are not discussed in this chapter. The reader interested in an overview of other systems should consult Pajak (2000). We have found that the creation of new tools or the adaptation of existing ones to fit the context or a specific need, especially if created in collaboration with the teacher, can greatly facilitate improvement.

You can view additional tools online if you search under the instructional focus or strategy that interests you. However, since most of the general sites dedicated to observational tools are oriented toward multifocal, monitoring, and evaluation purposes, we caution you to analyze a tool carefully before using or adapting it.

This chapter begins with a transcript of an actual sixth-grade lesson that will be referred to throughout the chapter. Quantitative and qualitative observation instruments highlight the remainder of the chapter. Each instrument is discussed in detail, and completed examples are provided for implementation in the chapter. Practice sheets can be found in Appendix D. Reflective practice activities will enhance your skill development.

SUPERVISION SCENARIO

Mario Tommasi has just completed his advanced certificate program at a local college and received his state certification as a school administrator and supervisor. A teacher for 10 years, Mario applies to a nearby township for a vice principalship. The board is impressed with his extensive teaching experience and letters of recommendation, as well as his keen insight into instructional improvement. Mario is hired.

The school to which he is assigned is William Heard Kilpatrick Middle School, which has a population of 1,200 pupils in grades 6 through 8. The school is located in an urban section of the Northeast, and the ethnic makeup of the student body is 45% African American, 40% Hispanic American, 10% Asian American, and 5% others. Mario discovers that teacher morale is quite low, in large measure due to the autocratic practices of the former vice principal, who used strict traditional methods of teacher evaluation and frequently observed teachers without notice. The former supervisor would write lengthy, albeit well-written reports criticizing the teachers' methods and urging them to comply with his recommendations.

Mario is sympathetic toward their resentment of the supervisory practices they have experienced. Initially, he decides to establish rapport with his teachers.

He begins by communicating a vision. He acts in a manner that is representative of an inclusive leader; he listens, validates teachers' feelings, includes teachers in the decision-making process, and collaborates. He sets goals that meet the needs of both supervisor and teachers.

Once trust in the form of a collegial relationship is established, he believes that instructional matters, such as observation and the improvement of teacher performance, will follow naturally.

Six months pass, and Mario feels proud of the rapport and mutual respect he has developed with his teachers. Teachers, too, are happy that the former assistant principal is gone, and they consider Mario to be congenial, articulate, and trustworthy. Mario is ready to model instruction.

At a recent sixth-grade conference, Mario presents an overview of his supervisory approach: "Student achievement can be enhanced only when we, as colleagues, discuss matters of instruction in an open, forthright manner." Mario continues,

The first step toward instructional improvement is for us to describe what is happening in the classroom when we teach. I'd like to present several observation tools and techniques that can help us begin to dialogue about instruction in a nonjudgmental, cooperative way. I'd like to introduce some of these tools to you and then conduct a demonstration lesson in which you will have the opportunity to observe me. You can use any of these techniques you want.

Microlab

Can you think of other ways to build trust and confidence with teachers? What do you think of Mario's approach to supervision?

Teachers enthusiastically listen to Mario, and several teachers welcome him into their classrooms.

Over the course of the next year and a half, Mario makes great progress in demonstrating that supervision is less about highlighting teacher deficiencies and more about collegial discussion of instructional matters. Both the principal and associate superintendent remark that a "culture of improvement" is clearly evident in the sixth grade. Teacher morale is high, pupil behavior is markedly improved, and test scores are on the rise.

Not all teachers, however, are partaking of Mario's "quiet revolution" at Kilpatrick Middle School. Clara Weingarten, a tenured social studies teacher with more than 28 years of classroom experience, is conspicuously absent during Mario's many staff development sessions and instructional workshops. At a recent after-school faculty conference, however, she lamented the change in the student body, claiming that "these kids today aren't the same as before. They're rowdy, lazy, and disrespectful of authority."

Clara, realizing Mario's growing popularity and effectiveness, finally confides to him that she is at her wits' end. "Can you help?" she asks Mario in a genuine manner. Mario and Clara meet several times during her prep periods to discuss not only instructional strategies but the changing student population and demographics of the community. Their informal chats continue over the next several weeks. Discussions include many different topics, such as observation techniques and teaching strategies. They share their experiences and expertise. Fully cognizant of the fact that Clara has 18 more years of teaching experience than he, Mario nevertheless suggests one day that Clara video a lesson on her own. Never having done so, she could then watch the video, and if she feels she would like "another set of eyes," she is free to call on him. Call on Mario she does. After watching the video, Mario feels it wise to transcribe the video before he meets with Clara.

The transcription follows (visual descriptions are added to enhance readability):

Class: Sixth grade; 16 girls and 16 boys; reading scores are on grade level

Teacher: Clara Weingarten, tenured with 28 years of experience

Description of room: Movable desks are arranged in concentric arcs for this lesson. Student work is exhibited around the room with headings for each topic. A daily plan is outlined on the right panel of the chalkboard. A map of the world is hanging from the center of the wall above the chalkboard.

Curriculum area: Social studies

Topic: The United Nations; lesson in current events given on December 10

Mrs. Weingarten:	What famous place in New York City is having its 68th birthday this year?
Ronald:	(volunteering) The United Nations.
Mrs. Weingarten:	What do you think we should discuss about the United Nations in class today?
Juanita:	(volunteering) Where it's located?
Warren:	(calling out) What it's supposed to do?
Mrs. Weingarten:	Class, what is it supposed to do?

(At this point she writes on the board: "Can the United Nations Prevent War?")

Huan:	(volunteering) I visited the U.N. with my class when I was in the fourth grade in the school that I came from.
Mrs. Weingarten:	What did you see there?
Huan:	It was a tall, flat building with a lot of windows. There was a smaller, round building, too.
Kevin:	I saw the Assembly on television when the president spoke to them on the 68th birthday of the U.N. It was on a news program.
Mrs. Weingarten:	Good. But let's get back to the question I wrote on the board at the beginning of the lesson.

(She asks the class to read the question aloud, which they do.)

Jessie:	(raising his hand) When countries want to go to war, they talk about it in the Assembly. I guess then they vote on what to do about it in the Security Council.
Natasha:	(raising her hand) But when Russia and the United States talk to each other about keeping the peace, they

	don't speak to each other at the United Nations. Like at Geneva. I saw that on television, too!
Mrs. Weingarten:	That's an excellent observation, Natasha. Class, what's the answer we could give for Natasha's question? (No one responds.) Because problems can be settled in many ways, including the United Nations. (pause) So what do we know about the United Nations? Do you think it can really prevent World War III?
Susan:	(volunteering) Yes, when it gets countries who want to go to war to stop.
Mrs. Weingarten:	That's right, when it gets countries that want to go to war to stop.
George:	(raising his hand) So how come Israel was at war with the Arabs? And what about Bosnia and other places?
Mrs. Weingarten:	Yes, but it's still not World War III. (pointing to the question on the chalkboard) Let's see whether we can answer this question today. How can we go about doing this?
Warren:	(volunteering) Well, we've had World War I and World War II, but so far we haven't had World War III.
Mrs. Weingarten:	Very good. World War I happened between 1914 and 1918, and World War II took place between 1939 and 1945. How do you know that World War II ended in 1945? We have all been given a clue to this question at the beginning of this lesson today.

(Teacher looks around the room, waits a short while, with no response forthcoming.) Because it was 68 years ago. Don't you remember what we talked about at the beginning of the lesson? (raising her voice) What did we talk about? Let's try to summarize what we have spoken about up to now.

Kevin:	(volunteering) The United Nations is 68 years old this year.
Mrs. Weingarten:	Rochelle, can you tell us what that means?
Rochelle:	I don't know.
Mrs. Weingarten:	It means that the United Nations got started at the end of World War II to make sure that World War III would never happen.
Tim:	(raising his hand) How can they do that?
Mrs. Weingarten:	They have two sections—the Security Council and the General Assembly. Their job is to try to make sure that we don't have World War III. (She then writes "Security Council" and "General Assembly" on the board.) Does anyone know how many members there are in the Security Council?

Tatiana: (volunteering) Russia and the United States, because they are the two biggest nations and they are the ones that could start World War III by attacking each other. I heard someone say that on television.

Mrs. Weingarten: No, there are 15 members in the Security Council, and 5 of them are there permanently, forever. The other 10 get elected by the General Assembly from time to time. The General Assembly has all the members, 159, each one of them having one vote. (pause) Class, class, which one— the General Assembly or the Security Council—votes on preventing war? Paul, we haven't heard from you yet.

Paul: I guess it's the General Assembly, because all the members are in it.

Mrs. Weingarten: No, it's the Security Council, because 5 of the 15 members are the great nations: the United States, Russia, China, England, and France. (She writes these countries' names on the board under the title "Permanent Members of the United Nations.") If one of these five says, "No," the United States can't take action against a nation that is making trouble. That is called the veto power. (pause) Here is an assignment to be done at home. I want you to look through newspapers and magazines and clip pictures and articles about the United Nations. You have one week to do this, and next Monday, when we have our next weekly current events lesson, we'll go over your clippings. You see, there is much more to learn about what the United Nations has done for the world. There are many other things it gets into besides trying to keep the peace. (pause) Now, let's sum up what we learned today.

Vivian: That the United Nations could stop World War III before it begins.

Mrs. Weingarten: Thank you. Good. Now, let's turn to the homework that was assigned to you last night. Take out your textbooks, as well as your homework.

Microlab

How do you think the former assistant principal would have handled the feedback conversation with Clara? What would he have said? How do you think Mario will handle the feedback conversation with Clara? What will he say? What concrete steps would he take to engage this teacher in instructional dialogue for improvement? How would you handle the feedback conversation?

Analysis

Based on our view of supervision, we maintain that Mario is not likely to make subjective judgments about Clara's style of teaching. She has been reluctant to engage in instructional improvement discussions, but now, for the first time she has requested some assistance. Mario sees this as an invaluable opportunity to encourage this teacher to become more reflective about her teaching practice. His goal is to facilitate Clara's reflection on her lesson—to focus more on her lesson aim, questioning techniques, or motivational strategies rather than attributing student lack of motivation and achievement to demographic changes in the community.

The next step Mario takes is to enable Clara to become aware of how her behavior and teaching style contribute to her classroom effectiveness. Mario realizes that this experienced teacher will view any feedback he might offer with suspicion and, possibly, resentment.

Seeing a film of oneself teaching is certainly an eye-opening experience. If you haven't had the opportunity to do so recently, we suggest you do.

> **Reflection**
>
> *How would you recommend that Mario approach Clara? Would you use video? Why or why not? What other ways could the videos be used?*

Practice

Videotape your next lesson and watch the video at home. What's your reaction? After you get over the initial shock, watch the tape the following week. Imagine that this lesson was not your own. What aspects of the lesson were effective, and which areas need improvement? What strategies would you employ to enable this teacher to help herself or himself? Record your reflections and share them in small groups in class. Please note that after you read the later chapters in this book, you'll have a better idea of how to analyze your lesson. Still, this activity is useful at this point.

Watching a video of your lesson, however, may not be very productive. Interactions in the lesson occur too quickly and are too complex for you or anyone else to pick up teaching subtleties such as effective use of wait time, number of higher-level questions asked, or distribution of questions to all ethnic groups in the class. We believe that videos are useful for enhancing instructional improvement only if specific teaching behaviors can be highlighted, analyzed, and discussed.

Being familiar with the use of various observation tools and techniques, Mario encourages Clara to choose an observation tool to increase her awareness of what is occurring in her classroom. The ultimate goal is for Clara to be able to self-reflect.

Before Clara is able to become self-reflective, she will have to learn how to collect evidence, know what behaviors to look for, and have a conceptual framework to guide her analysis. The remainder of this chapter is devoted to introducing observation instruments that Mario could use with Clara, or with any teacher for that matter. Each observation tool is presented, applied to Clara's lesson, if applicable, and practiced through the use of reflective activities and practice sessions.

Before we introduce and explicate each tool, see Figure 3.1 for several guiding principles about observation should be kept in mind.

> **Reflection**
>
> *How might your biases affect how you interpret what you see, for example, in Clara's classroom? Discuss your answers with a colleague.*

FORTY-TWO TOOLS AND TECHNIQUES FOR OBSERVATION

As we mentioned earlier, many excellent observation systems exist. Our intention is not to review all the systems for observation; rather, it is to introduce

Figure 3.1 Ten Guidelines of Observations

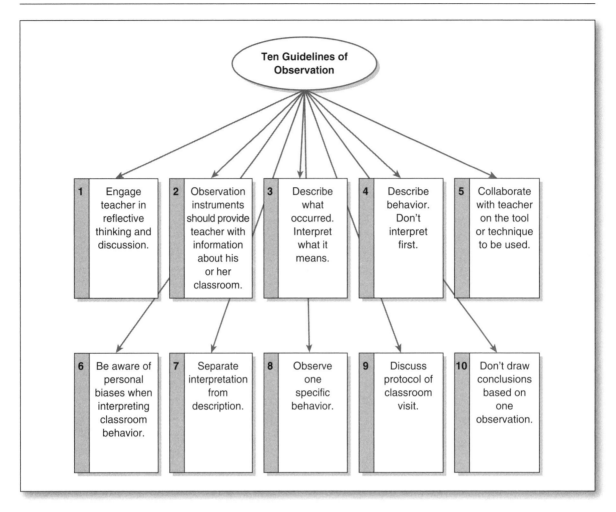

those tools for observation that we personally have used and think can be incorporated easily into almost any classroom situation. The teachers in our classes constantly adapt the tools provided and create new ones, often during the planning conference in collaboration with the teachers they are observing for the course.

Two major categories of observation tools exist: quantitative and qualitative. *Quantitative* approaches reveal the *number* and the ratios of teacher–student behaviors; *qualitative* approaches reveal the *nature* of the observed behaviors. In other words, one category of tools reduces data into fixed or preestablished groups, and the other category describes a situation so that common themes may emerge. In fact, we sometimes offer a qualitative and a quantitative tool for the same focus.[2]

Both approaches are valid. Each provides a different and unique lens for viewing a situation or a classroom. Look at Figure 3.2. What do you see? . . . Ah, so there may be more to "see" and "understand" from a different perspective! Well, that's what each approach offers—just a different, not better, perspective from which to view a classroom.

Figure 3.2 Do You See a Musician or a Girl's Face?

From Girl or Musician, http://www.sandeepkejriwal.com/illusions.htm. Used with permission.

We have also organized as many tools as possible in two parts: 1) Primary focus on teacher, and 2) Primary focus on students—two different perspectives on teaching and learning.

Table 3.1 provides an outline of the tools and techniques we discuss next.

Table 3.1 Summary of Observation Tools

Tool #	Table or Figure	Description of Instrument
Quantitative Tools		
1a	Table 3.2	Teacher Verbal Behaviors
1b	Table 3.3	Student Responses to Verbal Behaviors
2a	Table 3.4	Teacher Questions Using Bloom's Taxonomy
2b	Table 3.5	Student Responses to Questions Indicating Bloom's Taxonomy
3a	Table 3.6	Teacher Questions Using Webb's Depth of Knowledge
3b	Table 3.7	Student Responses to Questions Indicating Webb's Depth of Knowledge
4a	Table 3.8	Student On-Task and Off-Task Behaviors
4b	Figure 3.3	Diagram of Verbal Interactions
5a	Table 3.9	Gardner's Multiple Intelligences
5b	Table 3.10	Student Use of Gardner's Multiple Intelligences
6	Table 3.11	Hunter's Steps in Lesson Planning
7a	Table 3.12	Group Work Criteria
7b	Table 3.13	Group Performance: Assessment of Individual Participation
8a	Figure 3.4	Diagram of Teacher Space Utilization
8b	Figure 3.5	Diagram of Student Space Utilization

(Continued)

(Continued)

9	Figure 3.6	Feedback
10	Table 3.14	Teacher–Pupil Interaction
11	Table 3.15	Indicators of Culturally Diverse Learners
12	Table 3.16	Strategies for Diverse Learners
13	Table 3.17	Accommodations and Modifications for English-Language Learners
14	Table 3.18	The Differentiated Classroom
15	Table 3.19	Students' Construction of Meaning on Their Own
16	Table 3.20	Learning Centers
17	Table 3.21	Co-teaching: Push-in Model (initial)
18	Table 3.22	Strategies for Students With Speech and Language Impairments
19	Table 3.23	Guided Reading
20	Table 3.24	Read-Aloud/Story Time
21	Table 3.25	Teacher Language During Center-Based Learning in Pre-Kindergarten Classrooms
22	Table 3.26	Teacher Encouragement of Students' Problem-Solving Skills and Reasoning (Mathematics Common Core Standards)
23	Table 3.27	Teacher Encouragement of Mathematical Communication During Problem Solving (Mathematics Common Core Standards)
24a	Table 3.28	Teacher Behaviors Keyed to Accountable Talk
24b	Table 3.29	Student Behaviors Keyed to Accountable Talk
Qualitative Tools		
25a		Detached Open-Ended Narrative
25b		Participant Open-Ended Observation
26		Child-Centered Learning Observation
27	Table 3.30	Nonverbal Techniques
28		Questioning Techniques
29		Strategies for Diverse Learners
30		Differentiated Instruction
31	Table 3.31	Guided Reading
32		Team Teaching in the Inclusion or General Education Classroom
33		Classroom Assessment in the Differentiated Classroom

Summary of Observation Tools by Focus

I. Categorical Frequency Tools

    1a. Teacher Verbal Behaviors (Table 3.2)

    1b. Student Responses to Teacher Verbal Behaviors (Table 3.3)

2a. Teacher Questions Using Bloom's Taxonomy (Table 3.4)

2b. Student Responses to Teacher Questions Using Bloom's Taxonomy (Table 3.5)

3a. Teacher Questions Using Webb's Depth of Knowledge (Table 3.6)

3b. Student Responses Using Webb's Depth of Knowledge (Table 3.7)

4a. Student On-Task and Off-Task Behaviors (Table 3.8)

II. Performance Indicator Tools

5a. Gardner's Multiple Intelligences (Table 3.9)

5b. Student Responses to Gardner's Multiple Intelligences (Table 3.10)

6. Hunter's Steps in Lesson Planning (Table 3.11)

7a. Group Work Criteria (Table 3.12)

7b. Group Performance: Assessment of Individual Participation (Table 3.13)

III. Visual Diagramming Tools

4b. Diagram of Verbal Interactions (Figure 3.3)

8a. Diagram of Teacher Space Utilization (Figures 3.4)

8b. Diagram of Student Space Utilization (Figures 3.5)

IV. Tailored Tools

9. Feedback (Figure 3.6)

10. Teacher–Pupil Interaction (Table 3.14)

11. Indicators of Culturally Diverse Learners (Table 3.15)

12. Strategies for Diverse Learners (Table 3.16)

13. Accommodations and Modifications for English-Language Learners (Table 3.17)

14. The Differentiated Classroom (Table 3.18)

15. Students' Construction of Meaning on Their Own (Table 3.19)

16. Learning Centers (Table 3.20)

17. Co-teaching: Push-in Model (initial) (Table 3.21)

18. Strategies for Students With Speech and Language Impairments (Table 3.22)

19. Guided Reading (Table 3.23)

20. Read-Aloud/Story Time (Table 3.24)

21. Teacher Language During Center-Based Learning in Pre-Kindergarten Classrooms (Table 3.25)

22. Teacher Encouragement of Students' Problem-Solving Skills and Reasoning (Mathematics Common Core Standards) (Table 3.26)

23. Teacher Encouragement of Mathematical Communication During Problem Solving (Mathematics Common Core Standards) (Table 3.27)

24a. Teacher Behaviors Keyed to Accountable Talk (Table 3.28)

25b. Student Behaviors Keyed to Accountable Talk (Table 3.29)

V. Qualitative Approaches

25a. Detached Open-Ended Narrative

25b. Participant Open-Ended Observation

26. Child-Centered Learning Observation

27. Nonverbal Techniques (Table 3.30)

28. Questioning Techniques

29. Strategies for Diverse Learners

30. Differentiated Instruction

31. Guided Reading (Table 3.31)

32. Team Teaching in the Inclusion or General Education Classroom

33. Classroom Assessment in the Differentiated Classroom

(Continued)

(Continued)

VI. The Differentiated Classroom

    5a. & 5b. Gardner's Multiple Intelligences (Tables 3.9 & 3.10)

         11. Indicators of Culturally Diverse Learners (Table 3.15)

         13. Accommodations and Modifications for English-Language Learners (Table 3.17)

    14. & 29. Strategies for Diverse Learners (Table 3.12)

         15. Students' Construction of Meaning on Their Own (Table 3.19)

         16. Learning Centers (Table 3.20)

          7. Co-teaching: Push-in Model (initial) (Table 3.21)

         18. Strategies for Students With Speech and Language Impairments (Table 3.22)

         31. Team Teaching in the Inclusion or General Education Classroom

         32. Classroom Assessment in the Differentiated Classroom

VII. Student-Centered Tools

         1b. Student Responses to Teacher Verbal Behaviors (Table 3.3)

         2b. Student Responses to Teacher Questions Using Bloom's Taxonomy (Table 3.5)

         3b. Student Responses Using Webb's Depth of Knowledge (Table 3.7)

         4a. Student On-Task and Off-Task Behaviors (Table 3.8)

         5b. Student Responses to Gardner's Multiple Intelligences (Table 3.10)

         7b. Group Performance: Assessment of Individual Participation (Table 3.13)

         8b. Diagram of Student Space Utilization (Figure 3.5)

       24b. Student Behaviors Keyed to Accountable Talk (Table 3.29)

       25b. Participant Open-Ended Observation

        26. Child-Centered Learning Observation

VIII. Math and Literacy Tools

    19. & 31. Guided Reading (Tables 3.23 & 3.31)

         20. Read-Aloud/Story Time (Table 3.24)

         22. Common Core Standards in Mathematics: Teacher's Encouragement of Students' Problem-Solving Skills and Reasoning (Table 3.26)

         23. Common Core Standards in Mathematics: Teacher's Encouragement of Mathematical Communication During Problem Solving (Table 3.27)

IX. Questioning Tools

         2a. Teacher Questions Using Bloom's Taxonomy (Table 3.3)

         2b. Student Responses to Teacher Questions Using Bloom's Taxonomy (Table 3.5)

         3a. Teacher Questions Using Webb's Depth of Knowledge (Table 3.6)

         3b. Student Responses Using Webb's Depth of Knowledge (Table 3.7)

         28. Questioning Techniques

Note: All of the other tools and techniques are either teacher centered or interactions between students and teachers.

QUANTITATIVE OBSERVATION TOOLS

There are several types of assessment instruments that fall under the umbrella of quantitative tools, for example, categorical frequency, performance indicator, visual diagramming, and tailored.

Categorical frequency tools define certain events or behaviors that can be checked off at frequency intervals and counted. Tables 3.2 through 3.5 are examples of categorical frequency tools.

Performance indicator tools allow the observer to record whether or not an action or activity listed on the instrument has been observed. Tables 3.9 through 3.12 are examples of performance indicator tools.

Visual diagramming tools portray what happens visually in the classroom. The use of videotaping is particularly useful here to provide visual evidence. Look at Figures 3.3 and 3.4 for visual diagramming tools.

Tailored tools are those that are specially developed based on a teacher's unique concerns. The teacher, in other words, wants the observer to focus on a specific area or areas. See Figures 3.8 and 3.9 for examples.

Practice

Using any of the tools,

- Find a colleague who will allow you to observe him or her for at least 15 minutes.
- Choose a chart together and keep a record of the results.
- Share the information with your colleague.
- What was his or her reaction?
- How did you find the experience of actually using the tool?
- What did you learn?
- Will you make any changes in your own instructional practices based on what you have learned?

Tool 1a: Teacher Verbal Behaviors

Explanation. Supervisor and teacher collaboratively develop a list of no more than seven teacher behaviors that will be checked off as they occur at frequency intervals of, for example, 1 minute. In Table 3.2, seven teacher behaviors have been agreed upon: information giving, questioning, teacher answering own questions, praising, direction giving, correcting, and reprimanding. You'll notice that during the first minute, the teacher gave information, questioned, answered her own questions, and corrected. Note that the frequency of each behavior is not recorded, merely the fact that the teacher behavior occurred within the time frame.

Postnote. Note that the observer and teacher may collaboratively decide on any kind of teacher verbal behavior, not just the ones listed in Table 3.2. Also, some teachers and observers like to note student questions to ascertain teacher–student interaction. Some observers prefer checking the total number of behaviors over a time period, not just checking if a behavior occurred during brief intervals during a time period.

Tool 1b: Student Responding to Verbal Behaviors

Explanation: It is important for the teacher to ascertain which students are the objects of the verbal behaviors noted on the Teacher Verbal Behaviors chart. The following tool (see Table 3.3) charts the students who are the recipients of the teacher's verbal behaviors. We include only the behaviors that indicate an interaction between the teacher and student(s). Every student interaction with the teacher is recorded.

Table 3.2   Teacher Verbal Behaviors

Class: 3-1

Date: 5/10

Time began: 9:25 a.m.

Time ended: 9:41 a.m.

Min.	Information Giving	Questioning	Teacher Answering Own Questions	Praising	Giving Direction	Correcting	Reprimanding
1	X	X	X			X	
2	X	X			X		
3		X			X		X
4	X			X	X		X
5	X				X		
6		X				X	
7	X						
8	X	X			X		
9							X
10	X						
11	X				X	X	
12							X
13							X
14	X						
15	X		X				
16	X				X		

Source: Glickman, Carl D.; Gordon, Stephen P.; Ross-Gordon, Jovita M., *SuperVision and Instructional Leadership: A Developmental Approach*, 8th Edition, © 2010. Reprinted by permission of Pearson Education, Inc., Upper Saddle River, NJ.

Table 3.3   Student Responses to Verbal Behaviors

Class: 3-1

Date: 5/10

Time began: 9:25 a.m.

Time ended: 9:41 a.m.

Students	Answered Questions	Praised	Corrected	Reprimanded	Comments
Tomas	X		X		
Bill	X			X X X	Shouted out answers without raising his hand
Veronica	X			X X	Talked a lot with Sasha

Students	Answered Questions	Praised	Corrected	Reprimanded	Comments
Sasha	X	X		X X	See above
Deirdre					
David	X		X		
Miguel					Head on table
Alene	X			X	
Natasha	X X X X		X X X	X	Participated enthusiastically
Liam					Looking out window
Tony			X		
Rhonda	X X X		X X X	X	Answered quickly without thinking
Erica				X	
Katie	X	X			
Beltran	X X X	X X	X		
Zamira					Didn't participate at all

Tool 2a: Teacher Questions Using Bloom's Taxonomy

Special Prerequisite Knowledge. Familiarity with Bloom's Taxonomy. Click on the following link to learn more about Bloom's Taxonomy: http://projects.coe.uga .edu/epltt/index.php?title=Bloom%27s_Taxonomy

Bloom's Original Taxonomy	Bloom's New Taxonomy
Level 6: Evaluation	Level 6: Creating
Level 5: Synthesis	Level 5: Evaluating
Level 4: Analysis	Level 4: Analyzing
Level 3: Application	Level 3: Applying
Level 2: Comprehension	Level 2: Understanding
Level 1: Knowledge	Level 1: Remembering
(Level 1 is the lowest level)	(Level 1 is the lowest level)

From http://www.odu.edu/educ/roverbau/Bloom/blooms_taxonomy.htm. Used with permission.

Explanation. Supervisor and teacher collaboratively decide to focus on only the number and quality of questions posed during a specified time period. In the case presented in Table 3.4, both teacher and supervisor agree that Bloom's Taxonomy will be used as the principal guide. The six levels of Bloom's revised Taxonomy are listed: remembering, understanding, applying, analyzing, evaluating, and creating. A tally is kept for each instance in which a question is posed. The observer listens to the question and decides into which of Bloom's categories the tally mark should be made. If your knowledge of Bloom's Taxonomy is rusty, the aforementioned Internet site and several others can refresh your and the teacher's memory. Just Google "Bloom's Taxonomy." Bring to the observation a copy of the categories, their definitions, and sample questions. At the completion of the observation, totals are computed and percentages are calculated, as noted in Table 3.4. Note that the frequency of each type of question is recorded, but the question itself is not. In addition, many teachers and observers want to observe if there is a progression in the level of questioning during the time period. If the teacher prefers a running record of each question posed and/or a record of the progression in the level of questioning, a tape recorder could be used.

Tool 2b: Student Responses to Questions Indicating Bloom's Taxonomy Levels

Explanation. A typical scenario where the use of Tool 2b might be appropriate is following the observation and discussion of the teacher's use of Bloom's

Table 3.4   Teacher Questions Using Bloom's Taxonomy

Class: 7-2

Date: 3/11

Time began: 10:15 a.m.

Time ended: 10:45 a.m.

Number of questions asked: 24

Question Category	Tally 5 min.	Tally 10 min.	Tally 15 min.	Total	Percent	Comments
Creating				0	0	Where could you have developed creative questions?
Evaluating		✓ ✓		2	.08	Discuss placement of evaluation questions.
Analyzing				0	0	Discuss possible analysis questions and where they could be placed.
Applying	✓ ✓ ✓	✓ ✓ ✓	✓ ✓	8	.33	How could some of these become analyzing questions?
Understanding	✓ ✓ ✓	✓ ✓	✓ ✓ ✓	8	.33	How could some of these be made higher-level questions?
Remembering	✓ ✓ ✓	✓ ✓	✓	6	.25	How could some of these be made higher-level questions?

Source: Glickman, Carl D.; Gordon, Stephen P.; Ross-Gordon, Jovita M., *SuperVision and Instructional Leadership: A Developmental Approach*, 8th Edition, © 2010. Reprinted by permission of Pearson Education, Inc., Upper Saddle River, NJ.

Taxonomy Levels. The observer will use Tool 2b (see Table 3.5) to determine which students respond to which levels of questions. The focus can be on a select group of students or on the whole class. A tally is kept of the level of question each student answers. Again, bring a copy of the categories, their definitions, and sample questions to the observation. The goal is to meet individual student needs based on the data derived from the tables. Thus, questioning will improve and individual students' needs can be met based on the data derived from the tables.

Tool 3a: Teacher Questions Using Webb's Depth of Knowledge

Special Prerequisite Knowledge. Familiarity with Webb's Depth of Knowledge (DOK). To view an interesting Depth of Knowledge chart, click on the following link: http://www.dese.mo.gov/divimprove/sia/msip/DOK_Chart.pdf.

Table 3.5 Student Responses to Questions Indicating Bloom's Taxonomy

Class: 7-2

Date: 3/18

Time began: 10:15 a.m.

Time ended: 10:45 a.m.

Student	1	2	3	4	5	6	Observations
Tom	✓ ✓ ✓	✓ ✓	✓		✓ X		Enthusiastically responds to levels 1 & 2
Marissa	✓ ✓	✓					
Vanessa		✓					Head down most of time
Nurit	✓	✓	✓	✓	X		Hand often raised
Joseph	✓						Pulled out of class
Adam	X	✓		X	X		Raises hand before thinking
Lin	✓ ✓	✓ X	✓ X	X	X	X	Frustrated when wrong answers are incorrect
Elena		✓ X	✓ ✓	✓		✓ ✓	
Esmeralda							Head down on desk
Wayne	✓ ✓	✓ ✓	✓ ✓	X	✓	✓	Enthusiastic. Shouts out

Key:

✓ = correct

X = incorrect

1=remembering

2=understanding

3=applying

4=analyzing

5=evaluating

6=creating

Explanation. Supervisor and teacher collaboratively decide to focus on only the number and quality of questions posed during a specified time period. In the case presented in Table 3.6, both teacher and supervisor agree that Webb's Depth of Knowledge will be used as the principal guide. Four of Webb's levels are listed: recall, basic application of skill/concept, strategic thinking, and extended thinking. A tally is kept for each instance in which a question is posed. The observer listens to the question and decides into which of Webb's categories the tally mark should be made. If your knowledge of Webb's Depth of Knowledge is rusty, the above-mentioned site and several other Internet sites can refresh your and the teacher's memory. Just Google "Webb's Depth of Knowledge." Bring to the observation a copy of the categories, their definitions, and sample questions. At the completion of the observation, totals are computed and percentages are calculated, as noted in Table 3.6. Note that the frequency of each type of question is recorded, but the question itself is not. In addition, many teachers and observers want to observe if there is a progression in the level of questioning during the time period. If the teacher prefers a running record of each question posed and/or a record of the progression in the level of questioning, a tape recorder could be used.

Reflect and Practice

Activity. Refer back to the lesson transcript at the beginning of this chapter. Using the Teacher Questions chart, record the *level* of Clara's questions using

Table 3.6   Teacher Questions Using Webb's Depth of Knowledge

Class: 7-1

Date: 5/21

Time began: 11:20 a.m.

Time ended: 11:50 a.m.

Question Category	Tally 5 min.	Tally 10 min.	Tally 15 min.	Total	Percentage	Comments
Extended Thinking		✓ ✓	✓ ✓	4	.15	What additional questions would result in extended thinking?
Strategic Thinking				0	0	What kind of question would have resulted in strategic thinking, and where in the lesson would you have put it?
Basic Applications of Skill/ Concept	✓ ✓ ✓ ✓ ✓	✓ ✓ ✓	✓ ✓	10	.35	How could some of these become strategic thinking questions?
Recall	✓ ✓ ✓ ✓ ✓	✓ ✓ ✓	✓ ✓ ✓ ✓ ✓	14	.50	How could these be made higher-level questions?

either Bloom's Taxonomy or Webb's Depth of Knowledge Categories. You can also choose to record her Verbal Behaviors. Discuss your findings with a colleague. Did your recordings match your colleague's observations?

Postnote. Note that this type of categorical frequency tool doesn't necessarily have to deal with teacher questions. Any behavior that can be tallied may be observed using this format. For a comparison of Bloom's Taxonomy and Webb's Depth of Knowledge categories, click on the following link: http://www.ehow.com/facts_5631749_webb-vs_-bloom-taxonomy.html.

Tool 3b: Student Responses Using Webb's Depth of Knowledge

Explanation. The following is a typical scenario appropriate for the use of Tool 3b: The teacher and observer agree to use the Webb's Depth of Knowledge tool to focus on classroom questioning. Following the observation and feedback conversation, the teacher and observer decide to use Tool 3b to determine which students respond to which levels of questions. The focus can be on a select group of students or on the whole class. A tally (see Table 3.7) is kept of

Table 3.7   Student Responses to Questions Indicating Webb's Depth of Knowledge

Class: 7-1

Date: 5/23

Time began: 11:20 a.m.

Time ended: 12:00 p.m.

Student	1	2	3	4	Observations
Tim	✓ ✓ ✓	✓ ✓	✓		
Mara	✓ X	X	X	✓	Seems to respond without thinking first
Mohammed	✓ ✓	✓ ✓	X	X	Volunteers; difficulty with higher level
Trevor	✓ ✓	✓ ✓	✓ ✓	✓ ✓	
Scott					Off task
Linda	✓	X	X		
Maria Elena			✓ ✓	✓ ✓	Seemed bored
Jesus	✓	✓	✓	✓	Only answered when sure
Anar		✓ ✓			Confused look on her face
Estella	✓ ✓ ✓ ✓	✓ ✓ ✓ ✓	✓ ✓	X	Answered without raising hand

Key:

✓ = correct

X = incorrect

1 = recall

2 = application of skill/concept

3 = strategic thinking

4 = extended thinking

the level of question each student answers. Again, bring a copy of the categories, their definitions, and sample questions to the observation. The goal is to meet individual student needs based on the data derived from the tables.

Tool 4a: Student On-Task and Off-Task Behaviors

Special Prerequisite Skills. We recommend that you practice identifying student on-task and off-task behaviors (Tool 4a) prior to actually using it in a classroom with a class. We suggest you memorize and practice using the key prior to any real observation.

Explanation. Supervisor and teacher collaboratively decide to focus on student on-task and off-task behaviors. A list of student names is made as noted in Table 3.8. The students' names are listed according to their seat order, beginning from the front row or table and going down each row or table. The observer should be situated to the side of the front of the room. Because the observer will be seen readily by the students, we suggest that the observer come into the class a couple of times prior to the observation to sit up front and make believe that he or she is taking notes to acquaint students with the observer's presence.

Table 3.8 Student On-Task and Off-Task Behaviors

Class: 3-2

Date: 9/9

Time when sweep began: 9:00 a.m.

Time ended: 9:35 a.m.

Student	9:00	9:05	9:10	9:15	9:20	9:25	9:30	9:35	Observations
Tania	A	A	A	A	A	A	O	A	
Manuel	A	A	A	A	A	O	A	A	
Vivian	A	TK	TK	A	A	TK	A	TK	
Nurit	O	O	P	P	OT	O	O	OT	
Joseph	OT	OT	A	P	A	A	P	P	
Michael	OT	OT	A	P	0	A	A	TK	
Loi	A	P	P	A	P	P	P	OT	
Helen	A	A	A	A	A	A	A	A	
Mari-Celi	A	A	A	A	O	A	A	A	
Wayne	P	P	A	A	P	P	O	O	
Virginia	P	A	A	A	P	A	A	A	
Colleen	O	A	A	A	TK	0	A	A	
Hajime	OT	OT	OT	OT	OT	OT	OT	OT	
Kahlid	TK	A	A	TK	TK	TK	A	A	
Maria	0	A	A	A	TK	A	A	A	

Key: A = at task; TK = talking (social); P = playing; O = out of seat; OT = off task

Source: Glickman, Carl D.; Gordon, Stephen P.; Ross-Gordon, Jovita M., *SuperVision and Instructional Leadership: A Developmental Approach*, 8th Edition, © 2010. Reprinted by permission of Pearson Education, Inc., Upper Saddle River, NJ.

Observations are made in 5-minute intervals (depending on the number of students observed). In our case, 15 students are being observed. Thus, each student will be watched for 20 seconds (5 minutes = 300 seconds divided by the number of total students being observed [15] = 20 seconds per student). In a large class, the novice observer may need to reduce the number of behaviors observed. Often, the teacher will choose to focus on a small number of specific students. The observer records what he or she sees using the key at the bottom of the chart. Again, familiarity with student on-task and off-task behaviors is essential for this technique to work properly. By the way, the precise on- and off-task behaviors also should be collaboratively developed between observer and teacher.

Reflect and Practice

The video segments on the website have three classroom scenes that you can use to practice this and other techniques. The New Teacher Center in Santa Cruz, California, also has a number of classroom DVDs designed to foster the development of coaching and observation skills. Contact products@newteachercenter .org for further information. You might also ask a colleague to videotape your own class. Practice and report your ability and comfort in using this technique.

Postnote. Note that this type of categorical frequency tool refers solely to student behavior. What are other examples of student behaviors for which this technique can be used?

Tool 4b: Diagram of Verbal Interactions

Explanation. This tool can be used as a follow-up to an observation of on-task and off-task behaviors. By clarifying with which students the teacher interacts and which students respond, the teacher can understand more clearly why certain students are on or off task and plan future interactions according to individual student needs. Using the diagram of verbal interactions after student on-task and off-task behaviors provides an example of how a student-centered tool can also precede a more teacher-centered observation. The observer and observee decide collaboratively the order of observations.

A specified period of time to observe the lesson is agreed upon. For purposes of analysis in this case, both supervisor and teacher have agreed on a 30-minute observation period. Six copies of Figure 3.3 in Resource D should be made for the observer to record verbal interactions in 5-minute increments, that is, one chart for *each* 5-minute period. Cross-hatching facilitates the recording of multiple interactions. One of our students effectively used multiple transparencies of the seating chart as overlays for each 5-minute interval. The clear plastic sheets can be superimposed later. She also used different colors of ink to represent each observation interval.

Each arrow indicates a complete statement directed to another individual, and the arrows are numbered in sequence. The observer should have extensive experience applying this technique so that recording can proceed smoothly and accurately. Figure 3.3 is provided as a training tool for interpreting the verbal interaction provided.

Figure 3.3 Diagram of Verbal Interactions

Class: 10-517

Date: 11/15

Time: 10:15 a.m.

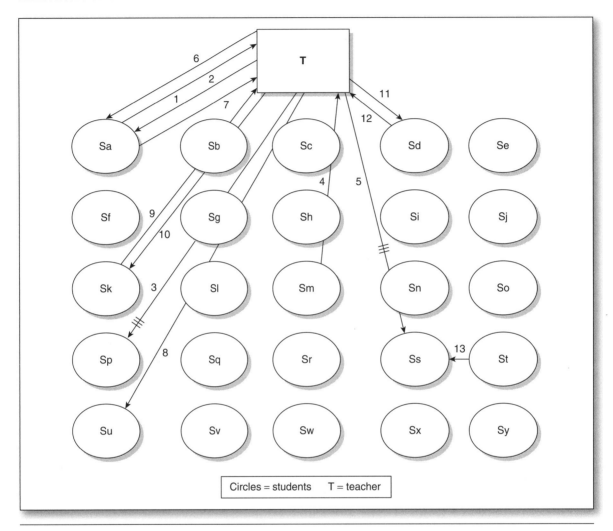

Source: Glickman, Carl D.; Gordon, Stephen P.; Ross-Gordon, Jovita M., *SuperVision and Instructional Leadership: A Developmental Approach*, 8th Edition, © 2010. Reprinted by permission of Pearson Education, Inc., Upper Saddle River, NJ.

Reflect and Practice

Postnote. How might the use of audiotaping assist or hinder interpretation of the nature of verbal interactions in a lesson?

Tool 5a: Gardner's Multiple Intelligences

Explanation. Well versed in Gardner's intelligences theory, both observer and observee have collaboratively decided to record the extent to which Gardner's intelligences are incorporated in a fifth-grade science lesson (see Table 3.9). A specified period of time to observe the lesson is agreed upon. The observer merely checks off whether or not the teacher addressed in any way each of Gardner's intelligences. The observer may comment on the nature or extent to which each intelligence was introduced and applied. Naturalistic and emotional intelligences are sometimes added to the list of multiple intelligences.

To learn more about Gardner's Multiple Intelligences or to find out what your own intelligence(s) is/are, click on http://www.tecweb.org/styles/gardner.html.

Table 3.9 Gardner's Multiple Intelligences

Class: 3-310

Date: 6/28

Time: 1:15 p.m.

Elements	Response Yes	No	N/A	Observations
Logical/mathematical	☑	☐	☐	Mathematical equation examples on board
Bodily/kinesthetic	☐	☑	☐	No references made
Visual	☑	☐	☐	Overhead transparencies used
Musical	☐	☑	☐	No references made
Interpersonal	☑	☐	☐	Small-group work
Intrapersonal	☐	☑	☐	No references made
Linguistic	☑	☐	☐	Problem-solving examples
Naturalistic	☐	☑	☐	No references made
Emotional	☐	☑	☐	No references made

Source: Glickman, Carl D.; Gordon, Stephen P.; Ross-Gordon, Jovita M., *SuperVision and Instructional Leadership: A Developmental Approach*, 8th Edition, © 2010. Reprinted by permission of Pearson Education, Inc., Upper Saddle River, NJ.

Reflect and Practice

Postnote. Howard Gardner's theory is only one example for which a performance indicator tool may be applied. What is another example of how you might use this tool?

Tool 5b: Student Use of Gardner's Multiple Intelligences

Explanation. Once the observer and observee have reflected on the nature and extent of the application of multiple intelligences to the lesson observed, they can discuss student response to the various intelligences (see Table 3.10). It is essential to determine which students use which intelligences and to decide how to modify lessons based on students' needs and intelligences. The focus can be on a select group of students or on the whole class. A tally is kept of the intelligences each student applies. You may want to bring to the classroom a copy of the definitions and sample applications of the intelligences. The goal is to meet individual student needs based on the data derived from the table.

Table 3.10   Student Use of Gardner's Multiple Intelligences

Class: 3-310

Date: 5/29

Time: 1:15 p.m.

Student	1	2	3	4	5	6	7	8	9	Observations
Teresa	✓		✓	✓	✓		✓			She used all the intelligences presented.
Marvin							✓			Talked a lot, but not usually on topic
Esperanza	✓		✓	✓						Worked quietly
Fatima	✓				✓		✓			Sometimes distracted by socializing
Jacob	✓			✓						Activities where he could work alone
Leslie			✓	✓	✓		✓			Volunteered a lot but difficulty with math problems
Tarik		✓								Only activities where he could move a lot

Key:

1. Logical/mathematical; 2. Bodily/kinesthetic; 3.Visual; 4. Musical; 5. Interpersonal; 6. Intrapersonal; 7. Linguistic; 8. Naturalistic; 9. Emotional

Tool 6: Hunter's Steps in Lesson Planning

Explanation. Well versed in Hunter's lesson plan model, both observer and observee have decided collaboratively to record the extent to which Hunter's steps are incorporated into a 12th-grade world-language lesson (see Table 3.11). A specified period of time to observe the lesson is agreed upon. The observer merely checks off whether or not the teacher in any way addressed each of Hunter's steps. The observer may comment on the nature or extent to which each of Hunter's steps were introduced and applied.

To read up on Hunter's Steps in Lesson Planning, click on http://www.personal.psu.edu/scs15/idweb/lessonplanning.htm.

Reflect and Practice

Postnote. Although Madeline Hunter created her steps many years ago, they are applicable to many current classroom strategies. To which ones can you apply these steps?

Tool 7a: Group Work Criteria[3]

Explanation. Well versed in Johnson and Johnson's cooperative learning format and Tomlinson's Group Work criteria, both observer and observee have decided collaboratively to record the extent to which the criteria of cooperative learning

Table 3.11 Hunter's Steps in Lesson Planning

Class: 10-406

Date: 5/18

Time: 11:15 a.m.

Elements	*Response*			*Comments*
	Yes	*No*	*N/A*	
Anticipatory set	☐	☑	☐	No references made
Objective and purpose	☐	☑	☐	Unstated, unclear
Input	☑	☐	☐	Group discussion employed
Modeling	☐	☑	☐	No references made
Checking for understanding	☐	☑	☐	Teacher asked "Do you understand?" but did not check
Guided practice	☑	☐	☐	Teacher circulates
Independent practice	☑	☐	☐	Sample sheets distributed

Source: Glickman, Carl D.; Gordon, Stephen P.; Ross-Gordon, Jovita M., *SuperVision and Instructional Leadership: A Developmental Approach*, 8th Edition, © 2010. Reprinted by permission of Pearson Education, Inc., Upper Saddle River, NJ.

are incorporated in a fourth-grade lesson (see Table 3.12). A specified period of time to observe the lesson is agreed upon. The observer merely checks off whether or not the teacher in any way addressed each of the group work criteria. The observer may comment on the nature or extent to which each group work criterion was introduced and applied.

Postnote. We are providing only some examples for which a performance indicator tool may be applied. Can you think of another example for which this tool may be applicable?

Tool 7b: Group Performance: Assessment of Individual Participation

Explanation. A performance indicator chart keyed to individual performance in group work is presented in Table 3.13. Again, once the cooperative learning process that the teacher has established has been observed and discussed, observer and observee can agree to look at individual student participation. They have decided to record the extent to which the agreed-upon criteria of individual participation are incorporated into the fourth-grade elementary school class. A specific period of time to observe the groups is agreed upon. Specific students or groups may be targeted. The observer checks off the level of participation of the individual students and adds comments to situate the involvement of the student and clarify the quality of the interaction.

Table 3.12   Group Work Criteria

Class: 4-417

Date: 3/15

Time: 9:15 a.m.

Elements	Response Yes	Response No	Response N/A	Comments
Students understand the task goals (academic and social)	☐	☑	☐	No explanation of either occurred—just went into lesson
The task matches the goals (leads students to what they should know, understand, and be able to do).	☑	☐	☐	
Students understand what is expected of individuals to make the group work function well (social skills taught).	☐	☑	☐	Teacher merely said, "Cooperate"—no instruction
Face-to-face interaction	☑	☐	☐	Students facing each other and conversing
The task requires an important contribution from each group member based on the students' skills and interests.	☑	☐	☐	One set of responses required from each group that requires individual skills
Individuals are accountable for their own understanding of all facets of the task.	☐	☑	☐	None evident—teacher walked around classroom minimally
There is a "way out" for students who are not succeeding with the group.	☐	☐	☑	
There is opportunity for teacher or peer coaching and in-process quality checks.	☑	☐	☐	Students paired and seated together to allow for peer coaching
Time lines are brisk but not rigid.	☐	☑	☐	No time to debrief at end
Group processing	☑	☐	☐	Students rated their performance
Students understand what to do next after they complete their work at a high level of quality.	☐	☐	☑	Group work not completed by end of class

Source: C. A. Tomlinson, *How to Differentiate Instruction in Mixed-Ability Classrooms* (2nd ed.). Copyright © 2001 by ASCD. Adapted by permission.

Table 3.13 Group Performance: Assessment of Individual Participation

Student: Jamal

Class: 4-417

Date: 3/16

Time: 9:20–11:00 a.m.

	Regularly	*Sometimes*	*Rarely*	*Comments*
A. Contribution to group goals				
1. Participates in the group's activities	X			
2. Does his or her share of work		X		Sometimes allows the more assertive students to control work
B. Staying on the topic				
3. Pays attention; listens	X			
4. Makes comments to help group get back on topic			X	Again, lets the more dominant students control
5. Stays on topic	X			
C. Offering useful ideas or information				
6. Gives helpful ideas & suggestions		X		
7. Offers helpful feedback & comments		X		Reticent to criticize
8. Influences group decisions & plans		X		
D. Consideration of others				
9. Makes positive, encouraging remarks about group members & their ideas			X	Reserved
10. Shows & expresses sensitivity to the feelings of others	X			Considerate of others
E. Involving, working, & sharing with others				
11. Tries to get the group working together to reach group agreements			X	Lets others lead the group
12. Considers the ideas of others; exchanges, rethinks, defends ideas		X		Participates at times
F. Communicating				
13. Speaks clearly; easy to hear & understand	X			When he participates, he speaks clearly, though softly
14. Expresses ideas clearly & effectively		X		Tries hard; seems to think before speaking

Source: Modified from the Connecticut State Department of Education; sponsored by the National Science Foundation.

Reflect and Practice

Postnote. We are providing a cooperative learning context for this tool. Can you think of how you could modify this tool for another use in the classroom? How could the use of videos enhance or impede this observation?

Tool 8a: Diagram of Teacher Utilization

Explanation. A specified period of time to observe the lesson is agreed upon. The observer charts teacher movement around the room and, at the same time, records the times.

Site Practice

Find a colleague who will allow you to observe him or her for an appropriate length of time. Using Figure 3.4, the Diagram of Space Utilization, keep a record of the teacher's movements during the lesson. Share information with

Figure 3.4   Diagram of Teacher Space Utilization

Class: 1.3

Date: 4/16

Time: 9:10–10:00 a.m.

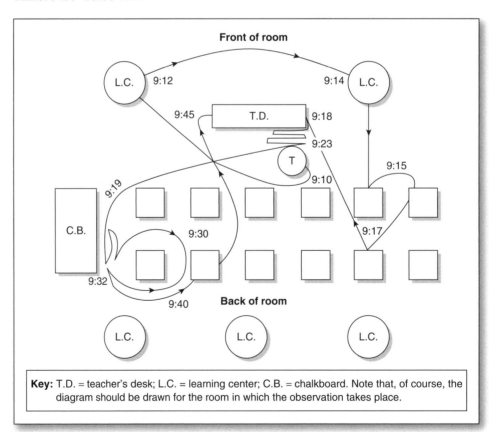

Key: T.D. = teacher's desk; L.C. = learning center; C.B. = chalkboard. Note that, of course, the diagram should be drawn for the room in which the observation takes place.

Source: Glickman, Carl D.; Gordon, Stephen P.; Ross-Gordon, Jovita M., *SuperVision and Instructional Leadership: A Developmental Approach*, 8th Edition, © 2010. Reprinted by permission of Pearson Education, Inc., Upper Saddle River, NJ.

Figure 3.5 Diagram of Student Space Utilization

Class: 3-402

Date: 4/18

Start Time: 9:05 a.m.

End Time: 9:35 a.m.

Source: Hillary Barranco-Casado, a New York City teacher and leadership candidate, adapted the form for student space utilization.

your colleague. What was her or his reaction? How did you find the experience of actually using this technique?

Postnote. How might the use of videos assist or hinder interpretation of the nature of teacher space utilization?

Tool 8b: Diagram of Student Space Utilization

Explanation: The Diagram of Student Space Utilization can be used in conjunction with the Diagram of Teacher Space Utilization or can easily be used separately. Observing a student's space utilization can have an impact on the teacher's choice of movement in class (see Figure 3.5).

1. *A* gets pillow, puts it on his head, moves it to sling it over his shoulder, crawls on knees to bookshelf.

2. Stops at bookshelf, chooses a book, stands and walks back to corner.

3. Reads quietly for about 3 minutes.

4. Crouches on knees and slides back and forth, glances around and spots *E*, another student.

5. Stands and walks over to bookshelf next to *E*, throws his book into a book bin, and sits next to *E*. *E* moves to the rug with a book, *A* grabs one and follows.

6. *A* lays down next to *E*, who is reading and watches him read. *E* stands up and returns book. *A* crawls on knees toward the closet.

7. *A* lies down again with book. *E* rejoins him. *A* closes his book and reads the back cover, then looks at *E* as he reads. They begin whispering—many interchanges. They begin reading after about 4 minutes. Seven minutes later class is asked to do a reading response in individual reading logs.

8. *A* crawls on knees while hugging pillow. Three boys come and try to pry him from pillow. *E* comes to lie next to him on it. Three boys return to tug pillow. Teacher redirects. *A* still does not move. Two girls come and pull pillow away from *A*. *A* stays on rug, others leave.

9. *A* stands and goes to sit in corner of rug where other pillows are kept.

Tool 9: Feedback

Explanation. A specified period of time to observe the lesson is agreed upon. At a planning conference, the teacher informs you that he or she is interested in whether or not he or she prompts, probes, and encourages student responses. He or she is also interested in how often positive reinforcement is used and how often pupils' responses are discouraged. A key then is developed collaboratively by the observer and the observee during the planning conference. Once categories and the key are approved, the observation may be scheduled. See Figure 3.6.

A reproducible version of Figure 3.6 is provided in Resource D as a training tool for interpreting the recorded feedback.

Figure 3.6 Feedback

Class: 6-2

Date: 9/27

Time: 2:20-3.00 p.m.

	D,D,Pr		Pr,D,D		E,Pb,Pb,O		Pb,Pb,E,O
	Jaime		**Renee**		**Peter**		**Michael**
	D		Pb,E		D,D,Pr		D
	Juan		**Natasha**		**Frances**		**William**

Key: Pr = prompted; Pb = probed; E = encouraged; O = positively reinforced; D = discouraged pupil

Source: Glickman, Carl D.; Gordon, Stephen P.; Ross-Gordon, Jovita M., *SuperVision and Instructional Leadership: A Developmental Approach*, 8th Edition, © 2010. Reprinted by permission of Pearson Education, Inc., Upper Saddle River, NJ.

Reflect and Practice

Refer back to the lesson transcript at the beginning of this chapter. Create a tailor-made technique to ascertain some aspect of the quality of Clara's teaching style. Discuss your findings with a colleague. Did your recordings match your colleague's observations?

Postnote. Can you develop another chart that might be keyed to another concern a teacher might have?

Tool 10: Teacher–Pupil Interaction

Explanation. In this case, the teacher wants the observer to focus on an individual student. The teacher informs you that he or she is having difficulty with Steve. The teacher complains that Steve's behavior gets progressively worse during a lesson and that the teacher is at his (or her) wits' end. A specified period of time to observe the lesson is agreed upon. The observer observes and records the student's behavior as well as noting the teacher's reaction.

A reproducible version of Table 3.14 is provided in Resource D as a training tool for interpreting the teacher–student interaction during this particular lesson.

Table 3.14 Teacher–Pupil Interaction

Student: Steve

Teacher: Clara Weingarten

Date: 9/13

Time: 9:05–9:30 a.m.

Time	Student Action	Teacher Action
9:05	Disturbing another student / Ceases misbehavior	Moves toward Steve
9:13	Leaves desk / Begins wandering around room / Returns to seat	Moves toward Steve
9:18	Playing with friend / Throws ruler	Establishes eye contact with Steve / Tells Steve to see her after class
9:30	Off-task/passive / Back on task	Approaches Steve, touches him on the shoulder, quietly asks him to go back to his seat

Source: Glickman, Carl D.; Gordon, Stephen P.; Ross-Gordon, Jovita M., *SuperVision and Instructional Leadership: A Developmental Approach*, 8th Edition, © 2010. Reprinted by permission of Pearson Education, Inc., Upper Saddle River, NJ.

Reflect and Practice

Postnote. How does this tool differ from the student space utilization tool? Compare the teacher's concerns in these two tools.

Tool 11: Indicators of Culturally Diverse Learners

Explanation. As much of the predominantly English-speaking world becomes culturally and linguistically diverse, supervisors need to attend to teachers' awareness of this diversity and their efforts to address it in the classroom. The performance indicator instrument shown in Table 3.15 can form the basis for that discussion and even lead to appropriate professional development.

Tool 12: Strategies for Diverse Learners

This tool has as a focus the teacher's strategies to reach all children in the classroom. It is applicable to all classrooms because diverse learners exist in any environment where people come together. Nonetheless, it is particularly pertinent to teachers who have students with disabilities integrated into the general population. The observer and observee can choose to limit the number of indicators to be observed or add others. See Table 3.16.

Table 3.15   Indicators of Culturally Diverse Learners

Class: 8-4

Date: 10/19

Time: 10:00–11:00 a.m.

Teacher Indicator	Response			Comments
	Yes	No	N/A	
Displays understanding of diverse cultures	☑	☐	☐	Spoke to student before class about parents
Displays personal regard for students of diverse cultures	☑	☐	☐	
Uses instructional materials free of cultural bias	☐	☐	☑	
Uses examples and materials that represent different cultures	☑	☐	☐	Asked for analogous examples from different cultures
Promotes examination of concepts and issues from different cultural perspectives	☑	☐	☐	
Intervenes to address acts of student intolerance	☑	☐	☐	Addressed student teasing
Uses "teachable moments" to address cultural issues	☑	☐	☐	
Reinforces student acts of respect for diverse cultures	☑	☐	☐	Asks related questions about students' cultures

Source: Glickman, Carl D.; Gordon, Stephen P.; Ross-Gordon, Jovita M., *SuperVision and Instructional Leadership: A Developmental Approach*, 8th Edition, © 2010. Reprinted by permission of Pearson Education, Inc., Upper Saddle River, NJ.

Table 3.16 Strategies for Diverse Learners

Class: 2-1

Date: 4/10

Time: 9:40–10:45 a.m.

Teacher Indicator	*Response*			Examples
	Yes	*No*	*N/A*	
Proximity to students	☑	☐	☐	Constantly walks around room to check on individual students
Different ways of encouraging students	☑	☐	☐	Uses different vocabulary to praise
Positive reinforcement techniques	☑	☐	☐	See above
Modifications for individual children or types of learners	☑	☐	☐	Use of paraprofessional to adapt for individual children
Use of children's strengths	☑	☐	☐	Multiple intelligences integrated
Multiple ways in which lesson is unfolding	☑	☐	☐	See above
Integration of grouping according to needs and skills	☑	☐	☐	Changes grouping for different subject areas
Scaffolding of instruction	☐	☑	☐	Not apparent

Tool 13: Accommodations and Modifications for English-Language Learners

Explanation. This tool (see Table 3.17) is essential for all the teachers who have English-language learners in their classrooms. It is crucial for ESL and bilingual classes; many of the strategies are also useful for students with disabilities.

Tool 14: The Differentiated Classroom

Explanation. The observer and the observee have chosen to focus on which classroom activities differentiate instruction. Differentiated instruction takes place when teachers are aware and able to consider and deal with different learning needs and abilities of their students. Table 3.18 contains many of the classroom activities that promote differentiated learning. No classroom can or should exhibit all of these characteristics at once, and others not included in the chart may be displayed. Observer and observee may choose to limit the focus to one or two of the strategies in the chart.

Postnote. This tool is appropriate for most classrooms. Can you think of specialized classrooms where these activities might be particularly important?

Table 3.17 Accommodations and Modifications for English-Language Learners

Class: ESL

Date: 3/10

Time: 11:05–11:30 a.m.

Accommodation Modification	Was This Element Present?			What Is the Evidence?
	Yes	No	N/A	
Teacher talk is modified: slower speech, careful choice of words, idioms, expressions	☐	☑	☐	
Teacher allows wait time and monitors teacher input vs. student output	☐	☑	☐	Sometimes moves too quickly to next volunteer
Definitions and language are embedded in content/context	☐	☑	☐	
Real-world artifacts present that support comprehension	☑	☐	☐	Constant use of visuals— either real world or virtual
Elicits and draws on students' backgrounds to build prior knowledge	☑	☐	☐	Refers to home life and everyday USA experiences
Teacher uses nonverbal cues to support comprehension	☑	☐	☐	Uses hands a lot

Table 3.18 The Differentiated Classroom

Class: 3-11 Language Arts

Date: 5/14

Time: 1:30–2:15 p.m.

Classroom Characteristics	Presence of Element			Comments/Description
	Yes	No	N/A	
1. Range of activities				
• whole-class instruction	☑	☐	☐	Mini-lesson
• small-group activities (pairs, triads, quads)	☑	☐	☐	Turn & talk at end of mini-lesson
• individualized activities (e.g., learning centers, independent study)	☑	☐	☐	Independent reading while teacher conferences with individual students
• student–teacher conferences	☑	☐	☐	
2. Students express themselves in diverse ways				
• artistically	☐	☑	☐	Class sang a song related to read-aloud
• musically	☐	☐	☐	
• technologically	☐	☐	☐	

Classroom Characteristics	Presence of Element			Comments/Description
	Yes	*No*	*N/A*	
• scientifically	☐	☑	☐	Some at computers during independent reading
• athletically	☑	☐	☐	
• through drama/speeches	☐	☑	☐	Stretching to song before independent work
• traditional compositions	☐	☑	☐	
• building models	☐	☑	☐	
• other	☑	☐	☐	
3. Students construct meaning on their own; take responsibility for their own learning; plan activities on their own	☑	☐	☐	Children chose their independent activity
4. Learning activities are provided for students who complete work before others	☑	☐	☐	Children could choose multiple independent activities
5. Peer tutoring to reinforce more advanced learners and support less advanced	☐	☑	☐	Might be a suggestion for future independent work time
6. Different types of assessment are ongoing and integrated	☑	☐	☐	Teacher assesses during conferences; independent activities contain self-assessments

Tool 15: Students' Construction of Meaning on Their Own

Explanation. This tool (see Table 3.19) zeroes in on one facet of student individual development: Students constructing meaning on their own. Although a few areas overlap with the general Differentiated Instruction Tool, this tool demonstrates how the teacher creates an environment that fosters student construction of meaning.

Tool 16: Learning Centers

Prerequisite knowledge. Familiarity with learning centers—different types serving different needs. Visit different learning centers in your school (or another site if possible) and online. For example, http://preschoolresource.tripod.com/classroom.html is a site focusing on options for the preschool classroom.

Explanation. Learning centers are effective for many ages. Their purposes and what they look like vary greatly according to the level of the student(s). Verify that you are familiar with the age- and skill-appropriate goals and activities for the centers you will be observing. Modify the tool according to the classroom

Table 3.19   Students' Construction of Meaning on Their Own

Class: 3.11

Date: 5/14

Time: 10:15–10:50 a.m.

Teacher Indicator	Response			Examples
	Yes	No	N/A	
Teacher preassesses student knowledge, skills, and interests	☑	☑	☐	Teacher asked who was familiar with book; only knowledge
Student activities: a. Centers • Provide clear guidelines • Promote self-construction of meaning b. Independent activities • Provide clear guidelines • Promote self-construction of meaning c. Anchor activities • Provide clear guidelines • Promote self-construction of meaning	 ☐ ☐ ☐ ☐ ☐ ☐	 ☑ ☑ ☑ ☑ ☑ ☑	 ☐ ☐ ☐ ☐ ☐ ☐	No center involvement
Groups vary with assignment—some homogeneous, some heterogeneous. Roles assigned according to learner needs	☑	☐	☐	Each student given a group role according to strengths and needs
Students self-assess & share feedback wherever possible	☑	☑	☐	No assessment but whole class debrief
Tiered activities: • match students' current understanding • challenge with higher-level thinking	 ☐ ☐	 ☑ ☑	 ☐ ☐	No guidance in creating questions for discussion
Students choose from a variety of activities and assignments wherever possible	☐	☐	☑	

Developed in collaboration with leaders from P.S. 145, Brooklyn, New York.

you will be visiting. Table 3.20 is oriented toward an upper-elementary class-room in a skills- and standards-oriented environment. A preschool chart would look very different.

Table 3.20 Learning Centers

Class: First Grade

Date: 11-11

Time began: 10:25 a.m.

Time ended: 11:05 a.m.

Learning Center Focus	Always Present	Somewhat Present	Not Present	Not Applicable	Comments
Learning centers are established and being used for every core curriculum subject.	☑	☐	☐	☐	Numerous rich centers
• Math	☑	☐	☐	☐	

• Literacy:
   o Reading
   o Writing
	☑
	☑
		☐
		☐
			☐
			☐
				☐
				☐	

• Science	☑	☐	☐	☐	
• Social Studies	☑	☐	☐	☐	
• Other	☑	☐	☐	☐	Music, Art, Store
Center work is interdisciplinary	☑	☐	☐	☐	Store, Art, & Music combine all skills; others, too
Tasks are standards based	☑	☐	☐	☐	Standards posted in simple language
Tasks are skill-driven	☑	☐	☐	☐	
Support independence by accessing prior knowledge of: • Strategies • Content • Other	☐	☑	☐	☐	
Tasks are matched to: • Readiness • Interests • Learning styles	☑	☐	☐	☐	A range of choices in every center
Provides system(s) for students' self-assessment and/or peer assessment: • Actual work at center or • Usage chart or	☑ ☑	☐ ☐	☐ ☐	☐ ☐	

(Continued)

(Continued)

• System for tracking students' product-choice and /or completion of product	☑	☐	☐	☐	
• Provides system(s) for students to record their own progress at centers.	☑	☐	☐	☐	
Development of technology skills is incorporated into tasks.	☐	☑	☐	☐	Where appropriate
Overall center rituals and routines are clearly defined and on display in the room:					Lots of visuals to support guidelines
• Guidelines for student behavior when doing center work	☑	☐	☐	☐	
• Guidelines for materials management, including storage of final products	☑	☐	☐	☐	

Developed in collaboration with leaders from P.S. 145, Brooklyn, New York.

Postnote. One of the authors provided professional development in a school where the faculty set up lower- and upper-grade "Center Fairs." The teachers shared their favorite centers. All staff visited both fairs where a suggestion box invited comments and suggestions at each center and a general suggestion box encouraged additional feedback.

The use of this type of chart can be divided into two parts:

1. An initial observation can focus on how the teacher has structured the centers.

2. A chart can be created to focus on the students' or a particular student's use of the center.

3. The order of observation could even be reversed. Observing student use of the centers could promote an examination of the setup and content of the centers.

4. A learning center chart is an excellent tool to use on an after-school Learning Walk or Instructional Rounds for teachers to observe the ideas in the centers created by their colleagues.

Tool 17: Co-teaching: Push-in Model (initial observation)

Explanation. As more and more classrooms are home to two teachers, it is essential that effective collaborations flourish. In Table 3.21 we have included this quantitative

Table 3.21 Co-teaching: Push-in Model (initial)

Class: Language Arts

Date: 11/11

Time: 9:00–9:50 a.m.

Observations	Frequently	Sometimes	Rarely	Notes
Both teachers are involved in the lesson (i.e., one teaches, one supports)	X			Both involved throughout lesson
Both teachers are instructing small groups; or both are conferring with students	X			
There is a note-taking system; both teachers are taking notes on students		X		Mostly push-in teacher taking notes
There is enough space/tables for each teacher to conduct a small group			X	Space is tight; recommend reconfiguration
Both teachers support the classroom rules	X			
Both teachers are using the classroom consequences	X			
The students seem to view both teachers as classroom teachers		X		Students tend to go to classroom teacher with questions
The ESL-certified teacher* is servicing students in small groups	X			
There is early evidence of two teachers in the room (charts, note taking, visuals in different handwriting)		X		Except for note taking, most visuals in classroom teacher's handwriting
Other ideas to help facilitate co-teaching, possible next steps and connections to support further co-teaching				

*Could be special education, speech, etc.

Adapted with permission from Maria della Ragione, New York City network leader.

tool and a qualitative one in the qualitative section that focus on the teachers' interactions in either a push-in or a collaborative team-teaching classroom.

Tool 18: Strategies for Students With Speech and Language Impairments

Explanation. Knowledge of speech therapy is a prerequisite for effective use of this instrument. Since speech therapists and other special service providers often share offices, this tool (see Table 3.22) or a variation for other specialists is very useful for informal or formal peer development.

Table 3.22 Strategies for Students With Speech and Language Impairments

Class: Social Studies

Date: 9/29

Time: 10:00–10:45 a.m.

Teacher/Therapist Indicator	Observed				Comments/Description
	Often	Sometimes	Rarely	N/A	
Is scaffolding of previous skills present?	☑	☐	☐	☐	Reviewed terminology from previous lesson; scaffolded "s" sound for Joseph
Does lesson include differentiation for the different learning styles (visual, auditory, tactile, kinesthetic)?	☑	☐	☐	☐	Visual: pictures & words on white board Tactile: hands-on objects Kinesthetic: students in size order
Are skills/strategies modeled for the students?	☑	☐	☐	☐	Modeled "big, bigger, biggest" with manipulatives, on white board, and with each other
Is the appropriate level of prompting used?	☐	☑	☐	☐	Give more time instead of giving phonemic prompt, i.e., "h" for house, "ye" for yellow
Are questions differentiated for each student's needs?	☑	☐	☐	☐	Each student had different vocabulary based on level
Is the appropriate wait time given to answer questions?	☐	☑	☐	☐	Alejandro not at same pace as others; OK to give him extra time & give others a new word/baggy
Is vocabulary reviewed prior to the lesson?	☑	☐	☐	☐	Reviewed "noun," "adjective," & several examples of each
Does teacher/therapist explain unknown vocabulary to the student during the lesson?	☑	☐	☐	☐	Explained "thick" using tactile objects
Are materials appropriate for the students?	☑	☐	☐	☐	Great hands-on materials; each student had own baggy full of materials
Does teacher/therapist address how session objectives are applied (generalized) to classroom activities?	☑	☐	☐	☐	Relates to curriculum by giving examples how students can use new vocabulary

This tool was adapted from one that Melissa Wildes, a speech therapist in Brooklyn, New York, and a leadership candidate, created.

Tool 19: Guided Reading

Explanation. The workshop model of teaching and learning provides natural opportunities for focusing on its discrete components. Whereas balanced literacy often uses the workshop model to organize the literacy classroom, we provide both quantitative and qualitative instruments for various literacy focuses (see Table 3.23). Can you think of student-focused tools to accompany them?

Table 3.23   Guided Reading

Class: 2-3

Date: 5/5

Time: Literacy Block

Guided Reading Teacher Indicator	Yes	No	N/A	Comments/Examples
Management				
Was the transition from the mini-lesson to group work implemented in an orderly fashion?	☑	☐	☐	• Children for guided reading were told in advance that they would meet • Independent work and book exchange were addressed before splitting up into groups
Were the other children on task while the teacher was in small-group instruction?	☑	☐	☐	• Teacher did not have to interrupt group to attend to other students until the very end of session, after about a 45-minute period • Teacher left guided reading group while they were reading independently to walk around and monitor/conference with others
Was the time allotted for the guided reading group appropriate?	☐	☑	☐	• Guided reading session lasted for 47 minutes • Recommended time is 15–20 minutes
Instruction (article for instruction: "Beverly Cleary")				
Was the text for guided reading introduced in a manner that provided knowledge? Was there support so that students could read independently and successfully?	☑	☐	☐	• Genre—a biographical article, columns, and how to read them • Activated prior to reading Beverly Cleary books • Nontext information—pictures, captions, lists

(Continued)

(Continued)

Were the children interested in and did they grasp the concepts being taught?	☑	☑	❑	• Girls seemed more interested than boys • 3 out of 4 students were able to touch on the main idea
Was the text appropriate for the group with respect to the level, content, and interest?	❑	☑	❑	• Level seemed too difficult • Interest—boys were not as interested as girls
Were support, challenges, and opportunities for problem solving provided?	☑	❑	❑	• Support—text was introduced with a variety of strategies, main idea was finalized as a group, teacher led students through each paragraph to find details
	❑	❑	☑	• Challenge—didn't seem appropriate. The text was challenging in itself as well as the activity
Did the students read independently?	☑	❑	❑	
Did assessment take place? What types?	☑	❑	❑	• Students wrote main idea in sentence form independently • Students highlighted details and were asked to justify their selections
Did the teacher allow students to be responsible for what they already know?	❑	❑	☑	
Did questions include the full range of Bloom's Taxonomy?	☑	❑	❑	• Knowledge • Comprehension • Evaluation—students had to support and justify answers
Did the teacher help students strengthen their strategies?	☑	❑	❑	• Students were asked to justify which details supported main idea. This developed the process behind the strategy. • Students were directed through each paragraph to break material into manageable chunks. This modeled how to approach the text. • Teacher told students how they could transfer what they did to other reading and writing

Source: This instrument was adapted from one that Suzanne Dimitri, a Brooklyn, New York, literacy coach, created. It is used with her permission.

Tool 20: Read-Aloud/Story Time

The following balanced literacy read-aloud tool (see Table 3.24) is adapted from a tool that Lorraine Call, a preschool teacher on Staten Island, created. With slight adaptations, it can be used for any read-aloud lesson. Which student-focused tools could be used as a follow-up to this observation?

Table 3.24   Read-Aloud/Story Time

Class: PreK

Date: 10/19

Time: 8:45 a.m.

Title of book: *The Busy Little Squirrel* Author: Nancy Tafuri

Type of book: Picture book story

New words: squeak, pumpkin, nibble

Other comments: Appropriate book choice and activities

Teacher Behaviors	Yes	No	N/A	Comments/Examples
Introduces book by showing cover and reading title. Encourages students to share thoughts about book based on these features.	☑	☐	☐	Teacher showed cover, asked who remembers what book is about. Encourages with "What else?"
Reads name(s) of author and illustrator. Asks students to point to title, author, illustrator, and encourages discussion about these features.	☑	☐	☐	Teacher asks, "Who can tell me what the author does? What the illustrator does?"
Introduces at least three words that will be in story by showing cards with words and pictures representing them.	☑	☐	☐	Teacher covers picture part of word cards and asks who remembers the word. Then shows picture.
Attempts to capture/maintain students' interest. Uses facial expression and changes in tone, pitch, and so on to represent different characters and emphasize words or facts.	☑	☐	☐	Teacher uses loud and soft voice throughout. Hesitates when vocabulary word appears, allowing children to fill in word.
Involves children throughout the story by encouraging comments and questions.	☑	☐	☐	Asks other children if they know response to classmate's question "What's the squirrel doing?"
Asks open-ended questions, such as What if? What would you do if? and so on, and provides wait time. When voluntary responses are limited, initiates discussion of facts, plot and/or characters.	☑	☐	☐	Teacher asks, "What would you do if you were a squirrel?" "What do you think it feels like to roll around in those leaves?"
Involves children in extension activities by creating charts or other visuals, for example, T charts, story maps, word/character webs.	☑	☐	☐	Evidence of extension: leaf rubbings, fall collages, KWL chart about fall
Invites children to retell story in their own words (through pretending to read the book to the class, using puppets, etc.).	☐	☑	☐	

Tool 21: Teacher Language During Center-Based Learning in Pre-Kindergarten Classrooms

Special Prerequisite Knowledge. Familiarity with the Early Childhood Environment Rating Scale–Revised (ECERS–R). This tool specifically addresses several indicators from the Language Reasoning subscale: Item #17: Using Language to Develop Reasoning Skills, and Item #18: Informal Use of Language. The ECERS–R includes other subscales that can be used as sources for early childhood observations.

Explanation. Supervisor and teacher collaboratively decide to focus on the language the teacher uses with the students during center time. As shown in Table 3.25, a tally is kept for each instance of the demonstrated language

Table 3.25   Teacher Language During Center-Based Learning in Pre-Kindergarten Classrooms

Site/Class: Bright Beginnings Early Learning Center

Date: 12-13

Beginning Time: 10:00 a.m.

Ending Time: 10:45 a.m.

Class: PreK

Teacher Language	*Tally*	*Examples*
Talk about logical relationships while children play with materials that stimulate reasoning i.e., sorting or sequencing materials	✓	Teacher asked why child put the round piece in the round hole and not the square hole
Encourage children to explain their reasoning when solving problems, i.e., why they sorted objects into different groups	✓ ✓ ✓	Teacher asked what the different materials felt like (smooth, rough, etc.) Teacher asked why the child put dishes on one side and food on the other Teacher discussed different types of foods with children
Add information or new vocabulary to expand on ideas presented by the children (not in the form of a question)	✓	Teacher introduced additional foods in each category
Ask questions to encourage students to give longer and more complex answers, i.e., "what," "where," "why," or "how"		Some prompting given, but more questions could be asked
Introduce concepts in response to children's interests or needs to solve problems, i.e., how to balance a tall block building		Discuss questioning and concept introduction

Adapted by Carol Berg, an early childhood instructional coordinator, from: Harms, T., Clifford, R. M., & Cryer, D. (2005). *Early Childhood Environment Rating Scale-Revised.* New York, NY: Teachers College Press.

behaviors from the chart, along with specific examples. The frequency of the language behavior is not recorded, rather its occurrence within the specific time frame. The tool may also be used to look at the language of both the head and assistant teacher during the same time frame. If necessary, the teachers' initials in the examples column would indicate whose language is noted. In addition, this tool might be used by the head teacher and/or the assistant teacher to observe and support each other's use of language during center-based learning.

Tools 22 and 23: Common Core Standards in Mathematics

Explanation. The mathematical practices identified in the *Common Core State Standards* are interpreted for students at various grade levels. However, the basic principles remain the same. These tools support the teacher in encouraging specific practices during her or his interaction with students. They ask that the observer record if the teacher encourages students to engage in specific mathematics problem-solving practices and to record examples. More detailed illustrations of what the practices look like at various grade levels can be found in the standards document http://www.corestandards.org/math. Teachers and observers may wish to create their own instruments to focus on one or two of the practices at any one time or do a general observation to see which of these are most frequent or least evident.

Tool 22 (see Table 3.26) focuses on encouraging student problem-solving processes.

Tool 23 (see Table 3.27) focuses on encouraging student communication in problem solving.

Tool 22: Teacher encouragement of students' problem solving skills and reasoning.

Table 3.26   Teacher Encouragement of Students' Problem-Solving Skills and Reasoning (Mathematics Common Core Standards)

Class: Grade 3

Focus: Relationship between area and perimeter

Date: 6/9

Time: 1:25 p.m.

Teacher Encourages Students:	Frequently	Sometimes	Rarely	Examples
To analyze givens, constraints, relationships, and goals.		X		After distributing tiles and posing problem, students had 1 minute "think" time to analyze the task and then share out.

(Continued)

(Continued)

Teacher Encourages Students:	Frequently	Sometimes	Rarely	Examples
To use mathematical models, such as simple addition equations, formulas, and flowcharts, to solve problems arising in everyday life.		X		Teacher posed playground problem and encouraged students to use tiles to represent playground layout. Graph paper was available to students.
To use appropriate tools, such as ruler, calculator, or website.		X		Students used rulers to draw an accurate sketch of their playground.
To attend to precision by: • using correct units of measure, • calculating accurately, and • using mathematical tools correctly.	X			Teacher required students to report area and perimeter measurements in correct units and use the correct terminology, i.e., square unit.
To find patterns and use them in solving problems, including looking for shortcuts to solve problems.	X		X (No short-cuts)	Students worked together to find relationships between the perimeters of the figures they created. As a class, students determined that the areas of all playgrounds were the same.

Tool 23: Teacher encouragement of mathematical communication during problem solving.

Table 3.27   Teacher Encouragement of Mathematical Communication During Problem Solving (Mathematics Common Core Standards)

Class: Grade 3

Focus: Relationship between area and perimeter

Date: 5/30

Time: 1:55 p.m.

Teacher encourages students:	Frequently	Sometimes	Rarely	Examples
To explain the meaning of the representation(s) they used to begin to solve a problem. (These representations may include numbers, words, pictures, concrete objects, graphs, etc.)	X			Students identified areas and perimeters of their playground from pictures they drew representing their tile models.

Teacher encourages students:	Frequently	Sometimes	Rarely	Examples
To explain: • what they are doing to solve the problem • why they are doing it.		X		Teacher walked around room and asked groups questions while they worked on task.
To make logical arguments while explaining their reasoning.	X			Students reported to class on the playground layout they chose as the team's favorite and why they chose that one.
To explain why the answer they have found is reasonable.			X	Teacher did not ask students if the areas and perimeters they found were reasonable.
To try to make sense of others' mathematical thinking.	X			Each group member was asked to examine fellow teammates' playground layouts.
To ask useful questions to clarify or improve others' reasoning.		X		Students asked presenting team questions about their layout.

Note: We thank Judy Walsh, an instructor of math methods at the College of Staten Island, City University of New York, and a former supervisor and teacher of mathematics, for her lead role in developing the math tools.

Tool 24a: Teacher Behaviors Keyed to Accountable Talk

Explanation. A learning concept that has recently emerged from the account-ability movement, and cooperative learning is accountable talk. It is based on the principle that classroom talk that is accountable to the learning community and to the academic disciplines is essential to learning. The following observation tools (see Tables 3.28 and 3.29) are based on the four ways that student talk should be accountable: accountable to the community (polite listeners), accountable to knowledge (use evidence), accountable to standards of reasoning, and accountable to standards of reasoning appropriate to a subject area. For further information on accountable talk, contact the Institute for Learning at the Learning Research and Development Center at the University of Pittsburgh or click on the following link: http://ifl.lrdc.pitt.edu/ifl/.

Tool 24b: Student Behaviors Keyed to Accountable Talk

Explanation. Once the teacher has analyzed and modified where appropriate his or her modeling of accountable talk, the observer can focus in on the students' use of accountable talk. This tool can serve as an assessment of the students as well as the effectiveness of the teacher's modeling (see Table 3.29).

Table 3.28   Teacher Behaviors Keyed to Accountable Talk

Class: 9-2

Date: 4/17/04

Time: Humanities Block

Teacher Indicators	Response Yes	No	N/A	Observations
Engages students in talk by: • Providing opportunities for students to speak about content knowledge, concepts, and issues • Using wait time/allowing silence to occur • Listening carefully • Providing opportunities for reflection on classroom talk	☑ ☑ ☑ ☑	☐ ☐ ☐ ☐	☐ ☐ ☐ ☐	Teacher consistently waited for students to answer. You could see her thinking about the response. At the end of the class, group reflectors reported on the process in their groups.
Assists students to listen carefully to each other by: • Creating seating arrangements that promote discussion • Providing clear expectations for how talk should occur • Requiring courtesy and respect • Reviewing major ideas and understandings from talk	 ☑ ☑ ☑ ☐	 ☐ ☐ ☐ ☑	 ☐ ☐ ☐ ☐	The class reviewed the guidelines for discussion before going into circles of small groups where a reflector and facilitator were chosen. No time remained at the end of class to review group work.
Assists students to elaborate and build on others' ideas by: • Modeling reading processes of predicting, looking for key words, engaging prior knowledge, and so on • Facilitating rather than dominating the talk • Listening carefully • Asking questions about discussion ideas and issues	 ☑ ☑ ☑ ☐	 ☐ ☐ ☐ ☑	 ☐ ☐ ☐ ☐	The introductory whole-class discussion of the topic allowed the teacher to model the skills the students needed in their small-group discussions. She asked the class what reading process she had just used at least three times. No time to debrief about the discussions at the end of class.
Assists in clarifying or expanding a proposition by: • Modeling methods of restating arguments and ideas and asking if they are expressed correctly • Modeling and providing practice at responding appropriately to criticism • Modeling expressing own puzzlement or confusion	 ☑ ☑ ☑	 ☐ ☐ ☐	 ☐ ☐ ☐	The teacher modeled all these methods in the introductory discussion and encouraged them as she walked from group to group.

Table 3.29   Student Behaviors Keyed to Accountable Talk

Class: Social Studies

Date: 2/2

Time: 2:15 p.m.

Student Indicators	Response			*Observations*
	Yes	*No*	*N/A*	
Students are engaged in talk when they: • Speak appropriately in a variety of classroom situations • Allow others to speak without interruption • Speak directly to other students	☑ ☐ ☑	☐ ☑ ☐	☐ ☐ ☐	The whole-class and small-group discussions were very lively. Many students spoke, primarily to each other. Sometimes they interrupted each other.
Students are listening attentively to one another when they: • Make eye contact with speaker • Refer to a previous speaker • Connect comments to previous ideas	☐ ☑ ☑	☐ ☐ ☐	☑ ☐ ☐	It was often difficult to determine if eye contact was being made. Students usually referred to the person whose ideas they were addressing.
Students elaborate and build on others' ideas when they: • Make comments related to the focus of the discussion • Introduce new, related issues • Listen carefully • Talk about issues rather than participants	☑ ☐ ☑ ☐	☐ ☑ ☐ ☑	☐ ☐ ☐ ☐	Students stayed on topic, listened to each other. They were so engrossed in the issue that they did not bring up any related or new issue. One or two students referred to each other.
Students work toward clarifying or expanding a proposition when they: • Model methods of restating arguments and ideas and ask if they are expressed correctly • Model and provide practice at responding appropriately to criticism • Model expressing own puzzlement or confusion	☑ ☑ ☑	☐ ☐ ☐	☐ ☐ ☐	Students actively reflected back what they heard and questioned what they didn't understand.

QUALITATIVE OBSERVATION TOOLS

Tool 25a: Detached Open-Ended Narrative

The observer records every person, event, or thing that attracts her or his attention, known as selective verbatim (Acheson & Gall, 1997) or script taping (Hunter, 1983). Whatever the observer considers significant is recorded. The observer simply records exactly what is said during the lesson; hence, a verbatim transcript is taken. Not all verbal communications are recorded but only those that the observer feels are significant or those communications agreed upon by both supervisor and teacher beforehand. Hence, only selected portions are recorded. Of course, no prearranged categories or questions are developed.

Selective Verbatim

Explanation. Supervisor and teacher collaboratively agree that anecdotal evidence will be collected during a specified period of time. The goal is to *describe*, as objectively as possible, the key events and actions that occur. It will be impossible to record everything. The observer must try to choose what he or she believes is indicative of the teaching and learning observed.

Open-Ended Narrative

Fifth-grade class; 13 boys and 12 girls; self-contained classroom; Amy Clayman, teacher; 9:45 a.m. I enter as Ms. Clayman tells class to take out their math books. As Ms. Clayman gives instructions for the math assignment, four students (two male and two female) are out of their seats, hanging their clothing in the rear classroom closet. A girl is talking. Ms. Clayman tells her to be quiet and sit down. Teacher takes attendance by reading class roster, name by name. After about 3 minutes, a monitor enters classroom, and teacher is recording daily attendance; noise level in class rises. Monitor leaves room. Teacher walks back and forth as students get quiet. At 9:53 a.m., Ms. Clayman asks a girl to tell the class what the answer to the first math problem is. Student responds; class attentive. Ms. Clayman asks a boy, "Can you answer question No. 2?" Student responds. Teacher calls on a boy who also responds, with a different answer. Ms. Clayman probes and asks boy to explain. Ms. Clayman asks another student to answer the question. Girl responds. Teacher asks another question to a boy and probes. Teacher proceeds this way for the next 15 minutes. Ms. Clayman then asks the class, "How may we figure out how much carpet to buy if the room is 10 feet by 15 feet?" No one raises a hand to answer. Ms. Clayman repeats the question. Still no response. Teacher draws a diagram on the board and then James calls out, "Oh, I know." Students giggle. Ms. Clayman tells class, "Now, stop that. Pay attention. Go ahead, James, tell us." James mumbles something. Ms. Clayman requests that he speak more clearly. James is silent. Teacher then explains to the class how to compute the area of a rectangle. She writes several examples on the board and then calls on several students to answer them.

Reflect and Practice

Obtain a video of a lesson and practice taking selected verbatim information. After recording is completed, share notes with a colleague.

Then view the video again, taking note of inaccuracies and missed information. Keep practicing until you're satisfied that you've recorded all that you wanted to.

Postnote. The ability of the observer to accurately and quickly record information is essential. Recording such information may appear simple, but much practice is required. Be certain to practice Activity 1 (page 137).

Tool 25b: Participant Open-Ended Observation

Explanation. Participant open-ended observation refers to a situation in which the observer takes part in the classroom activities. The observer may assist in the instruction by working with a group or helping individual students. We are including this technique as a student-centered one because it can follow a teacher-focused observation to determine how the students are responding to a particular teacher strategy. It can also be used as a stand-alone narrative of a lesson from a participant's point of view.

The observer may take notes or just jot down some ideas for later recall. The advantage of having the observer participate in the class is that many insights may be culled from direct participation that might otherwise be missed from detached observations.

The types of observation possible are similar to detached open-ended narratives. Using this procedure, the observer either makes notes during the activities or simply summarizes events after the observation period. The essential element here is that the observer is in a unique position to better understand classroom interactions because he or she actively is involved.

Observers should feel free to vary their approaches (detached or participant), depending on a given situation. For example, sometimes a teacher may feel uncomfortable having the supervisor participate, explaining that it may be distracting. We strongly suggest arranging the format of observation with the teacher in advance.

Practice participant open-ended observation as you did previously with the detached open-ended narrative.

Tool 26: Child-Centered Learning Observation

Based on constructivist learning theory, *child-centered learning observation* focuses primarily on the learner, the student, rather than on the instructor. By incorporating a qualitative approach, the observer may record observations in response to these and other learner-centered questions:

1. Were the children learning/thinking? What indications were there that the children were learning/thinking?

2. What kinds of questions were being asked (e.g., open ended)? How did the children respond?

3. How were the children treated? How did they respond?

4. What opportunities were provided for the children to learn in different ways?

5. Who is the source of knowledge?

(Continued)

(Continued)

6. Were the children talking to other children?

7. Were the children designing their own learning?

8. How was learning assessed? What was the role of the student?

9. What did we learn about the children?

Tool 27: Nonverbal Techniques

Explanation. Proxemics is the teacher's use of perception and space. The closer a teacher is to a student, the less likely the student is to behave inappropriately. For example, the teacher may stand near or move toward a potentially disruptive student as a behavior control strategy. This technique works best with teachers who customarily stand and move about. Another use of proxemics is to arrange classroom furniture in such a way as to convey warmth and closeness.

Kinesics is the teacher's use of facial and body cues, such as smiling, frowning, staring, pointing, or hands on hips. These cues communicate strong messages, work well from a distance, and help signal individuals and groups when they are disrupting others. Kinesic cues should be considered as an aid to conventional classroom management methods. The best way to learn these cues is to practice them with others and in front of a mirror.

Prosody is concerned with tone, pitch, and rhythm of the teacher's voice, and communicates the importance of what is being said. Teachers who use this tool know that yelling and high-pitched voices tend to excite rather than calm students. Effective use of prosody can convey caring, empathy, and warmth as well as a love of teaching and students.

Immediacy is the degree of perceived or psychological closeness between people. Teachers who use this technique are physically close to students, use socially appropriate touching, exhibit warmth, and use open body postures while communicating. For example, lightly touching a student's shoulder or upper arm while explaining an assignment tells that student the teacher cares and wants him or her to be successful.

Explanation. Observations are collaboratively arranged and made in a series of short visits at various times during one day or over several days. Although a checklist can be used noting each time the teacher uses a particular nonverbal technique, we prefer that the observer keep a running record of the types of nonverbal interactions used, along with annotations describing the nature and impact of those interventions. See Table 3.30.

Table 3.10 in Resource D is provided as a training tool for interpreting the teacher–student interaction during this particular lesson.

Tool 28: Questioning Techniques

Explanation. Questions play an important role in the development of a lesson. Effective questioning starts students thinking and guides the class from one important concept to another. In the Quantitative Tools section, two tools are

Table 3.30 Nonverbal Techniques

Class: 9th grade English

Date: 11/4

Time: 8:35 a.m.

Nonverbal Technique	Frequency	Anecdotal Observations/Student Responses
Proxemics • Standing near student(s) • Moving toward student(s) • Touching student(s) • Moving about room	✓ ✓ ✓ ✓ ✓ ✓ ✓ ✓ ✓ ✓ ✓ ✓	Teacher frequently moving around room, especially during independent work
Kinesics a. Affirmation • Eye contact • Touching • Smiling • Nodding • Open arm movements	✓ ✓ ✓ ✓ ✓ ✓ ✓ ✓ ✓ ✓ ✓	Eye contact during mini-lesson and discussion; frequent smiling Tendency to keep arms crossed
b. Disapproval • Frowning • Stern look • Finger to lips • Pointing • Arms crossed • Hands on hips	✓ ✓ ✓	Finger to lips to quiet students during independent work See above
Prosody • Varies voice tone • Varies pitch • Varies rhythm	✓ ✓ ✓	Clearly aware of need to vary tone, pitch, and rhythm during mini-lesson
Immediacy • Responds with warmth	✓	Generally responds with warmth without touching

Source: Glickman, Carl D.; Gordon, Stephen P.; Ross-Gordon, Jovita M., *Supervision of Instruction: A Developmental Approach*, 4th Edition, © 1998. Reprinted by permission of Pearson Education, Inc., Upper Saddle River, NJ.

provided to assess the teacher's level of questioning according to Bloom's Taxonomy and Webb's Depth of Knowledge. In this qualitative questionnaire, we look at how questions are asked and how the teacher responds to the answer, two equally important but different skills from the level of the questions themselves.

1. What classroom rules exist for students asking and answering questions?

2. How does the teacher direct questions?

3. How does the teacher address wait time for students to think about answers?

(Continued)

(Continued)

4. How does the teacher address a lack of response to a question?

5. Are questions directed to both volunteers and nonvolunteers?

6. How does the teacher handle other students' comments to student responses?

7. How does the teacher handle praise and other reactions to questions?

8. How were students encouraged to ask questions? Or discouraged?

9. How did the teacher's position in the room affect class participation?

10. How many questions beginning with "how," "why," "explain," or "compare" were asked?

These questions were adapted with permission from the New York City Teacher Academy Fieldwork Guide.

Tool 29: Strategies for Diverse Learners

Explanation. This focused questionnaire can be used as a basis for ascertaining how the teacher is meeting the needs of all the children. The following brief questionnaire is an adaptation of the Indicators of Culturally Diverse Learners chart (Tool 13) in the quantitative section.

1. How does the teacher encourage students?

2. What positive reinforcement techniques does he or she use?

3. What kinds of modifications for individual children or types of learners are evident?

4. How does the teacher use the children's strengths?

5. Where are the students situated in the room and why?

6. What are the opportunities for small-group work?

7. How does the teacher address grouping according to needs and skills?

8. What evidence is there of scaffolding of instruction?

9. How does the teacher adapt materials and instruction to different student learning styles?

10. What is the teacher's proximity to the students?

11. How are the children interacting?

12. What else is special about the treatment of the children?

We hope that these examples of two tools—one quantitative and one qualitative—for the same focus will facilitate your ability to create your own tools.

Tool 30: Differentiated Instruction

Explanation. Differentiated instruction can occur when teachers are aware of and able to consider and deal with different learning needs and abilities of their students. The following questionnaire addresses many of the classroom activities that promote differentiated learning. No classroom can or should exhibit all of these characteristics at once, and others not included in the questions may be displayed. This questionnaire can be adapted to include activities mentioned in the quantitative Differentiated Classroom tool and vice versa.

1. What preassessments of student knowledge are included prior to instruction?

2. How does the teacher incorporate multiple intelligences into the lesson?

3. How are different learning styles addressed?

4. What assessment strategies are used and when?

5. What homework options are offered?

6. Are all students prompted and probed equitably during questioning?

7. How is wait time for different students addressed?

8. What kind of grouping procedures are used (whole class, diads, triads, quads)?

9. Is peer tutoring used? If so, how?

Tool 31: Guided Reading

A Staten Island staff developer, Maria Casales, created a series of balanced literacy tools for her work with teachers. See Table 3.31 for an example.

Tool 32: Team Teaching in the Inclusion or General Education Classroom

Explanation. The integrated or inclusion classroom usually includes a general and a special education teacher. In addition, team teaching has increased with the expansion of the integrated curriculum and longer and flexible time periods. Effective use of two teachers in one classroom is difficult to achieve. The following questionnaire can support collaborative team teaching. You can also create a performance indicator instrument to describe the teachers' roles. Note the overlap between this instrument and the Push-in Categorical Frequency Chart in the quantitative section (Tool 17; Table 3.21). You can adapt your tools by combining some elements from both tools and adding your own.

1. Describe the involvement of the general education teacher and the special education teacher with the whole class, with small groups, and with individual children.

2. What is the role of each teacher in the classroom? How is instruction organized between the two teachers?

3. Who guides the curriculum?

(Continued)

(Continued)

4. What is the curricular role of each teacher?

5. Who attends to the individual needs of the children?

6. What accommodations are available for special needs students?

7. How are the accommodations for children with special needs handled?

8. How is responsibility for children with special needs divided between the teachers?

Note. Thanks to Claire Wurtzel, a special education consultant based in New York City, for her suggestions for the inclusion tools.

Table 3.31   Guided Reading

Time: Literacy Block

Selects appropriate text for small-group instruction Teacher uses book *The Birthday Cake,* written by Joy Cowley. Six students, 4 boys, 2 girls, receive a copy of the same book. They look at the cover of the book with curiosity and await teacher direction.	*Helps children to think, talk, and question through the story* The teacher encourages her students to take a "picture walk" through the story. As they preview the text, Amanda questions an illustration, and Mark questions some of the words in print. Teacher briefly discusses their concerns.
Introduces story to the group as well as vocabulary concepts and text features The teacher brings the students' attention to new vocabulary words and to the ending punctuation. Children give the teacher sentences using the new vocabulary words. Teacher reviews telling sentences and question sentences.	*Allows small groups to read independently with minimum teacher support* The teacher allows the group to read the book independently. She lends support rarely and her students read the whole book (12 pages).
Provides or reinforces reading strategies and provides students with the opportunity to use the strategy Upon completion of reading the story, the teacher asks the students, "How many of you noticed the end of some sentences? Why are some sentences telling sentences and others question sentences?" Children are able to respond to teacher-posed questions. The teacher encourages the children to reread the story, focusing on ending punctuation and pauses.	
Records reflections on the students' reading behaviors during and after reading The teacher logs their reading behaviors as they relate to the skill and fluency. After they read, she adds some quick notes.	*Engages students in a brief discussion after reading the story* The teacher asks the students if they enjoyed reading the book. The students reply "yes." She then asks what they enjoyed the most and why.

Tool 33: Classroom Assessment in the Differentiated Classroom

Adaptation. Assessment has taken center stage in the efforts to raise achievement for all children. Ongoing and multiple forms of assessment provide crucial knowledge for differentiating instruction. The following questions will assist the teacher in determining whether multiple forms of assessment are facilitating learning.

1. How does the teacher preassess students?

2. What different forms of assessments are used?

3. What is the role of the student in classroom assessment?

4. Is peer assessment used? If so, how?

5. How is it determined that the students are ready to proceed to the next step or level?

6. How does the teacher adjust and/or modify the lesson in response to student needs and varying mastery levels?

7. How do assessments address multiple intelligences and learning styles?

8. How do students demonstrate to the teacher and to one another that they have achieved the goals of the lesson (quiz, test, written assignment, project, discussion, a variety of media, exit pass, etc.)?

Adapted with permission from the New York City Teacher Academy Fieldwork Guide.

Reflect and Practice

We have presented 42 practical tools and techniques to assist your observations of classrooms. Some tools are certainly more appropriate than others in various situations. You know best what may be needed in a given situation. For instance, a teacher may request that you examine her verbal interactions with students since she tends to lecture too much at times and answer her own questions. You might suggest, therefore, the tool dealing with Teacher Verbal Behaviors. For this activity, use the following list of the 42 tools and create a scenario or situation in which each tool might be most appropriate. Share your list with a colleague. You will notice that different colleagues may have varied uses for even the same tool. Discuss the advantages and disadvantages of each tool selection.

1a. Teacher Verbal Behaviors

1b. Student Responses to Verbal Behaviors

2a. Teacher Questions Using Bloom's Taxonomy

2b. Student Responses to Questions Indicating Bloom's Taxonomy

3a. Teacher Questions Using Webb's Depth of Knowledge

3b. Student Responses to Questions Indicating Webb's Depth of Knowledge

4a. Student On-Task and Off-Task Behaviors

4b. Diagram of Verbal Interactions

5a. Gardner's Multiple Intelligences

5b. Student Use of Gardner's Multiple Intelligences

6. Hunter's Steps in Lesson Planning

7a. Group Work Criteria

7b. Group Performance: Assessment of Individual Participation

8a. Diagram of Teacher Space Utilization

8b. Diagram of Student Space Utilization

9. Feedback

10. Teacher–Pupil Interaction

11. Indicators of Culturally Diverse Learners

12. Strategies for Diverse Learners

13. Accommodations and Modifications for English-Language Learners

14. The Differentiated Classroom

15. Students' Construction of Meaning on Their Own

16. Learning Centers

17. Co-teaching: Push-in Model (initial)

18. Strategies for Students With Speech and Language Impairments

19. Guided Reading

20. Read-Aloud/Story Time

21. Teacher Language During Center-Based Learning in Pre-Kindergarten Classrooms

22. Teacher Encouragement of Students' Problem-Solving Skills and Reasoning (Mathematics Common Core Standards)

23. Teacher Encouragement of Mathematical Communication During Problem Solving (Mathematics Common Core Standards)

24a. Teacher Behaviors Keyed to Accountable Talk

24b. Student Behaviors Keyed to Accountable Talk

25a. Detached Open-Ended Narrative

25b. Participant Open-Ended Observation

26. Child-Centered Learning Observation

27. Nonverbal Techniques

28. Questioning Techniques

29. Strategies for Diverse Learners

30. Differentiated Instruction

31. Guided Reading

32. Team Teaching in the Inclusion or General Education Classroom

33. Classroom Assessment in the Differentiated Classroom

Site Practice

We have found that observers and observees often gain the most when they adapt or create their own tools. Therefore, we highly recommend that you collaboratively choose a focus with a colleague and either adapt one of the tools in the chapter or, preferably, create your own to use in an observation.

SUMMARY

We have described two approaches to observation: quantitative and qualitative. A total of 42 tools and techniques were reviewed and practiced. Wherever possible, we have provided two instruments: one focusing on teacher behaviors and another on student behaviors related to the teacher behaviors. We have not included videotaping as a separate tool; rather, it is a valuable instrument that can be used with any of the tools and techniques described in this chapter. According to Acheson and Gall (1997),

> Videos and audiotapes are among the most objective observation techniques. . . . They allow teachers to see themselves as students see them. . . . [T]hey can pick up a great deal of what teachers and students are doing and saying. A good recording captures the "feel" of classroom interaction. (p. 111)

Videos and audiotapes, according to Acheson and Gall (1997), are examples of "wide lenses" that are particularly useful "in supervising teachers who are defensive or who are not yet ready to select particular teaching behaviors for improvement" (p. 107). Acheson and Gall conclude, "After reviewing wide-lens data, these teachers may be more ready to reflect on their teaching, identify specific teaching behaviors for focused observations, and set self-improvement goals" (pp. 107–108). We agree.

At this juncture, we would also like to offer our perspective on the use of the tools and techniques presented in this chapter within a standards-based environment. In the 2000 edition of his book on different approaches to clinical supervision, Edward Pajak asks "whether clinical supervision is compatible with the principles of systemic reform and exactly how clinical supervision is being implemented in standards-based contexts" (p. 295). In our own work in the field and through feedback teachers and administrators have given us, our impressions are that the revised observation forms that districts often require are variations on the same old theme. Instead of an arbitrary list of categories of behaviors to be observed, the "new" standards-based formats address a range of standards. The supervisor fills out a rubric that does not differ much from the old checklists or short narratives or a combination of both. The result for the teacher is the same: He or she scans the form in relief and files it, or reacts in disbelief to the areas requiring attention. The postobservation conference may provide valuable feedback, but the form itself is of limited value. Too many areas are observed simultaneously. The teacher becomes frustrated because he or she cannot focus on multiple areas effectively at the same time.

We propose that supervisors and coaches use the principles of the reflective clinical supervision cycle in a standards-based environment. Rather than create complicated rubrics to verify if learning outcomes are being met, we suggest that each observation focus on one learning outcome, standard, or teaching skill. Many schools or districts mandate a comprehensive form. We cannot change that practice even though we know, as discussed in this text, that it is not effective supervision. However, we recommend that after the list is completed as required, focused observations, along with other strategies we discuss, should remain the primary approach for teacher development.

In this chapter, we have provided some sample tools that are already in use or that we have created to meet some of the current learning outcomes and standards. The overarching standard, currently expressed as "leave no child behind," is the underlying theme of most of these tools. The inclusion of many student-centered instruments enables observers and observees the opportunity to collect student evidence based on classroom learning. We have found that performance indicator instruments, categorical frequency instruments, and focused questionnaires can be easily adapted to meet most outcomes and standards. The samples that we have provided are primarily based on these three types of instruments, so that you can see the facility with which you and the teacher can discuss a focus, choose and adapt these tools, or create your own. We address diversity of backgrounds, learning styles, math standards, balanced literacy, differentiated instruction and assessment, and other strategies for enabling all children to reach their potential. Since most of these tools are variations of performance indicator instruments, categorical frequency instruments, and focused questionnaire tools, we have not included postnotes for all of these tools.

Another practice in the standards-based environment that we will address is the "walk-through," traditionally termed the *informal observation.* The walk-through, learning walk, or instructional round, which was developed as a means to improve instruction through teacher collaboration, will be presented in Chapter 5 as an alternative to traditional supervision. We believe that supervisors often use the walk-through or informal "pop-in" primarily as a monitoring method. In the best-case scenario, the supervisor has met with the teacher at the beginning of the year to talk about goals. Subsequently, the supervisor makes brief visits to a set of classes at regular intervals to ascertain if the agreed-upon goals are being implemented. More often, supervisors pop into classrooms unannounced and follow up the visit with a commendation or recommendation. We believe these informal or formal short visits are evaluation or monitoring practices that do not promote teacher-centered improvement of instruction. Supervisors should be present daily in classrooms and even take on teaching assignments. The goal, however, should be to get to know the children and how they are learning and to build a community of learners.

CONCLUSION

Research demonstrates that teachers are likely to change their instructional behaviors on their own after their classroom has been described to them by an observer. Observation is a mirror and thus a stimulus for change. Effective supervision is about engaging teachers in reflective thinking and discussion based on insightful and useful observation tools and techniques. In the next chapter, we place these observation tools within the context of a reflective clinical supervision program.

NOTES

1. We would like to acknowledge Glickman et al. (2010) for their excellent discussion of observation instruments. Our framework is drawn, in large measure, from their work. Their division of instruments into quantitative and qualitative approaches makes the most sense.

2. These categories were developed by Glickman et al. (2010).

3. From *How to Differentiate Instruction in Mixed-Ability Classrooms*, 2nd edition (p. 24), by Carol Ann Tomlinson, Alexandria, VA: ASCD. © 2001 by ASCD. Reprinted with permission. Learn more about ASCD at www.ascd.org.

4

An Introduction to Reflective Clinical Supervision

The way in which supervisors try to bring about change largely determines how teachers respond to the challenge. Supervisors can mandate change externally; or they can, together with teachers, build collaborative cultures that encourage the seeds of change to take root and grow.

—Grimmet, Rostad, & Ford, 1992, p. 185

CHAPTER OVERVIEW

1. Definition of Clinical Supervision

2. The Reflective Clinical Supervision Cycle

   a. The Planning Conference

      o Scenario A

      o Scenario B

   b. The Observation

   c. The Feedback Conversation

      o Scenario A (directive informational approach)

      o Scenario B (collaborative approach)

      o Scenario C (self-directed approach)

   d. Collaborative Reflection

3. Conclusion

The first chapter traced the emergence of clinical supervision in the 1960s. In this chapter, we first present and explain our definition of clinical supervision and then offer an adaptation of clinical supervision we call *reflective clinical supervision.* An outline of the steps for each part of the cycle (except the actual observation) is accompanied by brief case studies. Opportunities to practice each phase are included. Finally, we detail how the whole process can be simulated in the course before trying it out on site. By the end of this chapter, you will be prepared to complete the key assignment of conducting a whole cycle in your schools.

A DEFINITION OF CLINICAL SUPERVISION

Although the sequence of a preconference, classroom observation, and feedback conference already existed in the 1920s, during the era of democratic supervision, Morris Cogan is credited with developing the elaborated concept and techniques of the clinical supervision cycle, which has emerged as a major force in educational supervision since the 1960s.

Edward Pajak (2000) said that Cogan "viewed clinical supervision as a vehicle for developing professional responsible teachers who were capable of analyzing their own performance, who were open to change and assistance from others, and who were above all, self-directing" (p. 76). This definition encompasses some of the assumptions that we believe underlie effective supervision: It does not explicitly restrict supervision to the supervisor, opening up the possibility that change and assistance can come from many sources; and it emphasizes self-analysis and self-direction, important components of reflective practice. We expand the definition to include classroom teaching and learning as the focuses of improvement and collaborative as well as individual analysis and reflection.

Before we define supervision, and learn and practice an adaptation of the clinical supervision cycle, it is important to understand that clinical supervision is not only a structure but a concept, and as such, it contains a series of assumptions. Goldhammer, Anderson, and Krajewski (1993) outlined nine major characteristics of clinical supervision that we believe are consistent with any of the approaches and structures in this book:

1. It is a technology for improving instruction.

2. It is a deliberate intervention into the instructional process.

3. It is goal oriented, combining the school's needs with the personal growth needs of those who work within the school.

4. It assumes a professional working relationship between teacher(s) and supervisor(s).

5. It requires a high degree of mutual trust, as reflected in understanding, support, and commitment to growth.

6. It is systematic, although it requires a flexible and continuously changing methodology.

7. It creates a productive (i.e., healthy) tension for bridging the gap between the real and the ideal.

8. It assumes that the supervisor knows a great deal about the analysis of instruction and learning and also about productive human interaction.

9. It requires both preservice training (for supervisors), especially in observation techniques, and continuous inservice reflection on effective approaches. (pp. 52–53)

**Reflection
(Individual and Shared)**

Formulate a definition of clinical supervision based on the preceding ideas and assumptions. Work in class in groups of three to five; share your definitions and come up with joint ones that designated group leaders will report to the whole class.

THE REFLECTIVE CLINICAL SUPERVISION CYCLE

Richard Weller's (1971) formal definition of clinical supervision provides a basis on which we can develop our reflective cycle of supervision:

Clinical supervision may be defined as supervision focused upon the improvement of instruction by means of systematic cycles of planning, observation, and intensive intellectual analysis of actual teaching performances in the interest of rational modification. (p. 11)

Weller referred to the three phases of the clinical supervision cycle as represented in Figure 4.1.

We add a fourth phase to the three activities of planning, observation, and analysis through a feedback conversation that includes a collaborative reflection and analysis of the process and its findings. The fourth phase is professional development. If you juxtapose the four steps that we propose with the four steps of the reflective practice cycle (see Figure 4.2), you will observe that they are correlated: The planning phase of the clinical supervision cycle is similar to the concrete experience or problematic or indeterminate situation of reflective practice (the goal is to pinpoint an experience for examination and analysis); we have also included professional development related to the observation focus as a possible part of the planning phase; the observation phase of clinical supervision, which is followed by individual analysis, is analogous to the observation and analysis stage of reflective

Figure 4.1   Three Phases of the Clinical Supervision Cycle

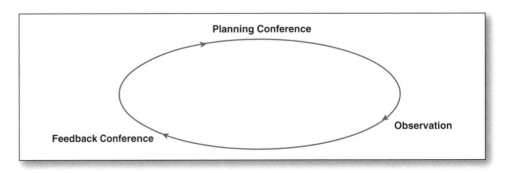

Figure 4.2   Comparison of Reflective Clinical Supervision With Reflective Practice

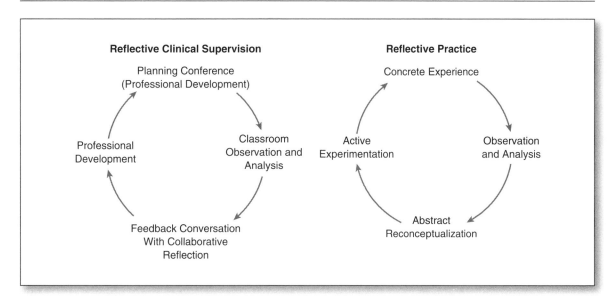

practice; the feedback conversation, which involves the joint analysis of the evidence and the reconceptualization and planning for the next cycle, is comparable to the abstract reconceptualization stage of reflective practice. The collaborative reflection concludes the third phase. It allows the supervisor and teacher to reflect on how the supervision process and its results worked before proceeding. In the fourth phase of the reflective practice model, the reconceptualized ideas are actually put into action, completing the cycle and simultaneously beginning another (Osterman & Kottkamp, 2004). In our fourth phase, professional development, the reconceptualized ideas are developed further. Thus, in the next cycle, the combination of the discussion of the observation and the further development through professional development prepare the teacher for a new planning cycle. If the observation does not result in a need for change in the practice, professional development can focus on a new instructional strategy.

It is apparent that in our model, the reflective process takes center stage in the clinical supervision cycle. Thus, our definition of supervision is: Supervision is the ongoing, nonjudgmental, collaborative process that engages teachers in dialogue that encourages deep reflective practices for the purpose of improving teaching and student learning.

The planning conference is the first step in the process and is crucial in determining the tone, content, and approach to the cycle. It can be the most important part of the cycle if, as in the Scenario B that follows, problem solving or professional development takes place before the observation.

The Planning Conference

Elena Santiago, the newly appointed principal of New Hope Middle School, whom we met in Chapter 2, began her first set of classroom observations as early as possible in the fall. She hoped to develop trusting relationships that would permit her and the teachers to focus on the improvement of teaching and learning, and not on the bureaucratic process of evaluation. Because her assistant principal could accomplish only some of the required observations and Elena wanted to be actively involved with what was going on in the classroom, she decided to meet with and observe herself the newest teachers first.

Elena set up a planning conference with a brand-new language arts teacher. She had heard that Sylvia, a recent graduate of a high-quality master's program, was having difficulty implementing her student-centered practices. Some of the students had not been exposed to cooperative learning groups before, and rumor had it that some of her classes were out of control. Nonetheless, Elena decided to query Sylvia about what she felt her concerns were. To make Sylvia comfortable, Elena set up a meeting in Sylvia's classroom, not in the principal's office.

We have found that the change process often begins during the planning conference. Therefore, we believe that two types of planning conferences can be effective. In the simpler form (see Scenario A), the teacher and supervisor identify the focus, choose an appropriate tool, and set the date and time of the observation and feedback conversation. The supervisor can choose either the directive informational, collaborative, or self-directed approach to determine focus and tool. In the second type of planning conference (see Scenario B), the change process actually begins in the initial conversation. The discussion and choice of focus frequently lead to a decision to try new strategies. The teacher can practice the innovations(s) before the actual observation or implement them for the first time during the observation. Again, the supervisor chooses one of the three interpersonal approaches to determine focus and tool. In either case, some kind of professional development may also take place before the actual observation. That professional development could be as simple as a conversation and an intervisitation with a teacher expert in the chosen focus area.

Scenario A

Elena: Hi, Sylvia. How's it going?

Sylvia: OK, I guess.

Elena: Since I will be beginning nontenured teacher observations, I thought we could discuss a particular area, interest, or concern that could be the focus of the observation.

Sylvia: Gosh, I wouldn't know where to start. You pick it.

Elena: I know that you use a lot of exciting innovative teaching methods. Is there any one in particular that you'd like some feedback on?

Sylvia: Mmm . . . I've been trying to have the students work in groups to discuss their writing, and it doesn't seem to be working in some classes. I have a rambunctious seventh-grade class that doesn't work well in groups at all, and I can't seem to get control of the process. Could you sit in on that class?

Elena: Sure. Let me show you a couple of tools I could use to observe the groups and see which one you think might pinpoint your concerns.

They decide to use the group work criteria instrument based on Tomlinson's Group Work Criteria (2001):

Elena: What is a convenient time for me to visit when you will be doing group work with the seventh graders?

Sylvia: How about third period next Tuesday? They're usually awake by then but not yet completely out of control.

Elena: Fine. Next Tuesday, October 1, third period. While we're at it, could we set a time to meet after the observation? How about during your professional period the following day?

Sylvia: Sounds OK to me.

Elena: Agreed. Third period on Tuesday and second period on Wednesday. By the way, if you have any other input that would be helpful before I visit, don't hesitate to stop in and share it with me. I'm looking forward to seeing students using this wonderful method.

> **Reflection**
>
> *What does Elena do to make Sylvia feel relaxed and at the same time focus on instruction? How does she get Sylvia to reflect on her own perceptions of her needs?*

Scenario B

Elena: Hi, Sylvia. How are you doing?

Sylvia: I'm at my wits' end.

Elena: You seem very frustrated. What's going on?

Sylvia: I've been trying to implement the group work criteria I learned in college, and it just doesn't seem to be working.

Elena: How long have you been doing group work with the seventh-grade class?

Sylvia: I began last week. I explained the process to them, handed out guidelines, and asked them to study the steps and rules for their homework assignment. We tried groups the next day, and they were so noisy. I made one more attempt the following day and had to abandon the process midway. It was so frustrating!

Elena: Did you model the process before you divided them in groups?

Sylvia: I thought that the sheets and my explanation would be sufficient. Maybe the change was too abrupt and extreme. Do you think one group could model without my losing control of the rest of the class?

Elena: Have you ever tried the fishbowl technique, where a volunteer group models the process in the middle of the classroom while the others watch and then comment at the end? If all the students keep their instructions in front of them, it will improve the fishbowl process and the ability of the rest of the class to comment.

Sylvia: Your suggestion could really help. It gives me another idea. I could have them make name plates for each role with a summary of the responsibilities on each card so the class would know who had each role in the fishbowl, and the list of steps on the other side would help everyone remember them. The list would also help them give feedback in the fishbowl and later in their small groups.

Elena: Your idea is very creative. Would you like me to visit when you do the fishbowl or when the whole class is in groups?

Sylvia: I think I could do both the fishbowl and groups in the double period we have the day after tomorrow. If I assign the name plates tomorrow, could you come the following day third and fourth periods?

Elena: I will make sure to be there. I'm very excited to see how it works.

They decide to use the Group Work Criteria performance indicator instrument, based on Tomlinson's criteria, to observe the fishbowl and the subsequent groups. They confirm the time and location and set up a feedback conversation time and place.

> ### Reflection
>
> *What are the major differences between Scenario A and Scenario B? What would help determine whether to use the approach depicted in Scenario A or Scenario B?*

Key Steps: Planning Conference

1. Decide the focus of the observation (choose a general approach: directive informational, collaborative, or self-directed).

2. Determine the method and form of observation. Problem solve or plan professional development prior to the observation where appropriate.

3. Set up the time of the observation and the feedback conversation.

The goals of the planning conference are:

- To identify teacher interests and concerns in an appropriate manner (directive informational, collaborative, or self-directed) and offer professional development prior to the observation where appropriate.
- To clarify that the primary purpose of the observation is to improve teaching and learning.
- To reduce stress and make the teacher feel comfortable about the process.
- To choose an observation tool and schedule the visit and feedback conversation.

The three steps of the planning conference are:

1. *Decide the focus of the observation.* Whereas the chief purpose of the observation is to improve instruction, it is essential to have the teacher's perspective on his or her concerns and interests. Even a new teacher can help identify the primary or most urgent concerns. Change occurs most easily if the teacher has a role in providing the focus. The supervisor will

use one of the three interpersonal approaches to guide the planning conference. Wherever possible, begin the problem-solving process related to the chosen focus of observation and include professional development prior to the observation.

2. *Determine the method and form of observation.* Once the focus is determined, the supervisor can discuss the appropriate tools. The supervisor will decide whether to include the teacher in making the choice of the observation instrument or in helping create an original one. A newer or less secure teacher may have enough to cope with without taking part in that decision.

3. *Set up the time of the observation and feedback conversation.* It is important, wherever possible, to provide the teacher with the opportunity to choose the day and time. The teacher knows in which class the focus that he or she has chosen can be observed best. Once he or she has had a role in deciding the focus, the choice is simplified. It becomes a learning experience with less likelihood that the visit will be an occasion to put on a show.

Class Practice

During the week, think about two teachers in your school: an experienced, confident teacher and a novice. Imagine a planning conference with each one, and write a short dialogue based on the imaginary planning conference. In class, you will practice at least one of the scenarios in groups of three using the reflective practice guidelines. Keep your key steps cards and practice guidelines handy. Volunteers will model at least one scenario, which can be videotaped for their personal use and reflection.

Site Practice

Begin to think about a teacher who would be receptive to participating in a reflective clinical supervision cycle with you. Once you have found a volunteer, you can rehearse the planning conference in class and then actually schedule the site planning conference.

The Observation

Key Steps: The Observation

1. Finalize the choice of observation tool.

2. Conduct the observation.

3. Verify the feedback conversation meeting time, and offer a copy of the observation tool to the teacher *before the feedback conversation.*

4. Analyze facts of the observation and begin thinking of interpretations.

5. Think about a feedback conversation interpersonal approach from Chapter 2 to be used after the observee has reflected on his or her analysis of the completed observation instrument.

1. *Finalize the choice of observation tool.* The supervisor finalizes the choice of observation tool from those described in Chapter 3, preferably in consultation with the teacher during the planning conference. The supervisor and the teacher may have created their own instrument or modified an existing one.

2. *Conduct the observation.* The observation takes place at the agreed-upon time. The teacher should be less anxious about your presence and your writing because he or she has chosen the focus and has been involved with the instrument development or choice of instrument being used to document it.

3. *Verify the feedback conversation meeting time, and offer a copy of the observation tool to the teacher.* At the end of the class, the supervisor reminds the teacher of their scheduled feedback conversation. The supervisor supplies the teacher with a copy of the completed observation tool so that they both can examine it individually before the conversation.

4. *Analyze facts of the observation and begin thinking of interpretations.* It is preferable for the supervisor to analyze and interpret the observation tool as soon as possible after the class, while the observation is fresh in his or her mind. Study and analyze the facts and then begin to think about an interpretation of the findings. Don't jump to conclusions before meeting with the teacher. It is important to get the teacher's perspective before finalizing an interpretation.

5. *Choose a feedback conversation interpersonal approach from Chapter 2.* Now that the supervisor has held the planning conference with the teacher and actually observed the teacher in the classroom, the supervisor should be able to determine which interpersonal approach is appropriate for the feedback conversation. Whereas the teacher has been given the completed tool prior to the feedback conversation, we highly recommend that the feedback conversation begin with the teacher's analysis and reflection on the results. A change in interpersonal approach can follow where needed.

The Feedback Conversation

We now provide three scenarios based on the interpersonal approaches presented in Chapter 2. Before briefly reviewing the steps, try to identify which approach the supervisor chose.

Scenario A

In the first scenario, we return to Elena and Sylvia. You will remember that Elena is the recently appointed principal of New Hope Middle School, and Sylvia is a new, young language arts teacher who is trying to implement the cooperative learning methodology she learned in college and who is running into some difficulties. She asked Elena to observe her rambunctious seventh-grade class during a cooperative learning workshop on the writing process. Elena chose

Group Work Criteria as the observation tool (Table 3.12) and shared a copy of the results with Sylvia immediately, so she could review it before the feedback conversation the following day. The scheduled meeting was in Sylvia's classroom during her professional period. This feedback conversation is based on Scenario A of the planning conference (no prior professional development).

Elena: Did you get a chance to look at the cooperative learning performance indicators?

Sylvia: I was devastated! Despite your attempts to write positive comments, it looks like I didn't get any of the responses right.

Elena: The students seemed to know what they were supposed to be doing because they kept on arguing about how they weren't following the rules! I didn't see them referring to written guidelines or following a clear sequence. How much preparation did they have before they began using the process?

Sylvia: I handed out a sheet one day for them to study at home, and then I had them try it out the next day.

Elena: Maybe it was too much too soon. Don't forget that some of these students haven't had much opportunity to work collaboratively. They are fortunate to have you as a teacher with all your current knowledge! This class in particular may need much more practice and role playing of the different roles before they can run their own groups. Have you ever tried the fishbowl technique, where a volunteer group models the process in the middle of the classroom while the others watch and then comment at the end? They also need to keep their instructions in front of them and make sure that the reflector has time to provide feedback at the end. Perhaps the reflectors can share who performed the roles most effectively in each group before the end of class. What do you think? Do you have any ideas?

Sylvia: I love your ideas, and they made me think of others. I can assign them as homework the job of making 3 × 5 cards for each job. They can then use the cards to direct their group work. And I could get a volunteer to videotape a group so they can see for themselves how they did.

Elena: Effective ideas! Let's review your plans and jot them down on the observation sheets so that we don't forget. First, you'll give them the 3 × 5 card assignment. The next day, a group will model the process using the fishbowl technique. Then you'll ask for a volunteer to videotape a group and ask the reflectors to identify who performed most effectively in each group. We can think of further incentives if these work. Do you want to go over them so we're sure we are on the same wavelength?

Sylvia: Sure. I can't wait to try these ideas. I'll give them the card assignment tomorrow. The next day, we'll do the fishbowl technique. Then I'll ask

Reflection

What does Elena do to take some of the heat off of Sylvia? What strategies does she use in giving suggestions? Why do you think Sylvia gets so excited? Which approach did Elena choose and why?

for videotaping volunteers. The following day, I'll explain the reflector's new role, and we'll try our first practice. How does that sound to you?

Elena: Terrific. How about meeting next week at the same time to touch base on how it's working? If it's going as planned, we can brainstorm some other refinements. Your feedback can help us decide if I need to revisit that class or if we can move on to another area.

Key Steps: Directive Informational Approach

1. Identify the problem or goal and solicit clarifying information.

2. Offer solutions. Ask for the teacher's input into the alternatives offered and request additional ideas.

3. Summarize chosen alternatives, ask for confirmation, and request that the teacher restate final choices.

4. Set up a follow-up plan and meeting.

Scenario B

Judy has been a French and Spanish teacher at New Hope for five years. As part of a state grant, all the world-language teachers have a bank of computers in their classrooms for the first time. Very little staff development accompanied the grant, so the teachers have been struggling to use the computers effectively. Elena is trying to get some funds to pay the world-language teachers to work on lessons for the wired world-language classroom.

In the meantime, Elena thought she might get the dialogue started by observing one of Judy's classes. At the planning conference, they decided that Elena would use the Student On-Task and Off-Task Behaviors tool (Table 3.8) to determine what is going on in the groups working on projects while Judy is helping the students on the computer. Elena gave a copy of the observation to Judy after class.

Elena: Did the on-task, off-task tool provide any helpful information?

Judy: It was actually pretty depressing. The students were off task much more than I had thought while I was helping at the computers. I guess that I was so immersed that I didn't realize how little work was getting done. On the other hand, when I left the computer group, they really stayed on task. I wonder what that means.

Elena: The students really can get involved in the computer work. It really has a lot of potential for world-language work. Your guiding them is so important. They are getting off on the right foot. What do you think you can do to get the rest of the class to stay on task while the computer group still needs assistance?

Judy: I guess I'm going to have to develop clear roles and processes for them to work together so I don't have to watch them all the time. I thought that writing and practicing scenes for a play they're going to perform would keep them on task. I have to remember that they're middle school students. Can you think of how I can organize them?

Elena: How about using some simple cooperative learning techniques—in French, of course—to keep the groups focused?

Judy: I guess they do need that structure. One could be the recorder for the scene and another could be the group leader. Do you think they need a reflector to report on how the group worked?

Elena: Maybe to start off with. Once you see that they are on task most or all of the time, you may or may not choose to do away with the reflector. If this strategy works well, do you think one of the other world language teachers could observe it?

Judy: I'd prefer not at this point. I'm not comfortable with either the technology or leaving the groups on their own. And I'm the least experienced of the world language teachers.

Elena: OK. We can wait till the funding for your meetings comes through and start from there. So, you'll start training the students in cooperative learning techniques so they can work more effectively while you're working at the computers. Do you need any literature on cooperative learning?

Judy: No, thanks, I've got plenty.

Elena: Can we meet again next week at the same time to see how it's going? I'd also like your input on how the observation process worked for you. Would you like me to observe the groups again before we meet?

Judy: Let's meet first and see how it's working. I wouldn't want you to observe until I've gotten some of the kinks out.

> ### Reflection
>
> *How does Elena respond to Judy's rejection of Elena's request? What do you think is Elena's ultimate goal? How can you tell which approach is being used?*

Key Steps: Collaborative Approach

1. The teacher identifies the problem; you solicit as much clarifying information as possible.

2. Reflect back on what you've heard for accuracy.

3. Begin collaborative brainstorming, asking the teacher for his or her ideas first.

4. Problem solve through a sharing and discussion of options.

5. Agree on a plan and follow-up meeting.

Scenario C

Several parents have already come in to complain to Elena about John O'Connell's class. A few have been trying to switch their children out of his class. As a result, Elena has decided she'd better see what's going on. It is going to be a difficult task because John has been teaching math at New Hope for more than 25 years, and from all accounts, he is teaching the exact same way he did 25 years ago.

Elena has an idea. At the planning conference, she asks John, as the senior math teacher, to try out some techniques that a math teacher in her previous school found exceedingly successful, especially in preparing students for the new state math test. Depending on how they work for him, they could discuss recommending them to the other math teachers, she says. Elena also offers John the opportunity to visit the math teacher from her previous school so he can see the techniques at work and talk about them with their originator. After much hesitation, John reluctantly takes her up on the suggestion. Elena then asks if she can observe him using the techniques and use the visit as her official observation. When Elena mentions observation tools, John immediately says that he prefers that she use the traditional narrative form. Elena convinces John to allow her to record verbatim as much as she sees, and he agrees that each of them will analyze the verbatim narrative separately.

Elena: Did you get a chance to look at the transcript of my observation?

John: No. I've been too busy. The visit to your old school really set my schedule off.

Elena: Can you take a few minutes now and give me your reactions?

John: (after a few minutes) Having the students work in twos to solve problems and then share their answers and processes with the closest set of twos just doesn't work for me. The desks got all messed up, the class was disorderly, and then it took me a long time to get them back to their regular work. It may work for your colleague, but not for me. Look at all the confusion and lost time.

Elena: I hear what you're saying. Besides the noise and confusion, how did the students work together?

John: They had a ball because they could talk away, but I had no way of knowing what was going on.

Elena: Do you have any ideas on how you could get rid of the glitches?

John: Your math teacher friend has the room set up differently, so she doesn't have to deal with students moving all over. I can't have them working at tables all the time. I can't teach that way.

Elena: How could you get around that?

John: Maybe I could have them rearrange the desks on Friday so the custodians could get them back in rows for Monday. But that would mean teaching the whole day with them in groups.

Elena: Could you arrange your schedule to do that?

John: I guess I could do problems on Friday and have them go over their tests for the rest of the period. They always have trouble concentrating on Friday anyway, so I won't have to deal with trying to make them listen all period.

Elena: Good suggestion. What do you think about getting feedback on their problem-solving processes and solutions?

John: I don't know. Your colleague has one student from each group write the solution and explain the process on the board. I'm afraid I'll lose control on a Friday if they're at tables. Maybe I'll have each table be responsible for writing one problem's solution and process on the board, and then ask for other suggestions. I don't know if it'll work. They may not stay as quiet as I like.

Elena: I think it's a terrific start. Let's go over what you're going to do. If it works, maybe some of the new math teachers can sit in on your class to see how it works.

John: I don't think so. They should concentrate on keeping order in their own classrooms. Some of the noise I hear coming out of those rooms. . . . So, I'm going to ask my homeroom to arrange the desks on Friday morning in tables of four. The students will first work in twos solving a problem, then they'll share their process and answer with the other two at the table. Then one person will put one process and solution on the board, and I'll ask for comments. Then they'll go to the next problem. If I have time at the end of the period, they can go over their weekly tests. The custodian will put the desks back in rows for Monday.

Elena: Fine. So Friday will be problem-solving day with the students at tables. If you make this an ongoing schedule, I could ask the custodian to rearrange the desks when he cleans on Thursdays. Can we meet a week from Monday to see how it's going?

John: Let's wait for two weeks. It'll give me a better idea if I want to continue with it. Since I get here early, you could come to my classroom on Monday before school starts.

> **Reflection**
>
> *What does Elena do to avoid feeding into John's negativism? How is she responding to the parents' complaints? How does she react to his resistance to doing certain things? Which approach did Elena choose and why?*

Key Steps: Self-Directed Approach

1. Listen carefully to the teacher's initial statement.
2. Reflect back on your understanding of the problem.
3. Constantly clarify and reflect until the real problem is identified.
4. Have the teacher problem solve and explore consequences of various actions.
5. The teacher commits to a decision and firms up a plan.
6. The supervisor restates the teacher's plan and sets up a follow-up meeting.

Collaborative Reflection

The purpose of the collaborative reflection is to think about the value of the reflective supervision cycle just completed. This discussion can take place toward the end of the feedback conversation, at a scheduled time after the feedback conversation, informally soon after the feedback conversation, or, if schedules are really tight, as written feedback. The questions asked are simple; in fact, they are a variation of the reflector's questions in the reflective practice guidelines presented in Chapter 2—What went well? What needs improvement? What would you do differently?—and are the prototype for most effective feedback processes. Remember that the focus of the collaborative reflection is the *process between the supervisor and the teacher, not the teaching that took place in the observation.*

Collaborative Reflection

1. What was valuable in the process we (just) completed?

2. What was of little value?

3. What changes would you suggest for the next cycle?

Class Practice

If you are able to schedule the planning conference or observation with your teacher volunteer before the next class meeting, be prepared to role-play the feedback conversation in class. Decide on an interpersonal approach to follow the teacher's analysis and create a description of the teacher with whom you met. Using the reflective practice guidelines, groups of three will practice as many of the scenarios as possible.

Site Practice

If the colleague on site with whom you practiced the planning conference is not the participant for the whole clinical supervision cycle, find another teacher who will volunteer to do the complete cycle. Complete the cycle on site and prepare the following written report:

A. Recount each phase of the cycle: planning conference, observation, feedback conversation, and collaborative reflection. A video can substitute for the written description.

B. Analyze the evidence from each approach choice you made and then interpret the evidence.

1. How much teacher input was there in the planning conference? Would you recommend a change in the approach to this teacher in another planning session? Why?

2. Did the observation tool reveal the behaviors on which you and your colleague agreed to focus? How or why not? Was the observation tool you chose appropriate and effective? Is it a tool you would use again? Why or why not? What other tool would you suggest?

3. Which interpersonal approach(es) did you use in the feedback conversation? Why? What was the teacher's response? How well did it (they) work?

4. What were the teacher's reactions to the process? How effective was the collaborative reflection? What did you learn?

C. Provide a final reflection on the whole process, that is, your personal evaluation of what worked and was of value and what you will think about doing differently in the future.

CONCLUSION

This chapter has permitted us to expand our understanding of clinical supervision and become acquainted with the authors' version of reflective clinical supervision. The cycle presented consists of four stages:

1. The planning conference

2. The observation

3. The feedback conversation

4. The collaborative reflection

Scenarios for some phases based on actual school contexts were presented, and exercises for practicing the stages in class and on site were created. Now that you are familiar with and have practiced various interpersonal approaches, tools and techniques of observation, and the reflective clinical supervision cycle, you can begin to think about the different ways that improvement of classroom instruction can be configured in a department, grade, team, or school. In Chapter 5, we present some of the significant alternatives to and variations on the traditional procedures for improving classroom instruction.

5

Alternative Approaches

Case Studies and
Implementation Guidelines

We have laid the foundation for a sound supervision program by discussing interpersonal approaches, reviewing observation instruments, and introducing a framework for a complete cycle of reflective clinical supervision. You also have had the opportunity to practice and reflect on each facet of this supervision program. In this chapter, we provide a unique compendium of alternative approaches to supervision. Each approach is presented through an actual case study[1] that highlights the successful implementation of an alternative approach to supervision of classroom instruction.

Stages for implementation accompany each approach. In addition, a few of the case studies focus primarily on the organizational processes that the individuals or group instituted to develop their procedures. Thus, these studies illustrate the way that instructional leaders introduce innovative supervisory strategies in the context of unique school settings. We are broadening the picture. Until now we have concentrated on the development of supervisory skills and practices; now we are beginning to look at supervision as one facet of instructional leadership.

We are introducing these strategies as food for thought. As Michael Fullan says, "transferability is complex . . . successful reforms in one place are partly a function of good ideas, and largely a function of the *conditions* under which the ideas flourished. . . . Successful innovations fail to be replicated because the wrong thing is being replicated—the reform itself, instead of the conditions which spawned its success" (Fullan, 1999, p. 64). We hope that these vignettes will provide a springboard for innovative strategies for your own schools.

In the final chapter, we will illustrate how supervision of instruction can be the basis of whole-school instructional leadership and reform. Again, these ideas can be a starting point for your own creativity.

INSTRUCTIONAL ROUNDS

The highest form of intelligence is the ability to observe without evaluating.

—Jiddu Krishnamurti

Case Study 1

At the beginning of the school year in a private high school in New York City, one of the authors was invited to introduce to the faculty the concept of faculty rounds. The faculty was mosaic. It was composed of accomplished teachers educated at some of the finest universities in the country. The faculty was diverse in age and background. There was a new principal in the school, and in the age of the Great Recession, the faculty shared, despite their diversity, an anxiety about their school's future as well as skepticism about the professor from outside who was going to help improve the school.

Indeed, the challenge for the author was formidable. The first concerns of the faculty had little to with instructional supervision. With a new principal, an aging building, and diminishing enrollment, the author had to overcome a distracted and skeptical faculty who had also become inured to viewing the observations of their classes as fundamentally evaluative and critical. It was this last challenge, engaging a faculty who had been programmed through experience to view teacher evaluation in fundamentally negative terms, which was going to be the most significant obstacle to encouraging the implementation of instructional rounds in this high school.

At their core, the author explained, instructional rounds adopted the successful practice of teaching hospitals. Groups of teachers would move from classroom to classroom to observe and supervise instruction. The teachers would then dialogue about the class and teachers whom they observed. The concept in principle and practice had so much potential, he explained. Before the professor could continue to explain the benefits of

(Continued)

(Continued)

instructional rounds, an experienced teacher raised his hand and asked with distrust and frustration, "Is my classroom being compared to a sick and dying patient?" This was the moment that the author had been hoping for. It was precisely this sense of distrust, and the belief that teacher observation was necessarily a judgmental process, that instructional rounds could help overcome.

The professor explained the key role of the instructional core in the educational process. He explained that the goals of instructional rounds involved the observation of the complex interaction of the student, the curriculum, and the teacher. Participants in the instructional rounds had the opportunity to learn about not only what good teaching looks like in practice but also what good learning looks like in action. He explained that the faculty would choose whether or not they wanted to participate in the project. He then engaged the faculty in a participatory role-play activity where colleagues challenged themselves to dialogue in nonjudgmental language. In one activity, the teachers were asked to act out the process of teaching and observing. One teacher playing an observer began with a few well-intentioned compliments: "Your lesson was very energetic. I liked the way you engaged the students by asking them questions." The person playing the observer was confident that the compliments that were rendered would win the approbation of the professor. The author explained that even compliments were counterproductive, suggesting a relationship of power and judgment. He suggested that we wanted to cultivate spirited dialogue and debate among colleagues who respected each other and their opinions. The teacher being observed was almost incidental to the value of witnessing all elements of the instructional core come together in one setting. The instructional rounds allowed the curriculum, the learning, and the teaching of a school to be observed in a context that produced the vital dialogue and cooperation essential to school improvement.

The presentation was received with mixed results. No doubt many members of the faculty went back to their usual teaching habits and did not reflect further on the opportunities of instructional rounds. Over the next weeks and months, though, the notion of instructional rounds blossomed in the high school in ways that were entirely unanticipated.

Two critical questions that Collins (2001) asks in his essential study on leadership, *From Good to Great: Why Some Companies Make the Leap . . . and Others Don't,* were gradually answered. "First who, then what": Gradually many of the finest faculty, the "who," began to engage in dialogue and debate about instructional rounds, the "what." They initiated their own protocols and discussions about how to adapt the rounds to the unique circumstances of their school. For example, they asked members of the administration to remove themselves from the process, as they wanted personal ownership of the process to ensure that the process remained untainted by evaluation. They met and discussed what objective standards would be used in the observations and what principles would guide the discussions before and after the observations. The core early adopters developed the protocols and tools necessary to engage in successful collaboration. Among the quality teachers who took initiative in starting this process, conversations about the nature of education, professional development, and school improvement flourished. Gradually, because teachers came together and were motivated by a powerful tool, instructional rounds became a vital component to the process of school improvement.

Some teachers were motivated and excited by the type of nonjudgmental, collaborative partnerships that are vital within successful organizations. The new administration helped to "shape the path." Most important, teachers were given the time and then the support they needed to engage in the process of educational rounds. In fact, though it took several months before the first instructional rounds were finally launched, they merely further crystallized the reflective, collaborative, and nonjudgmental practice that is at the heart of effective classroom supervision.

A Definition

Instructional rounds provide the opportunity for a faculty, through a classroom-centered approach, to observe and impact the instructional core in a nonjudgmental, collaborative approach to classroom observation. The rounds are distinguished in important ways from more traditional classroom walk-throughs, which are often evaluative. In contrast to a walk-through in which faculty members or administrators may attempt to identify and "fix" apparently defective teaching practices, the role and emphasis of rounds in the educational process are quite different. In instructional rounds, all members of the team are engaged in an active process of reflection, not just about the teacher but about all aspects of the instructional core. The students, the curriculum, and their complex interaction with the teacher are viewed by a team of educators with the goal of fostering the critical dialogue and debate that are a precondition of school improvement. Rather than existing in isolation, instructional rounds, when properly implemented, become part of and reinforce the overall objectives of a school improvement plan.

Stages for Implementation

In advance of the implementation of instructional rounds, have faculty members who want to be involved meet and discuss their concerns and ideas about the process. Teachers who voice any concerns or discomfort about the process of instructional rounds should be listened to and their point of view respected. Faculty members who are uncomfortable with the process should withdraw from participation. The process must be noncoercive and positive in order to succeed. Teachers should be asked to identify a few core challenges and opportunities that they would like to see as the focal points of their observations. The early adopters should conduct a few mini-rounds and deliberate about that experience before they launch the full project.

The implementation for instructional rounds is usually considered a four-step process that in many respects resembles the definition of all good empirical observation since Francis Bacon.

1. The first step in implementing rounds is to identify a concrete problem or practice within the instructional core on which the school is focusing.

2. Conduct the rounds with well-trained groups of observers entering classrooms to create the empirical data that can be recorded and used as evidence to foster further dialogue and debate.

3. Build and debrief the evidence that was collected through the observations in ways that are neither evaluative nor judgmental.

4. Use the evidence that was collected prescriptively, to learn new classroom approaches, affirm effective practices, and make recommendations about how elements of the instructional core can be improved. This process is based upon the nonjudgmental, collaborative conversations that remain at the heart of open, healthy institutions. (City, Elmore, Fiarman, & Teitel, 2009)

Reflective Practice

Activity 1

Groups of two or more conduct research on instructional rounds. Can you find a school to visit that has implemented faculty instructional rounds? If so, interview the participants. What do you think are its advantages and disadvantages? How might you implement an instructional round with a colleague or an entire faculty at a given grade level?

Activity 2

Make the comparison with the three-minute walk-throughs and traditional informal observations. Have faculty members discuss their experiences of being observed in the past. What did they learn from this experience? Have faculty members discuss the important operative differences between the instructional rounds model and traditional evaluative and judgmental teacher observation. Have faculty members role play and model the type of nonjudgmental, collaborative observations that are at the heart of positive and healthy school supervision.

BOOK STUDY GROUPS

Involvement in Book Study really raises our level of professionalism as we meet to share our views and experiences in the classroom . . . invaluable opportunities to exchange ideas with colleagues in an easygoing and nonthreatening manner to learn from each other.

—Stuart Rozen, chair of a book study
group in a high school in the Northeast

Case Study 2

Dr. Maya Jaboe, a young and vivacious educator with a résumé as eclectic as it was extensive, was invited to become headmaster of a new private school now entering its fourth year in the heart of Greenwich, Connecticut. The school's board and PTA hoped that her wide range of expertise would gain her appeal in connecting with her faculty, student and parent body, and certainly impress the school's major benefactors. Though she would be younger than a good number of the teachers, her background as informal adult educator meant she was prepared to effectively guide them. Her experience in mass media coverage for a local news station meant her communication skills were sharp and she would network well when it came to organizing professional development events at the academy. So too, her volunteer charity work showed compassion and innovative event planning, while her decade-long membership in a young quilters circle revealed her meticulous attention to detail, creativity, and spirited team membership. Finally, her educational background in English literature and her doctorate in Shakespearean studies would certainly gain her respect as an academic and educational leader.

Having done their homework on laying the groundwork for developing a new private school, the board members expected that by virtue of her possessing these skills and having amassed these experiences, Dr. Jaboe would naturally bridge the gaps among the varying personality types and even educational, professional, and cultural backgrounds of the teachers. They knew how important it would be for her to accomplish that in order for them to succeed as a school community. As lofty as their missions for the educational programs they promised their member families were, it would only manifest well if cultivated and supported by a united faculty. The hope was that a united faculty would naturally engage in ongoing discussion about teaching and learning, gaining insight and new knowledge from one another. The expectation that this would happen on its own, however, was quite unrealistic.

As this became apparent in the first year of the school's inception, Dr. Jaboe realized she needed to utilize her creative talents to devise a game plan that would facilitate the achievement of the school's mission.

Inspired by some summer research she had done in consultation with one of the authors, she developed a strategy she would implement the following year. She decided the first step would be to get teachers talking with one another across age gaps, disciplines, and schedules. She would also have to guide them to maximize that talking time by focusing on constructive and forward-thinking teaching methods, especially those that would encourage reflective teaching models. She wanted not only for them to learn from one another but also for each teacher to become inspired to think more reflectively about his or her own teaching. That way she could also integrate her own professional goal to integrate a collaborative and nonjudgmental approach to supervision and instruction. The more the teachers would reflect upon their own teaching, the less she would need to direct them and the more self-directed they would become.

Dr. Jaboe understood that theorizing a game plan was only half the work and that she needed the right tools to actualize it. Dr. Jaboe again reached out to the author for suggestions, and together they came up with the idea to try establishing a book study group. The goal for this group would be to provide teachers with a forum to engage in discussion about teaching and to consider their roles as teachers, thereby promoting unity among staff as well as independent and reflective professional growth.

Dr. Jaboe pitched the idea to her faculty during an orientation staff development meeting as follows:

> The book study group will be a professional development opportunity for you to engage in on a regular basis. As members of the group, you will have the opportunity to select the books you will be reading and then discuss them with one another in terms of both theory and practical application in your teaching. The chair of the group will be responsible for setting meeting times, obviously done in consensus with the other members. They will also be asked to summarize each meeting to keep me in the loop and so that I too may benefit from your learning and be prepared for any further related consultation. I would recommend monthly meetings which would allow members sufficient time to read and that they take place during lunchtime so that both morning and afternoon teachers can participate. I would also recommend that members take turns choosing the monthly reading so that all will have an opportunity to present on an area they feel most connected to or interested in. Please feel free to be creative in your choices—the criterion is just that they relate to education.

The idea of a book study group generated strong interest from faculty. Within a week's time, there were seven members, including the chair, who was a morning English teacher. Other members included a morning social studies teacher, a morning psychology teacher, an afternoon creative arts teacher, an afternoon reading specialist, an afternoon economics teacher, and the school librarian. They ranged not only by department but also in age and years of teaching experience. So too their book selections crossed a wide spectrum from topics on teaching children with special needs, to bringing technology into the classroom, to esoteric philosophical works on the meaning of education. At the last meeting of the year, a survey was distributed to book club members asking them to reflect on benefits they felt they derived from the group and ways they would suggest improving the group for the coming year. Here are some responses:

Perceived Benefits:

- A feeling of camaraderie among teachers that would not normally cross paths during the school day, let alone to discuss their teaching.
- Having a forum in which to exchange ideas and collectively pool those ideas together.
- The development of a very easygoing and nonthreatening way to find out about what is going on in other classrooms.
- A renewed sense of school community.
- A broadened base of education by expanding each member's breadth of knowledge about new educational methods and ideas.

(Continued)

(Continued)

When asked about what recommendation they would make for the coming year's group, here is a synopsis of what they said:

- Too much time was expended on teachers presenting options on book selections and requesting feedback from fellow members on which to assign. Next year the member whose turn it is to choose should just assign one book and everyone agree to accept it.
- The group felt too insular. Perhaps we should consider ways to share lessons learned from group discussions with the rest of the faculty.
- Teachers may have left their book study meetings with more practical ideas for application of ideas discussed if there was a designated time for reflection on how those ideas would directly relate to their teaching.
- Technology books were very provocative and should be encouraged.

At end-of-year conferences, Dr. Jaboe reflected on the survey responses from book study participants and felt very proud of their collective accomplishments. The main goal she had set for teachers involved was for them to "become better teachers," without offering specific content-related guidance or measures beyond that. It was clear that by virtue of being allotted choice and leadership opportunities within the group, members developed a sense of empowerment and not only willingness but also genuine interest in learning and growing as individuals and as a school community. In recognition of the group's success and interest in taking their recommendations to heart, Dr. Jaboe intends to have members of the book study club share their practices in small groups at several faculty meetings instead of as talking heads.

A Definition

Book Study offers a formalized opportunity for teachers to convene on a regular basis to engage in ongoing discussion about teaching and learning. As in a book club, members take turns choosing books to be the subjects of conversation. Book choices can range from theoretical to practical, technical to academic, as long as they relate to education. The book is intended as a springboard for discussion to inspire improved teaching skills and attitudes. Book Study functions as a collaborative, nonintimidating, and often self-motivated means to share ideas about teaching and to stay current in the field. It also facilitates professional growth and development in becoming more dynamic and well-read educators.

Book Study is a unique alternative approach in that it is led by teachers and for teachers. The range of book choices allows for teachers to shine in researching and presenting on their own strengths while simultaneously inviting fellow teachers to learn, analyze, and challenge underlying ideas and concepts. Book Study also fosters the building of a sense of community by coordinating schedules, reading lists, and a venue in which to reflect on different educational models and perspectives. This approach also welcomes teachers from varied teaching disciplines and backgrounds to join together cohesively to work toward becoming better educators. Its casual structure elicits self-motivation and initiative and offers members a sense of empowerment in shaping their own professional development.

Stages for Implementation

1. Appoint a chair for the group to keep track of scheduling and communication in preparation for upcoming meetings. The chair will also be responsible for summarizing meetings to keep administrators informed of major topics and themes discussed.

2. Encourage teachers from different departments and schedules to join. Accordingly, designate a time that will be convenient for different teachers with different teaching schedules, possibly lunchtime.

3. Meetings should convene on a regular basis, ideally once per month.

4. Participants will take turns choosing books, to be announced at the close of the previous meetings. This will allow a full month to read and prepare for the next meeting.

5. Members should agree to accept each other's book choices for the sake of time efficiency and as a means of offering respect for each other's interests and recommendations.

6. School administrators should be responsible for the cost of the books so as to eliminate financial obligation or strain from teachers.

7. Either a school administrator or the Book Study chair can be held responsible for purchasing the books to ensure that all members receive it in time to have sufficient preparation for the next meeting.

8. Members should be encouraged to take notes on their readings and come to the meetings with some of their own ideas and reflections regarding practical implications on their teaching.

9. Be mindful of the nature of book selections in order to promote a balance between practical and theoretical knowledge. Encourage diversity.

10. Meetings should include time to enumerate major themes or ideas, exchange thoughts and opinions about them, and finally—and most important—time for personal reflection.

11. Teachers involved in a Book Study group should meet with nonmembers to facilitate a discussion (i.e., shared, open time for instructional conversations).

Reflective Practice

Imagine you are creating a Book Study in your school. Would it work? Why or why not? Those of you who can, set up a Book Study group at your school. Maintain and develop it. Report to colleagues on its progress and impact. Challenges?

LESSON STUDY GROUPS

Teachers doing lesson study practice cognitive empathy and work to make student thinking visible.

—Cerbin and Kopp, 2006, p. 251

Research lessons are designed to bring to life in a lesson a particular goal or vision of education.

—Lewis, 2000, p. 5

Case Study 3

The Stenton Middle School is a typical suburban school in the Northeast part of the country with 950 students in grades 6–8. New state guidelines required the incorporation of curriculum that is devoted to the history and understanding of the state and local community in which students live. Departments affected by the new rules are English language and social studies, as well as specialty courses like art and music. Whereas the state-designed curriculum was general, autonomy was given to individual school districts to adjust the local section of the curriculum to fit the needs of the locale. Initial attempts produced quality lessons; however, the lessons were isolated from and failed to harmonize with the rest of the subject material. Furthermore, there was a lack of integration among disciplines. Teachers felt they had little input in either creation or implementation decisions, the lessons did not match course content, and the lessons were created by a curriculum coordinator or individual teacher working in a vacuum unaware of the dynamic needs of a particular classroom.

At a recent conference, the principal, Dr. Dan Dunton, attended a workshop demonstrating the lesson studies model given by a teacher who studied in Japan. Upon returning to school, Dr. Dunton presented the concept of lesson study, a method that is used extensively in Japanese schools, and how it could be effectively incorporated into the school to resolve many of the challenges emerging from the new state mandate. Two social studies teachers, one English teacher, and the art teacher volunteered to be part of the pilot group. Meryl McIntire, an 11-year veteran English teacher, commented:

> I had mixed emotions about joining the lesson study team. On the one hand, I was excited for the opportunity that we, the teachers, would be responsible for setting the agenda. Yet on the other hand, I was apprehensive about the process and nervous if I would be judged on the results. Although I have been teaching for many years, I rarely have had a chance to be involved in substantive conversations on education with colleagues from a different department. However, the vote of confidence that Dr. Dunton expressed in me and my colleagues, by empowering us to create the lesson study, was what turned the tide for me.

The five-member lesson study team met during lunch on Fridays, while the assistant principal covered their lunchroom duties. The initial meetings were devoted to the first step in the process, the research theme, which is a statement outlining the broad long-term goals for student learning that would serve as the focus for the lesson study cycle. Working together and collaboratively, the team as a whole focused on three ideal student characteristics for its research theme:

1. Identifying and understanding different elements that comprise a community.

2. Evaluating source material and how it contributes to the overall understanding of the community.

3. Working collaboratively to solve problems.

An outside facilitator hired by the school was instrumental in guiding the team through the process, assisting in developing communication skills among team members, focusing the team on student learning rather than on lesson content, and assisting the team in becoming self-sufficient in its own professional development.

The second step of the lesson study was the lesson plan, or research lesson, in which an in-depth lesson is researched, designed, and planned. In preparing the lesson study, the team used the goals developed in the research theme as a guide and referred back to them periodically to remain on task and be sure the lesson was enhancing the unit and overarching goals. An eighth-grade history lesson about identifying characteristics of the local government was selected because research showed that students were weak in this area. Jason Numre, a third-year social studies teacher, remarked on the process:

It was exciting researching new methods of how to present the material. Hearing different point of views and sharing prior experiences challenged me to realize that I had biases that I wasn't aware of. The process of planning the lesson provided a greater mastery of the material. In creating a detailed, almost scripted lesson, I found it most challenging to try and anticipate student responses and how I would react to them. Viewing the lesson from the perspective of an eighth-grade student allowed me to focus on how students learn and not just on presenting the material.

The third step in the lesson model process was the observation. The team members each reviewed their role for the observation and prepared to collect data and evidence to determine if the lesson goals were met. The team invited the assistant principal, Dr. Berkman, to observe the class as she was considered an expert in gauging student "on-task, off-task" behavior. Mr. Hall, the social studies teacher who gave the lesson, observed:

The independent observation by Dr. Berkman was valuable in highlighting areas that the team wasn't familiar with. In retrospect, we should also have invited Mrs. Eckman, the history chair, to serve as a knowledgeable other and bring her content expertise on subject matter. One aspect that was not factored in during the preplanning was that the students were very rambunctious in the beginning when they saw the team enter the classroom; this could be solved by preparing the students beforehand in the future.

The team members and independent observers met later that afternoon while the lesson was still fresh in their minds to debrief each other and analyze the evidence gathered, which is the fourth step in the lesson study process. The meeting was held in the same classroom as the lesson to enable everyone to highlight aspects and teaching tools used during the lesson. Ms. Fox, the art teacher, noted:

The debriefing session was conducted in an open, nonjudgmental manner, since the focus was on student learning, not on the instructor. Having a moderator helped keep the discussion moving and involved everyone. The team realized that having time to independently self-reflect prior to the debriefing would have enriched the discussion.

As the team was preparing to revise and re-teach the lesson, they encountered an unforeseen obstacle. Both eighth-grade classes were learning the local government lesson at the same time, thereby preventing the revised lesson from being re-taught. Mr. Hall solved the problem when he remembered that a colleague in a neighboring school district had not yet covered a similar unit. After going through the appropriate channels, Mr. Hall was able to give the revised lesson at the neighboring school with the observation team in attendance.

The final step of the lesson study process is to reflect and share. The team published a report that contained the lesson and the team's reflections. Mrs. McIntire concluded:

The lesson study process allowed me to reflect on the educational process, focus on student learning, and develop my professional abilities. Although I teach a different discipline, it was enriching to see that many of the same skills and methods are used in English similar to the way they are used in social studies. The research lesson allowed us to test our hypotheses and make sure the lesson related back to the big picture and long-term goals that we established. The process was teacher initiated and gave us the ability to integrate the previously disjointed local community unit in a method that enhanced the overall curriculum. Our next lesson study cycle will continue the theme, but from the vantage point of English. The discussion will revolve around introducing local authors to our students and using the new methods and strategies that were discovered in the social studies lesson to improve the understanding and learning for this English unit.

The success of the lesson study team encouraged other teachers to join the program. The faculty decided, in conjunction with the administration, that they would alternate years between doing lesson studies based on single departments and inter-disciplinary lessons. The neighboring school that provided the class for the research lesson became interested in lesson studies and contacted teachers from the Stenton School to assist them in incorporating the program as part of their professional development program.

Definition

Lesson study is a cycle of teaching improvement in which three to six teachers collaboratively establish goals, plan a lesson, implement it in the classroom, observe the lesson, and analyze and refine the lesson for future implementation. The process focuses on understanding student learning and not on evaluating teacher performance. Lesson study has its origins in Japan, where it is practiced on multiple levels by individual schools, local districts, and across the national stage (Murata & Takahashi, 2002). Stigler and Hiebert's (1999) book, *The Teaching Gap: Best Ideas From the World's Teachers for Improving Education in the Classroom,* and the work of Catherine Lewis are responsible for bringing this method to the attention of American educators. Lesson studies are more effective than traditional forms of professional development in that they are teacher driven and collaborative and establish an ongoing process that allows teachers to continually self-reflect and focus on how well the content is learned. The process is not about creating a bank of perfect lessons but about understanding the instructional teaching process. The actual implementation of lessons in the classroom provides practitioners with the ability to mesh theory with practice. This is what makes lesson studies unique.

Stages for Implementation

To implement lesson studies effectively, the reader is advised to read *Leading Lesson Study: A Practical Guide for Teachers and Facilitators* by Stepanek, Appel, Leong, Turner Mangan, and Mitchell (2007). It outlines five stages in the process:

1. Identify a research theme that sets long-term goals that are broad in nature and focus on student learning.

2. Plan the research lesson that includes researching the topic, developing a highly detailed lesson, which includes anticipated student responses, and determining a method of evaluation to analyze if the goals have been met.

3. Teaching the lesson in which one member of the team presents the lesson while the other members of the team observe and collect data on student learning.

4. Debrief and revise—team members discuss the observation evidence, refine the lesson and, if necessary, reteach the lesson.

5. Reflect and share—the group members reflect on the process and publish a report that includes the lesson and the team's reflection, both of which can serve to improve other lessons and serve as the basis for future lesson study cycles.

Reflective Practice

Students will recruit two to four colleagues to discuss designing a lesson study in their school. The group members should discuss and list anticipated benefits and obstacles they will encounter in implementing the program. They should also chart out the pros and cons of using a lesson study that focuses on a single subject versus one that is multidisciplinary.

PEER COACHING

*When two teachers observe each other; the one teaching is the "coach" and
the one observing is the "coached."*

—Showers & Joyce, 1996, p. 15

Case Study 4

The International Institute is one of four mini-schools or institutes that are part of a large New York City middle school. It was previously one of the lowest-performing middle schools in the district. Nancy Brogan, an assertive, go-getter principal, was brought in to improve both achievement and image. Open to innovation and aggressive in pursuing funds, she broke up the 1,200-plus students into four theme institutes. The International Institute is composed primarily of Haitian, Russian, Spanish, Chinese, Bengali, and Urdu bilingual students. Because of the bilingual focus, the staff of the institute mirrors the diversity of the student body.

Through one of her outreach efforts, Nancy secured the assistance of one of the authors of this text. My (the author's) initial project was to help organize the governance committee of the institute. This task completed, our conversations veered more toward curriculum and teaching and learning issues. All of the teachers on the steering committee were committed, enthusiastic, effective, and creative teachers and, along with the institute director, Lynne Pagano, were open to anything that would promote student achievement. Because peer coaching was an approved choice in the new union contract's weekly period for professional development for each teacher, we decided to pursue the possibility of using this staff period to develop and implement the skills and practices of peer coaching. A second, recently approved union provision included the option of alternative assessment for tenured teachers. The director's reaction was,

> These teachers are the best. They can all use the peer coaching as their official observations—even the one who is just shy of tenure. This way I can concentrate on the teachers who really need help. By the way, would you mind if I sat in on your meetings?

The prospective participants and I then made a site visit to a school that had developed a very sophisticated system of peer assessment. The teachers came back excited and ready to take on the challenge.

Next, we had to decide the focus of the peer coaching. Two of the teachers had been trained during the summer in the new standards required by the city and the state, and one teacher had been involved in developing the Spanish curriculum and city adaptation for the standards. Their enthusiasm about the work they had been doing and the need for implementation triggered conversation about two possible coaching models:

1. Peer observations, based on the implementation of the curriculum for the new standards

2. Coaching, where teachers would discuss classroom challenges or interests and conduct interclass visitations

Mannor Wong, the English as a Second Language (ESL) teacher, commented, "Since I'm not tenured yet, I'd prefer honing my general instructional techniques. I'd like someone to be able to give me feedback on the strategies I'm working on in the classroom and how the students are responding to them."

Farooqui Nasreen, the Urdu bilingual teacher, had the following conversation with Madeline Castaneda, the Spanish bilingual teacher:

Farooqui: Since you've already developed a curriculum in Spanish for the new standards, could I see how you're going to implement it in the classroom? Then maybe you could observe me as I try to use the adapted curriculum in my Urdu classes.

Madeline: That's a good idea. And the students will feel comfortable with you there because of the multicultural sharing we've been doing.

(Continued)

(Continued)

Lynn Lavner, an English language arts teacher with a strong performing arts background, began sitting in on our meetings unofficially. Her reactions were somewhat different: "I could use help as I try to develop our Facing History Through the Arts curriculum this spring, but I don't know about observing another teacher's class. I don't think that's for me."

The plan that emerged was for the participants to learn and practice interpersonal, observation, and feedback skills through observations of videotaped classroom instruction and role plays of interpersonal techniques and feedback approaches. They would then be prepared to help each other more effectively and become turnkey trainers for future coaching groups. A date for the first orientation and training meeting was set. In the interim, the volunteer group was to be finalized.

The Best-Laid Plans of Mice and Teachers

We began meeting in the director's office during the teachers' 40-minute lunch period. There were constant interruptions, time lost getting lunch, and teachers arriving late or not at all. Lynn Lavner hadn't been in on the original planning, which may have been the reason for her initial spotty attendance. Mannor Wong had not been involved in the early meetings either and may have had some initial apprehension. I decided that we needed to go back to the drawing board to look for a longer block of time at a different point in the day. Luckily, this particular group was involved in implementing a grant with some flexible funding. The coordinator of the grant, Elke Savoy (one of the participants), figured out that she could compensate the teachers to come after school for a series of two-hour workshops.

We had one more setback before launching the after-school workshops. Through her ongoing outreach efforts, Nancy Brogan had procured additional professional development help to increase achievement scores. One strategy included daily brief observations by the directors in all classrooms and completion of checklists for each teacher. All staff were to follow certain procedures that the directors would verify in their visits. I met with the principal and Lynne Pagano to explain that this method was at odds with our peer-coaching goals. They agreed that the teachers involved in our project would be exempt from this requirement. In fact, Lynne was relieved because she was "going crazy" trying to keep up with the marathon visiting schedule.

Uninterrupted quality time, snacks, and compensation were a few of the elements that fostered time on task. The following weeks were spent perfecting the participants' interpersonal and feedback skills and using various techniques to observe videos of teachers and students. As the group simulated and role-played the skills in class, they began to practice observing colleagues' classes. Finally, they went through the clinical observation cycle with each other and other volunteers in the International Institute. Discussions and feedback took place at each session to fine-tune the process as we went along. Open communication about reactions to the process was encouraged.

Once the participants were comfortable with their observing and feedback skills, the next step was to set up individual or paired plans for their dialogues around curriculum implementation. The initial plans were set up at the last workshop because it was the last opportunity for quality time. We decided that each teacher or pair of teachers would write an action plan for his or her focus. Brief meetings would take place every two weeks for sharing experiences, providing feedback on what was and was not working, troubleshooting, and modifying plans as needed.

I kept a running record of the process and provided both a qualitative and quantitative evaluation at the end of the semester. The participants were so enthusiastic that it was decided to involve more volunteers the following fall and share the experience with another institute.

Reflection

What are the lessons to be learned from the initial meetings of the coaching group? What are a couple of underlying assumptions that the facilitators of this type of project must maintain for successful implementation?

A Definition

Peer coaching is an umbrella term for the many different configurations of teachers helping teachers that have emerged primarily since the 1980s. Some of the other terms often used interchangeably with peer coaching are *peer assistance, collegial coaching, technical coaching, cognitive coaching, challenge coaching,* and *peer supervision.* Most of these models pertain to variations of peer-to-peer assistance of equals and do not involve evaluation. Mentoring programs that consist of master teachers helping less experienced or less-well-trained colleagues are not included in our categorization. In this case study, peer coaching is defined as teachers helping teachers reflect on and improve teaching practices or implement particular instructional skills introduced through staff or curriculum development. Joyce and Showers (1980) specified the process as two or more teachers who meet regularly for problem solving using planning, observation, feedback, and creative thinking for the development of a specific skill.

Stages for Implementation

Goals for peer coaching include:

- Refine teaching practices
- Stimulate self-initiating, autonomous teacher thought
- Improve school culture
- Increase collegiality and professional dialogue
- Share in the implementation of new or common instructional skills

Key Steps

Teresa Benedetti (1997) outlined a simple set of procedures for teachers to initiate a peer-coaching system in their schools. The following procedures are an adaptation of her recommendations:

1. After obtaining permission from the appropriate administrators, suggest that your colleagues choose a peer whom they trust and with whom they feel they will work well.

2. Make sure that everyone is familiar with and able to engage in the cycle of clinical supervision. Ask assistance from supervisors or others familiar with clinical supervision.

3. Peers may have to help each other cover classes while their colleagues observe each other. Interested supervisors can also facilitate the freeing-up of teachers. If scheduling conflicts occur, videotaping a class can provide the additional experience of viewing the class together. If both teachers teach the same content to similar classes, combining classes and observing each other's application of skills or team teaching can be very effective.

4. Organize weekly or biweekly seminars for peer coaching. The first sessions can be used to learn and review observation and feedback techniques. The opportunity to share experiences and brainstorm new ideas as well as modify the existing structure is essential.

Through the ongoing discussion of teaching and learning, curriculum development, and implementation, peer coaching can become the heart of professional development.

Reflective Practice

Site Practice

Each student will recruit a colleague who is interested in exploring peer coaching. Brainstorm with the teacher or teachers, if possible, about how peer coaching could be developed at your site. Record your ideas on chart paper and bring the actual sheets to class.

Class Practice

Divide the class into groups. Share the brainstormed ideas. Make a group list of the most promising ideas. The list can be developed by having each participant choose two or three favorites. The final choices will be the strategies that receive the most votes. Each group will report its results to the whole class. Students will then record their preferred strategies.

A JOURNEY: FROM PEER COACHING TO CRITICAL FRIENDS

In a Critical Friends Group context, critical means "important," "key," "essential," or "urgent" such as in "critical care."

—http://www.nsrfharmony.org/

Case Study 5

New Milford Middle School, a large intermediate school in a Northeastern urban school district, has seen a recent and rapidly increasing number of English-language learners (ELLs) enter the school over the past five years. Many of the new arrivals are Latino, but there is a sprinkling of Asians, Albanians, and several other nationalities. Unfortunately, the ESL teacher is not deemed an effective resource, adding to the teachers' frustration. Veteran staff members are not used to addressing the needs of non-English-speaking students, and the large number of new faculty are struggling just to survive in a large, somewhat anonymous environment. An ESL consultant, who had worked with one of the authors on a peer-coaching project, suggested that faculty work with the author on a peer-coaching model that would allow them to focus on their English-language learners. Soon after, the end-of-the-year district report cited the school for poor results on standardized tests of its English-language learners. Something had to be done! Thus was launched a new adventure in learning community building through alternatives to traditional supervision.

Professional development began with a series of meetings during which the participating group of teachers learned and practiced planning, observation, and feedback skills as a foundation for peer coaching. Practice scenarios were based as much as possible on real English-language learner classroom dilemmas the teachers were facing. After each workshop, teachers practiced their new skills with each other and other colleagues. One teacher commented, "Practicing with each other using real classroom challenges is not only teaching us new skills, but we are actually solving problems in our workshop sessions." Another noted, "The lists of strategies that we have been building together are providing some of the support for ELLs that we have been lacking." The coaches then began to observe each other's classes using the Reflective Clinical Cycle.

As a result of their peer coaching, the participants realized that they still didn't have a grasp on the skills of certain ELL students. The author told them about Critical Friends Groups, professional learning communities consisting of approximately 8–12 educators who come together voluntarily at least once a month for about two hours. Critical Friends Group members are committed to improving their practice through collaborative learning (www.nsrfharmony.org/). She explained that problem-solving protocols or tools are often the basis of Critical Friends meetings and that they might try to use some student work protocols to examine the student work of the ELL students. She also thought that the protocols might serve as a springboard to creating a Critical Friends Group. The participants were willing, and two teachers volunteered to bring in the student work of two struggling English-language learners for the next meeting. Since the participants were quite familiar with each other's students, they decided that names would be left off to allow for a more objective description of the work.

At the next meeting, I introduced the protocol "Describing Students' Work." We began with a brief description exercise to prepare us for describing the student work. I gave the group the word "typhoon," to which each teacher responded with free association in a round-robin style. Next, the first teacher/presenter shared the student work describing the assignment. We then began descriptive rounds of the work, beginning with general impressions and physical description, continuing with "what the student is working on" rounds, which involves asking oneself what the student is trying to accomplish, what she or he values, knows how to do, and so on. Then we looked at the implications for teaching this child and what changes the teacher might make in working with this student. The culmination of the protocol was a round of "I wonder . . ." The teachers came up with perceptive thoughts and ideas. When we talked about what we learned about this student, we realized that the student had more knowledge and skills than the teacher had previously thought. The presenting teacher commented, "I really feel now that I can have higher expectations for Jorge and will try to challenge him more."

We described another piece of student work, and to our surprise, we came to a similar conclusion. Looking objectively and anonymously at the student letter that was shared, we were able to describe patterns of skills that no one had realized this student possessed. The teacher came away with a fresh, positive perspective of the accomplishments and potential of both of these students who the teacher had previously thought had few English skills.

The unexpectedly felicitous outcomes of the protocol led the group to decide to continue analyzing student work at the next meeting. I also decided to share the "Text Rendering Experience Protocol" with the group. Besides providing the opportunity to introduce another protocol, I felt that this protocol could be a bridge between using protocols for adults and children. The purpose of this protocol is "to collaboratively construct meaning, clarify and expand our thinking about a text or document" (National School Reform Faculty CFG Institutes 2004–2005). We used a text to which I had been introduced at a training session for Critical Friends facilitators, *Turning to One Another,* by Margaret Wheatley (Wheatley, 2002). I chose this text because it talks about perspectives and change—our willingness to be disturbed—in our complex world. I thought it appropriate for a school in transition and an empowering model for working with English-language learners. Each participant chooses and shares first a sentence, then a phrase, and finally a word from the text. The facilitator then reads the group-created text. Upon completion of the process, the group discussed their reactions to the protocol and brainstormed ways to use this protocol in a class with ELLs.

At the conclusion of this session, our last for the year, the participants made three recommendations: (1) to request to use peer coaching as their alternative evaluation process (a choice in their union contract), (2) to create a Critical Friends Group where they would problem solve student, grade, and academy dilemmas, using additional protocols, and (3) to eventually turnkey their new skills to other faculty. In addition, the end-of-the-year tests revealed that it is the special education English-language learners who are having particular difficulty. The assistant principal in charge of our project recommended expanding the skill building to the faculty working with this targeted group of students.

(Continued)

(Continued)

However, the creation of a Critical Friends Group requires more than an outside facilitator on whom the group would be dependent and a small number of members familiar with only a few protocols. The author and the assistant principal, with the group's support, went to the principal with the two immediate requests: (1) a heads-up on the peer-coaching evaluation option and (2) professional development financial support to allow some of the group members to be trained as Critical Friends facilitators. The author, a trained Critical Friends facilitator, along with a recently relocated well-known facilitator, could incorporate the available members of the group into a seminar they would be running in the fall. The principal had recently been introduced to the concept of Critical Friends by a district leader who was encouraging the development of Critical Friends Groups in district schools. As a newly appointed principal in a large school with little sense of collaboration, she thought Critical Friends Groups could help begin the building of a learning community. Therefore, the principal arranged to release three teachers for three Friday sessions, and three teachers agreed to attend two Saturday sessions to fulfill the required week of training. The school would then have a core of three trained teachers to promote the success of the first group and the expertise to turnkey to other faculty down the road. Finally, the principal also lent her support to the peer-coaching process as another means to build a professional learning community.

> **Reflection**
>
> *What attitudes do facilitators and leaders need when trying to develop new and/or alternative programs or projects? How does Michael Fullan's belief that "It is one thing to see an innovation 'up and running,' it is entirely another matter to figure out the pathways of how to get there in your own organization" (Fullan, 1999, p. 14) apply to this case study?*

A Definition[2]

A *Critical Friends Group* is a professional learning community consisting of approximately 8–12 educators who have made the commitment to come together voluntarily at least once a month for about two hours to improve their practice through collaborative learning.

Stages for Implementation

The primary goals of a Critical Friends Group (CFG) are to:

- Create a professional learning community
- Make teaching practice explicit and public by "talking about teaching"
- Help people involved in schools to work collaboratively in democratic, reflective communities
- Establish a foundation for sustained professional development based on a spirit of inquiry
- Provide a consistent, ongoing context to understand work with students, relationships with peers, and thoughts, assumptions, and beliefs about teaching and learning
- Help educators help each other turn theories into practice and standards into actual student learning
- Improve learning and teaching

What does a CFG session look like?

Ideally, each session is approximately two hours. However, many protocols range from one to two hours, providing flexibility in busy schedules. The session often begins with a "check-in"—an ice breaker, an exercise that previews the protocol, or a reflective question, such as, "So, what has transpired that's new or interesting as a result of the last meeting?" The coach may facilitate one of several protocols for examining a participant's student work (similar to the one in the case study). One of the members may bring in teacher work that the group can examine with teacher protocols. A text-based discussion of a topic of concern or interest to the group may take place, preferably with the use of a text-rendering protocol. Peer coaching may emerge among members in an ongoing or episodic manner.

Reflective Practice

Site Practice

Each student will recruit a colleague who is interested in exploring "Critical Friends." Go to the website of the National School Reform Faculty (NSRF; http://www.nsrfharmony.org/), and share the information with the teacher or teachers, if possible, about how a Critical Friends Group could be developed at your site. Record your ideas on chart paper and bring the actual sheets to class.

Class Practice

Divide the class into groups. Share the brainstormed ideas. Make a group list of the most promising ideas. The list can be developed by having each participant choose two or three favorites. The final choices will be the strategies that receive the most votes. Each group will report its results to the whole class. Students will then record their preferred strategies.

PORTFOLIOS FOR DIFFERENTIATED SUPERVISION

Case Study 5

When Carmen Farina became principal of the New York City elementary school PS 6, she faced many challenges, some more familiar to suburban principals than to urban ones.[4] She entered a school long renowned for academic excellence, located in one of the most elegant neighborhoods in the city. The previous principal presided over a building known as the private public school. Many of the parents had the means to send their children to private schools but preferred to send them to PS 6, generously funding the PTA to provide some of the extras that wealthy districts and independent schools often provide.

(Continued)

(Continued)

In her previous positions as a building principal and district staff developer, Carmen had transformed her school's language arts/social studies curriculum into an exciting interdisciplinary program called Making Connections and had overseen its implementation in the whole district. Carmen described the challenge at PS 6:

My dilemma upon assuming the principalship was that the students scored high on the standardized tests while little student-centered learning was going on. Veteran teachers, for the most part, ran traditional classrooms. How could I effect change in an environment where many parents and teachers were content with the status quo?

The approach I took was to begin visiting teachers on a daily basis and engaging them in conversations around their teaching practices. These visits allowed me to assess school strengths and weaknesses. Through constant class visits and discussion of successes and challenges, areas of concern and/or interest began to emerge. By the end of the year, we had been able to designate three priorities around curriculum needs and an area of interest for each teacher.

At that point, Carmen selected 10 teachers to participate in the first-year implementation of Portfolios for Differentiated Supervision. Although it was emphasized that participation was open to all faculty, a total of 16 teachers volunteered and subsequently took part in the process.

Laura Kotch, a staff developer, was key to the successful development and implementation of the model. The following remarks are some of the thoughts she shared in greeting a group of visitors to the school:

Each participating teacher is involved in creating a portfolio, a container for his or her area of inquiry. The decisions about which topics to study came from questions teachers had, their areas of interest, their curiosity, and experimentation with new classroom strategies and techniques. Some questions have lingered over time. A first-grade teacher's investigation originated with her question about a practice that wasn't working. Her inquiry led to research on the most effective way to create competent and curious first-grade spellers. Other teachers began their portfolios by taking a risk and experimenting with new ways to integrate curriculum, such as Making Connections, author studies, and math/cooperative learning.

Laura concluded a workshop with these thoughts:

Teachers have been spending time talking together, reading articles and books written by the experts, and reflecting on their beliefs and practices. The task of writing ideas down in a portfolio requires us to clarify thoughts and ideas, refine our language, and find our writer's voice. The process of creating text has been both challenging and exciting. Writing together has allowed us the wonderful opportunity of forming a writing network, relating to each other not only as teachers but as authors as well. It will be worth all the hard work if the portfolio serves as a practical resource, while continuing to change and grow as our learning continues. As a facilitator, adviser, and friend working alongside the dedicated, hardworking, and talented professionals of PS 6, I am proud to be part of this exciting and innovative model of staff development.

A Definition

A *professional portfolio* can serve many different purposes. It can be, as it is at PS 6, a container for a particular area of inquiry. At PS 6, the portfolio not only documents the development of innovative and effective practices but is also a central vehicle for the growth of the teacher through self-reflection, analysis, and sharing with colleagues through discussion and writing. Although each PS 6 portfolio is different, each one includes teacher resources and references, professional articles, and practical suggestions.

Portfolios also can be used to support and enrich mentoring and coaching relationships. Although the portfolio does not replace the classroom observation, it extends and enhances the professional discussion by going beyond what is observed in the classroom on a given day. The advent of the electronic portfolio opens even more opportunities for sharing practices within a school, between schools, and beyond the teacher's district. When a teacher is applying for another position, an annotated collection of materials on a teacher's best classroom practices and work with colleagues supplements and strengthens the interview process (Danielson, 1996). One of us has repeatedly witnessed the influence that a well-crafted portfolio has on hiring committees.

Stages for Implementation (based on the PS 6 process)[3]

Phase 1

A. Curriculum prioritizing

    1. Assess the school's strengths and weaknesses and develop a set of prioritized curriculum needs.

B. Portfolios for differentiated supervision

    1. Designate an area of expertise in each teacher's classroom, built through intensive class visitation and conversation around teaching practices.

    2. Solicit a group of volunteers or select staff to reflect on an area of expertise and share and provide materials for the school faculty and visiting colleagues.

    3. Criteria for inclusion of participants:

        a. Outstanding expertise in a certain area.

        b. A teacher who has not refined or reflected on a special talent.

        c. Teachers likely to respond to a collegial environment for self-improvement.

    4. Institute professional development to lay the groundwork for the creation of portfolios. Possible outcomes of the workshops are:

        a. Reflection on and analysis of the areas of expertise.

        b. Decision of some teachers to collaborate on their efforts and create a joint portfolio.

        c. Use of a letter format as a means of beginning faculty journals.

    5. First drafts of the portfolios are submitted the following fall, and an administrator reviews the drafts and gives oral and written comments and suggestions.

    6. When portfolios are completed, the principal writes a "dear author" letter to each participant.

Phase II

A. New portfolio cycle

    1. Additional teachers choose to participate in the process.

    2. Specialty faculty, such as ESL teachers, can complete their portfolios by adding to individual portfolios.

B. The reflective teacher

    1. The process now involves semiannual "conversations" with the principal for a minimum of one uninterrupted hour to discuss portfolios and other areas of interest.

    2. Teachers receive a summary of their conversation with the principal.

Advantages and Limitations of Process (according to PS 6)

A. Advantages

    1. Affords the staff the opportunity to be reflective and analytical.

    2. Encourages the teachers to work cooperatively together.

    3. Allows the administration to get to know the teachers better and to encourage their growth in many areas.

    4. Encourages the staff to read professional journals.

    5. Gives a purpose for intervisitations.

    6. Fosters professionalism in teachers.

    7. Encourages teachers to apply for grants in areas of their expertise.

    8. Enhances parents' view of the school.

    9. Provides a focus for the two-way conversation with teachers.

    10. Gives teachers more input.

    11. Produces the "Hawthorne effect" when visitors come to the school.

    12. Provides a vehicle for continuous inclusion of strategies (e.g., ESL, multiculturalism).

B. Challenges

    1. Administration must develop a trusting relationship with the staff.

    2. A lot of time is required.

    3. Principal must be aware of what is going on in the classroom.

    4. Teachers must be accepting of the process.

    5. Inordinate amount of time is required for planning and writing.

Reflection

How does this process differ from peer coaching? What are the similarities?

6. Materials must be available.

7. Change is not immediate—it takes time.

Reflective Practice

Each student reflects on an area of classroom practice in which he or she has expertise or talent, about which he or she has questions, or with which he or she would like to experiment. Once everyone has come up with an idea, the class divides into small groups. After each person shares his or her area, the other members of the group offer suggestions of resources, professional articles and references, and strategies for creation of the portfolio.

ACTION RESEARCH

Although action research is not a quick fix for all school problems, it represents a process that . . . can focus the brain-power of the entire instructional staff on maximizing learning.

—McLean, 1995, p. 5

Case Study 7

Doris Harrington is a tenured math teacher at Northern Valley Regional High School, a school that comprises 1,100 students. Having taught in the school for 18 years, Doris is excited about the new program that Principal Bert Ammerman spearheaded to enhance professional development and instructional improvement: "I think it's neat that we now have a system in place in which we feel empowered. I mean, having an option, a choice in determining my professional development is certainly new and much appreciated."

Doris selects an action research plan as a part of the supervisory program that teachers, supervisors, and administrators collaboratively developed. "I've read so much about action research," she says, "and am so excited that others now appreciate how important it is to provide time for teachers to reflect about what we do every day in the classroom." Doris's observations confirm the views of many educators, who maintain that encouraging reflective teaching is one of the most important responsibilities of instructional supervisors (Schon, 1988).

Familiarizing herself with the literature on action research (Elliott, 1991; Glanz, 2003; Stringer, 1999), Doris reviews the four basic steps:

1. Selecting a focus for study

2. Collecting data

3. Analyzing and interpreting the data

4. Taking action

She wonders about her classroom. "What has been successful? How do I know these strategies are successful? What needs improvement? What mistakes have I made? In what ways can I improve my instructional program?" In collaborative conversations with her assistant principal, Jim McDonnell, Doris frames her project.

(Continued)

(Continued)

She wonders whether or not the time and energies expended on cooperative learning activities are worth the effort. Although she is familiar with the extensive research on the subject (D. W. Johnson & Johnson, 1989), Doris decides to compare her fourth-period math class with her sixth-period class in terms of how cooperative learning strategies affect student achievement and attitudes toward problem solving in mathematics. She chooses these two classes because they are somewhat equivalent in mathematical problem-solving ability. She selects a nonequivalent control group design commonly associated with *ex post facto* research because the study involves the use of intact classes (see Glanz, 2003, for an explanation of this research design).

She randomly assigns cooperative learning as the primary instructional strategy to be used with the fourth-period class, whereas the other class will work on mathematical problem solving through the traditional textbook method. After six weeks of implementing this plan, she administers a posttest math exam and discovers, after applying a *t*-test statistic, that the group exposed to cooperative learning attained significantly higher mathematical problem-solving scores than the group that was taught math traditionally. Doris keeps an anecdotal record throughout the research project on how students seemed to get along socially in both classes. Independent observers are utilized to ensure more reliable findings. She also administers an attitude questionnaire to ascertain how students felt about learning math using cooperative learning groups as compared to learning math in the more traditional format.

Based on her findings, Doris decides to incorporate cooperative learning procedures into all her classes. She still wonders whether or not, for example, cooperative learning will work for all math topics and whether cooperative learning is uniquely effective for problem-solving activities. In consultation with Jim McDonnell, she develops a plan to continue assessments throughout the year. Jim asks Doris to present her findings at both grade and faculty conferences.

Doris's enthusiasm for action research was emphatic:

Employing action research engenders greater feelings of competence in solving problems and making instructional decisions. In the past, I never really thought about the efficacy of my teaching methods to any great extent. The time spent in this project directly impacts my classroom practice. I'm much more skeptical of what really works and am certainly more reflective about what I do. Action research should, I believe, be an integral part of any instructional improvement effort. No one has to convince you to change an instructional strategy. Once you gather and analyze your own data, you'll be in a position to make your own judgments about what should or should not be done. Action research empowers teachers!

A Definition

Action research is a type of applied research that has reemerged as a popular way to involve educators in reflective activities about their work. Action research is not a narrow, limited practice but, rather, can use a range of methodologies, simple and complex, to better understand one's work and even solve specific problems. Action research, properly used, can have immeasurable benefits, such as:

- Creating a systemwide mind-set for school improvement—a professional problem-solving ethos
- Enhancing decision making
- Promoting reflection and self-improvement
- Instilling a commitment to continuous instructional improvement
- Creating a more positive school climate in which teaching and learning are foremost concerns

- Empowering those who participate
- Promoting professional development

Action research is an ongoing process of reflection that involves four basic cyclical steps:

A. Selecting a focus

1. Know what you want to investigate.

2. Develop some initial questions.

3. Establish a plan to answer or better understand these questions.

B. Collecting data

1. Primary
   a. Questionnaires
   b. Observations
   c. Interviews
   d. Tests
   e. Focus groups

2. Secondary
   a. School profile sheets
   b. Multimedia
   c. Portfolios
   d. Records
   e. Others

C. Analyzing and interpreting data

D. Taking action

Stages for Implementation

To effectively implement action research, the reader is advised to read Glanz's (2003) *Action Research: An Educational Leader's Guide to School Improvement*, view videos produced by the Association for Supervision and Curriculum Development (1995) on action research, and even take a course at a local university or attend a workshop. Another resource is Hubbard and Power's (1993) *The Art of Classroom Inquiry: A Handbook for Teacher-Researchers*. The following stages for implementation were developed at Northern Valley Regional High School District (1996) and are paraphrased from a handout titled *Differentiated Supervision*.

Action Research

Description. The model allows the educator the chance to increase his or her scholarly background by encouraging him or her to examine and analyze pertinent documents. The educator might complete this independent study in one year. To complete the project, the educator will have periods designated for research and development during the year.

Before the beginning of the action research project, the educator will discuss the project with his or her supervisor, reviewing goals and objectives and questions to be researched. Discussion of research methods should also be discussed to ensure that ethical guidelines for conducting research are maintained (see, e.g., Glanz, 2003).

At the end of the year, the researcher will submit a report to the supervisor. The report will highlight the project's significance, content, and conclusions, as well as pedagogically sound methods to teach the materials.

If the project's scope warrants an extension, the supervisor can recommend granting an additional academic year to complete the project. This model is applicable to all tenured staff and, in an exceptional case, could apply to an experienced but nontenured staff member.

Approach

1. Identify the importance of the research and suggest ways the project will enhance students' knowledge or improve services offered by the school district.

2. Identify the specific materials (primary and secondary sources) the educator will research.

3. Develop a schedule.

4. Limit the project's scope. Such delimitation will promote thorough rather than superficial research.

5. Study and analyze all materials for the project.

6. Develop and implement a unit or program based on the project.

The Northern Valley Regional High School District uses a prescribed set of guidelines that have resulted in a number of valuable research projects. In our experiences, without a formal structure to support such efforts, action research projects rarely, if ever, are successful. The implementation of this alternative means of instructional improvement in Northern Valley has furthered the efficacy of action research as an invaluable means to promote professional development. Action research as used at Northern Valley does not necessarily replace other traditional forms of supervision.

Reflective Practice

Groups of three to six students will consult Glanz's (2003) book, *Action Research: An Educational Leader's Guide to School Improvement,* and develop a workable research project whose aim is to improve classroom teaching. Describe the project and be as specific as possible. Incorporate both quantitative and qualitative approaches. Each group will present its project in a fishbowl. Sitting in a circle surrounded by the rest of the class, members of the group will describe different facets of the project. At the end of the presentation, the observers, or outer circle, will provide feedback, ask questions, and offer suggestions.

CONCLUSION

With these seven case studies of alternative approaches and the guidelines for creating a supervisory program that encompass alternatives to traditional supervision, you are now ready to consider how you might approach improving the supervision of classroom instruction in your school and district. We will first present a case study of how one school transformed its visions and processes of improving teaching and learning. Finally, we will challenge you to develop your own platform of "super-vision" and develop your own next steps.

NOTES

1. Most of the faculty in the schools involved in the case studies have encouraged us to use their real names.

2. Most of the information in this section has been quoted or adapted from the website of the National School Reform Faculty (NSRF): http://www.nsrfharmony.org/.

3. The information for this case study was gathered from materials distributed at workshops held at PS 6 and through conversations with the then-principal, Carmen Farina. Names have not been changed.

6

Creating Transformational Change Through a Focus on Instructional Supervision

To exercise leadership in this climate of change will require deep convictions, strong commitments, and clear ideas about directions for changes.

—Robert J. Starratt

Thus far, we have covered much territory in exploring innovative ways of conceiving of instructional supervision. It certainly requires a new paradigm of thinking. Mention the word "supervision" to most people, including educators, and they will respond: "oversight," "hierarchical control," "monitoring," "observation by a higher-up," "evaluation," and so on. We conceive of supervision differently. We turn the term and concept of supervision on its proverbial head. Supervision is the ongoing, nonjudgmental, collaborative process that engages teachers in dialogue that encourages deep reflective practices for the purpose of improving teaching and student learning. It's *not* the one doing the observation (be it a supervisor or fellow teacher) who has "supervision," but rather it is the one being observed who develops "SUPER-VISION" as a result of having engaged in the process defined above.

Our students and working professionals (i.e., principals, assistant principals, and others responsible for instructional leadership in schools) often have difficulty grappling with this different vision of "doing" supervision. First, it is hard to break old habits. Teachers have been conditioned to respond as automatons, as nonparticipants in an overly prescriptive and dogmatic way of doing supervision. Therefore, when they are challenged to actively engage in conversations about their teaching in nonjudgmental ways, they can find it very difficult. At first, they are suspicious, and rightly so. Few, if any, of their past supervisors have encouraged them to truly reflect and take charge of improving instruction. Supervisors too have been conditioned, trained to conduct supervision using the outdated hierarchical model wherein an individual with "SUPER-VISION" (due in large measure to one's higher status in the organizational framework) dictates measures the teacher must follow to improve his or her teaching.

When we teach our perspectives and innovative methods, it takes months for students to first "believe" that this approach is preferable and makes a difference in terms of thinking about one's teaching and improving student achievement. Then, once they believe that the approach makes sense, it takes time to develop the skills we highlighted earlier in the book: skills of communication, observation, using the observation instruments, choosing appropriate language during the planning conference and feedback sessions, and incorporating alternative approaches such as peer coaching, action research, or instructional rounds. Near the end of our course, students appreciate the new approach to supervision and all it has to offer, but the one question that troubles them is, "How can we ever implement these strategies in our schools?"

This chapter presents a case study of one school grappling with implementing some new supervisory approaches to improving teaching and learning. The case is not meant to represent or capture all likely scenarios, but merely one to bring some important issues to light when implementing instructional change.

Before we present the case study, we provide a few of the many theories and ideas that inform our work leading to instructional change and improvement.

> **Reflection**
>
> *What sorts of problems do you suspect a school might encounter in trying to implement these innovative approaches to instructional improvement?*

FRAMEWORK

According to Blase and Blase (2004), the three primary elements of successful instructional leadership are as follows:

1. Conducting instructional conferences: Whether involved in planning or feedback conversations, informal or more formal grade conferences, effective principals, according to Blase and Blase (2004), make suggestions, give feedback, model, use inquiry, and solicit opinions from teachers.

2. Providing staff development: According to Blase and Blase (2004), "Behaviors associated with providing staff development include emphasizing the study of teaching and learning, support for collaboration, development of coaching relationships, use of action research, provision of resources, and application of the principles of adult growth and development to all phases of the staff development program" (p. 162).

3. Encouraging teacher reflection: Effective principals purposefully engage teachers in articulating feelings, sharing attitudes, and deep thinking about instructional issues (Carroll, Featherstone, Featherstone, Feiman-Nemser, & Roosevelt, 2007; Farrell, 2003; Lasley, 1992; Schon, 1987).

Instructional supervision, as best practice, is a schoolwide process in which teaching and learning become the core of the school's mission. Principals and other administrators work to develop a professional learning community that supports such work (Burke & Krey, 2005; Hord, Roussin, & Sommers, 2009; Morrissey, 2000; Sullivan & Glanz, 2006; Ubben, Hughes, & Norris, 2004). A professional learning community has five dimensions: (1) supportive and shared leadership (e.g., school administrators participate democratically with teachers, sharing power, authority, and decision making); (2) shared values and vision (e.g., the principal or head and staff decide on the values and vision of the school and support its realization); (3) collective learning (e.g., staff and the administration come together to learn how best to improve student performance); (4) supportive conditions (e.g., principals and teachers possess adequate resources to promote instructional excellence and create structures that facilitate learning for all); and (5) shared personal practice (e.g., peer review and feedback are school norms, as is feedback given to administrators by teachers in informal and formal ways) (Hord, 1997 as cited by Morrissey, 2000, pp. 4, 32–33). Instructional leaders within professional learning communities keep instructional quality as their main focus.

In order to provide a theoretical frame for discussion of instructional quality, see Figure 6.1 below, which addresses a critical factor in understanding that instructional supervision, to be effective, must focus on the "instructional core" (see City, Elmore, Fiarman, & Teitel, 2009). The instructional core (see Figure 6.1 below) is "composed of the teacher and the student in the presence of the content" (p. 22). A reciprocal relationship exists between each component (i.e., between student and teacher; teacher and student, student and content, and teacher and content). The aforementioned authors explain:

> Simply stated, the instructional task is the actual work that students are asked to do in the process of instruction—*not* what teachers *think* they are asking students to do, or what the official curriculum *says* . . . , but what they are *actually* doing. (p. 23; italics in original)

Learning occurs in the interaction among these three vital components. For instance, if we match the level of content to the students' ability level, then learning is more likely to occur. As teachers' knowledge of the content and skills in delivering it increases, students are more likely to learn. If students themselves are engaged in learning (e.g., on task, challenged, monitored), then

Figure 6.1 The Instructional Core

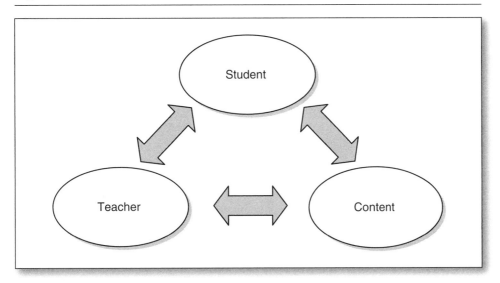

learning is more likely to occur than without such attention to student engagement. City, Elmore, Fiarman, and Teitel (2009) say it plainly: "If you are not doing one of these three things, you are not improving instruction and learning" (p. 24). It is important to emphasize that the structures we employ to encourage learning (e.g., learning communities, differentiation, grouping, supervision, block scheduling, individualization, instructional prompts, professional development) do not, by and in themselves, improve learning. Rather, these structures must influence the instructional core for learning to occur. For example, if professional development is aimed at changing teacher behaviors in the classroom and appropriate follow-up is employed to help the teacher gain a better understanding of the two other elements of the instructional core, students and content, then learning will be enhanced (C. C. Johnson & Fargo, 2010). City, Elmore, Fiarman, and Teitel (2009) explain:

> At the very best, when they are working well, they *create conditions* that influence what goes on inside the instructional core. The primary work of schooling occurs inside the classrooms, *not* in the organizations and institutions that surround the classroom. Schools don't improve through political and managerial incantation; they improve through the complex and demanding work of teaching and learning. (p. 25; italics in original)

More pointedly, whether we are employing supervision, professional development, or any of the other structures, activities, or processes that impact teacher behavior and student learning, four questions in the instructional process must be considered at all times:

1. How will this affect teachers' knowledge and skills?

2. How will this affect the level of content in classrooms?

3. How will this affect the role of the student in the instructional process?

4. How will this affect the relationship between [and among] the teacher, the student, and content? (City, Elmore, Fiarman, & Teitel, 2009, p. 27)

When teachers are observed by peers or supervisors, the observer, if he or she wants to know if learning is occurring, must examine the instructional core and ask:

1. What are the teachers doing and saying?

2. What are the students doing and saying? (in response to teacher behavior)

3. What is the task? (City, Elmore, Fiarman, & Teitel, 2009, p. 88)

Assessment of instructional quality, then, must consider the above theoretical frames.

A major theme of this chapter is our belief in the urgency for school leaders to accentuate their role as instructional leaders by focusing the majority of their efforts on the instructional core. Moreover, school leaders need to strengthen their role as instructional leaders as they also balance managerial, political, financial, operational, and communal imperatives. Too many leaders eschew instructional leadership responsibilities for a variety of reasons, including perceived time constraints, increase in administrative report keeping from the central office, management of schoolwide student behavioral issues, lack of knowledge on how to best engage experienced teachers in discussions about teaching practice, among others. To do so, however, is myopic and detrimental toward spearheading student academic growth and overall social and emotional growth. School leaders need to balance managerial responsibilities with quality time to improve teaching in classrooms and schoolwide.

> **Reflection**
>
> *Explain why you think a focus on the instructional core is so essential for improving classroom instruction. How might you employ it as a supervisor in working with a teacher during a feedback session?*

THE CASE AND TWO QUESTIONS

The following questions guide our discussion in this chapter:

1. How did the school actually begin to transform the way it conducts supervision and evaluation?

2. What challenges did the school face in its attempt to transform its instructional program?

Part I: A New Vision for Excellence

Janet Ironside is the recently promoted principal of Summerville Middle School, with 400 students in grades 5–8. The school has experienced significant changes in demographics over the years, resulting in diverse teacher and student populations. While the teachers range quite significantly in age, teaching experience, and years of employment at Summerville, together they have created an atmosphere of professionalism and dedication to teaching and learning. The majority of teachers have been in the school from 5 to 10 years, and several teachers who function as "the old guard" have been in the school for over 20 years. The school is steeped in tradition, with teachers having their required yearly observations and four or five professional development (PD) days throughout the year. Newly titled Principal Ironside appreciates many of the traditions of Summerville that initially lured her to the school, such as the school's acceptance and appreciation of diversity. Still, her forward-thinking nature and integrity as a reflective teacher motivate her to redefine the school's vision for instructional leadership and supervision. She knows that introducing this change will surely elicit excitement from some and resistance from others. She hopes her sincerity and commitment to the task and to her role as instructional leader at Summerville will inspire as many teachers as possible to come on board and join her in this initiative.

Ms. Ironside has long been known for her attention to detail, her empathetic listening skills, and her exuberance toward education. Whether in her role as history teacher for 15 years, during which she twice received awards as Outstanding Teacher of the Year, her promotion to chair of the history department, or in her more recent post as assistant principal of a nearby elementary school, Ms. Ironside has shown consistent growth and achievement in her field. She has also expressed her passion for education through her pursuit of her master's degree in educational leadership. During her coursework, she was exposed to cutting-edge, research-based approaches to instructional supervision and was particularly intrigued by the main text in her supervision class, Sullivan and Glanz's *Supervision That Improves Teaching and Learning.* It helped her to appreciate the importance of self-reflection and gave her the vocabulary and related tools to actualize collaborative reflection in the supervisory cycle. Embracing this new wave in educational psychology would certainly help her to usher Summerville's educational leadership team into the 21st century.

Ms. Ironside is cognizant of the skepticism that many of her faculty members have toward any change process that seems to potentially affect their teaching style. Moreover, she is particularly aware of the reality that the supervisory cycle in the past has been performed in a perfunctory fashion that has often left her faculty feeling derided and judged. She was totally caught off guard, though, when she was called into Vice Principal McAfee's office. Truth be told, she had been warned that Vice Principal McAfee ran a tight ship where law and order was the rule. She knocked timidly at the door awaiting permission to enter. Finally, she heard a gruff voice saying "Come in already!" Vice Principal McAfee barely looked up from the papers on his desk that he had been reading and motioned with a dismissive wave of his hand that she should take a seat.

"So, I hear that you are thinking of changing the way things run here at Summerville," Vice Principal McAfee began. "Tell me, Janet, what makes you think that some newfangled idea that you heard from some big-shot professor can change the many decades of success that we have enjoyed here at Summerville?"

Ms. Ironside swallowed hard. "Well, sir, please do not misunderstand." She was aware that her nervousness was making her swallow her words. "I have heard of the many accomplishments that have been achieved over the years here at Summerville. It was for that very reason that I enthusiastically applied for this job. However, as I've been getting a taste of things firsthand and observing current supervisory patterns, I think there are some creative ways that we can enhance the existing programming here at Summerville, excellent as it is."

Ms. Ironside picked up her eyes and searched Vice Principal McAfee's face for any signs of disapproval. Finally, Vice Principal McAfee replied, "Like what, pray tell?"

"Well sir, . . . I would like to implement this change in several stages."

"Change??? I wasn't aware that we were in need of a change," said the Vice Principal.

"I have noticed that several of the new teachers are having trouble adapting to the teaching requirements here at Summerville."

"Ms. Ironside, with all due respect, that is precisely why we brought you here. It was my understanding that you would instruct these teachers in the proper ways to deal with the students in their classes. Am I missing something?"

Ms. Ironside became increasingly aware that the challenge of bringing instructional leadership to Summerville could not happen all at once and that it would take time to change the culture. She also realized that she would have to find a way to get Vice Principal McAfee to see the value of instructional leadership if she was going to succeed at all.

"Vice Principal McAfee, do you mind if I ask you a question?" She had decided to go for broke. She would either convince Vice Principal McAfee of the value of instructional leadership or she might as well begin to pack her bags now.

"You have been the vice principal here at Summerville for the last 23 years. Is there any one principle that you can point to that has shaped Summerville into the very respectable institution that it is today?"

"Well, come to think of it, it has always been my belief that a strong command of the material will produce the desired results in students. I daresay that our high graduation record proves that my assertion is correct. Summerville graduates are among the highest-scoring students in the state."

"That is great. I am so excited to be working with you and your fine faculty that has such an impressive track record of success. But I would like to ask you how much of our time do you feel is spent managing your faculty?"

"Sometimes I feel like it is an impossible job. I try to get to every class each day. I want the teachers to know and feel that they are being watched and that they are being held to a high standard."

"That must be difficult to get to every class each day."

"Yes, I work hard. My teachers know this, and in turn they know that I expect that they work hard."

"And how do you measure this success, may I ask?"

"Our success speaks for itself. We have students going to the top schools every year."

"But how do you know if the process of school supervision is contributing to this success? Have you discussed the instructional core and the supervisory cycle with your faculty?"

"I try to give instructions and not ask my faculty for input lest I be perceived as weak and ineffective. I am not trying to win a popularity contest. I am trying to run a great school."

"Indeed, I appreciate the dedication that you have to your school and that you have assembled such a creative, talented, and dedicated faculty. However, as we are colleagues now, and as I have been brought to the school by the Board to advance this school, I need to be honest with you. So although we agree that we have a great faculty and a very good school, the mission of any institution must be continual improvement. As a school, if we are not advancing we are falling behind."

"Yes."

"And we agree that most of our faculty are the right players."

"Yes."

"If that is the case, why do you feel such a need to hold the reins so tightly? Knowing that we have a hardworking, dedicated faculty of the right people, do you appreciate that the right people do not need to be 'snoopervised'?"

"Well, I guess I understand what you mean, but everybody needs to feel accountable."

"That, sir, is precisely the point. Our faculty needs accountability. They also need instructional leadership. If our faculty feels constantly watched with daily checkup visits to their classes, they will never take on new initiatives or experiment with new ideas in educational research in their classes. They will play it safe."

"You know between you and me, I do have so much respect for this faculty. I just feel like as their leader they need to be led."

"I'd like to challenge you to reflect on when you were a teacher. What relationship did you have with your principal?"

"I tried to stay out of his way. I knew he was tough and would make sure that I was on time and doing my job. I never wanted to meet with him because I knew that a meeting with him would always be critical, so I would do everything I could to stay out of his way."

"What if that same person were interested not just in the school but in you and your own personal professional growth? What if that principal gave a young teacher the opportunity to reflect on his or her teaching? What if that principal, with his valuable experience, could serve as a resource in guiding that teacher to develop his or her own successful strategies? Imagine if a teacher could have an extra pair of eyes in the classroom from a fellow teacher objectively observing the student learning and not judging his or her teaching performance. Wouldn't that have made a world of a difference for a new teacher?"

"It is an interesting point. Again, the last place I wanted to be was in my principal's office. When I was with him I felt not much different from one of the students who was getting in trouble."

"Could that be how some of your faculty feel today?"

"Ms. Ironside, you make some interesting points and have got me really thinking, but before I become a believer I have to tangibly see this in action. What suggestions do you have?"

"Since this is a novel way of looking at professional development that teachers are not used to, I suggest we start small. We should ask for small groups of volunteers. Since two of the new teachers have asked me for help in adjusting to the school, two senior teachers could volunteer to serve as mentors. This will be group one and consist of four teachers. Groups two and three would be composed of three to six volunteers who could choose to implement either a book study or lesson study. Giving them a choice of which project to choose will empower them and illustrate that the goal is to create teachers who think about and make educational decisions. With the success of these initial groups, hopefully, other teachers will buy into this strategy, and it can expand. This will allow the teachers to build trust and not feel threatened by one another and the administration. Then we can introduce the reflective clinical supervision cycle as the method of classroom supervision throughout the school."

Ms. Ironside reviews the cycle with Vice Principal McAfee.

"With that many teachers, how do you plan on having them meet so often? The school day is pretty packed; this will become a scheduling nightmare."

"Finding the time is a big concern, but in my old school we found creative ways to adjust the schedule that allowed teachers to meet. I noticed that a lot of the teachers have lunch duty at the same time. If I or someone else covers it, then they could meet during lunch. Perhaps, we can even offer free lunch as an incentive. I am not sure if we have that in the budget, but maybe we could offer teachers a cash stipend to attend an extra workshop/meeting time after school. Finally, we can ask teachers for their input on these suggestions and to offer their own."

Vice Principal McAfee concluded, "I will see what I can do about scheduling and finding some extra finances. I look forward to seeing how this idea is implemented with the faculty."

At one of the early faculty meetings, Ms. Ironside discussed research on instructional leadership. She emphasized that "what really matters is attention to the instructional core. That is, no matter what we do we won't significantly change anything unless our efforts are aimed at addressing issues and problems centered around the instructional core." At the meeting, she introduced the new model of supervision and introduced the concept of self-reflection to the faculty. In engaging the faculty she encountered several hurdles. The faculty was skeptical and viewed this as just the latest in "new" initiatives that claimed to work wonders but usually lasted a few months at most. In the past, teachers' perception was that when their opinion was solicited, it was merely perfunctory and lip service. Finally, there were four teachers in the English department who were called the "the old guard" because they had been in the school from its founding and were known not to be receptive to new ideas.

Part II: The Change Process

Ms. Ironside began the meeting, "I know that I sit in the company of many talented faculty members. If we are going to continue to develop our school, we need to keep challenging ourselves to find ways to improve our educational model. Although you hopefully already know this, I want to make it very clear that we respect the hard work you do and appreciate the high level of professionalism that you bring to your job. Rather than imposing a new initiative upon you, we would like to invite you to join us in creating a new model of supervision that is based on encouraging dialogue about our teaching practices in a nonjudgmental and self-reflective manner. Information that highlights mentoring, book study, and lesson study can be found in the packet that you received at the beginning of this meeting. We would like to ask for volunteers to pilot these programs. I'll present a brief overview of each in a few minutes. If you would be interested in joining one of these initiatives, please leave a note for Dr. Harris, chairman of the math department, who has graciously accepted to organize the groups."

Ms. Ironside chose to ask Dr. Harris to organize the groups so teachers wouldn't feel pressured into joining. She wanted volunteers who were committed to making a change.

Not surprisingly, many teachers took a wait-and-see attitude, not willing to go out on a limb until they saw if Vice Principal McAfee was on board. However, there were enough teachers who volunteered to enable the formation of the pilot groups. Three teachers even had to be wait-listed. One teacher who responded said, "We always complain that we lack a voice, and this sounds like an opportunity to try and change that. How could I not try it? The fact that the principal wouldn't be controlling the group or sitting in on the sessions showed me that it would not become another method to judge my performance."

Following the pilot program, teacher feedback was extremely positive. Mr. Ilariya commented, "Although there was a period of adjustment in learning how to communicate openly with each other, it was so refreshing to hear the opinions of my colleagues in discussing the issues. It made me really think how much in common the English department had with my subject, history. We collaborated on a lesson project that integrated the readings used in English that came from the period of the Civil War that we were studying in history class."

One of the mentored teachers reported, "Working with a senior mentor allowed me to easily integrate into the school and adjust to the high expectations here at Summerville. The process allowed me to reflect on my teaching practices. My mentor helped me explore new methods to teach a topic, and I see now it was because he wasn't judging or rating my performance. Rather, it was an objective record of what I was really doing. At the end of the year, another first-year teacher from the math department asked me if it was really true that my mentor didn't serve as a spy for the principal to evaluate me. He was so amazed that it was a safe and teacher-centered process that he joined the program the following year."

After the success of the first-year pilot program, the initiatives were expanded the following year. With more participation, however, scheduling became more difficult, and more creative ways had to be found to increase funding. Each volunteer faculty member was going to engage a team of colleagues to participate in one form of instructional supervision (see Chapter 5). In turn each of these teams would share on at least one occasion their findings and observations from participating in the alternative supervisory model.

Change is a process that works in ways that are sometimes subtle and even imperceptible. This was the case at Summerville Middle School. What began as a process to measure and document instructional supervision over time became a process for a more broad-based program of school improvement that touched every aspect of the institution. As people heard about and saw classrooms engaged in new initiatives, and when colleagues heard the exciting conversations about pedagogy that became more and more the focal point of the faculty room, more people were brought on board and joined in these new initiatives. Gradually the momentum of success was felt in the entire school.

The principal engaged the faculty directly to understand why there was some resistance to change. She began by arranging informal one-on-one meetings with individual faculty members to discuss the new initiatives. These private meetings were intended to be a forum for teachers to respond and for the principal to have an opportunity to thoughtfully consider their individual reactions. This would also offer an opportunity to the principal to probe their responses in order to get at the core issues underlying their willingness or unwillingness to participate. She could then individualize her approach by reflecting on teacher responses and considering how to make this program not only less intimidating but even appealing to them.

Mrs. Lane, for example, is someone we can certainly call a veteran teacher. Already teaching second-generation students at the school, Mrs. Lane runs her classes like a well-oiled machine. She has been walking the walk and talking the talk of seventh-grade social studies for longer than any other faculty member at the school can remember. While in some respects her seniority has garnered a great deal of respect and admiration from colleagues and school administrators, she has become very resistant to the renewed vision of instructional supervision and school leadership. Ms. Ironside braced herself for an anticipated difficult conversation—expected the worst, hoped for the best, and realistically anticipated something somewhere in between.

"Mrs. Lane, please come in, and have a seat. Can I offer you some coffee?"

"Yes, thank you. I have been up grading papers since 5:00 this morning. You wouldn't believe how hard of a time some of these students have following directions. I have been assigning the same project for the last—well—don't want to date myself—so I know my assignment is clear. You would think they would understand what I mean when I say no online resources!"

Trying to offer a supportive smile, Ms. Ironside responded, "Please help yourself to coffee and make yourself comfortable. In the last few months, I have been engaging teachers in conversations about teaching and learning in light of a newly defined notion of instructional supervision. I realize that this model is only as strong as my faculty's commitment to this process. I value your tenure at this school and appreciate that you have seen it undergo quite a number of transformations during your years here. I was wondering if you might have any questions about the model and how you anticipate it affecting your role at the school—both inside and outside the classroom."

"Well, to be honest, I appreciate you asking—I thought I knew where this was going and I can't say I liked it, but now while I'm here—let me ask you a few questions. I want to make sure I understand this correctly."

In the course of the discussion, Ms. Ironside realized that Mrs. Lane was insecure because of her fear of not belonging and living up to the high standards of the school, as well as her unfamiliarity with technology.

"Mrs. Lane, I can appreciate how daunting the new technology can be. Just when you think you understand how one aspect works, the world has moved on to the next one. I remember when I first started teaching I was considered advanced because I used an overhead projector. Today, the students know the interactive whiteboard better than we do."

"I agree; that is how I feel sometimes."

"One of the supervision ideas we would like to implement is a book club on technology. I was wondering if you would like be the chair of the project. You and your team members will collaboratively select a book on the topic and use the protocols to discuss it. I think it will be a great opportunity for the faculty to familiarize itself with the latest trends in technology as well as begin to openly analyze and discuss educational issues that relate to technology."

"Wow, this sounds like a daunting task, but I think it could really help me better understand technology. It will also be great to hear what my colleagues are experiencing and to share strategies. Thank you for selecting me."

Mrs. Lane chairing the book club encouraged another one of the "old guard" English teachers to join the book club, that eventually led her to start a book club for the English teachers. However, the two other old guard teachers did not change their ways and could not adjust to the new paradigm of thinking. These two teachers felt increasingly marginalized not by the administration but by their fellow teachers.

Through empowering and giving faculty choices and a sense of personal efficacy, the administration found that the faculty did not need to be watched over or hounded in order to do their jobs. In fact, the best and most inspired faculty grabbed the opportunity of openness being fostered by the new administrator to demonstrate clearly that they were an effective and diligent staff. Gradually, the process of faculty empowerment that was made manifest in the implementation of the supervisory cycle created a clear delineation among the faculty. There were those faculty members that embraced change and were self-motivated. These faculty managed themselves and held themselves to a high standard of accountability. It was precisely these teachers who became increasingly frustrated by those teachers who were not diligent, who were not "A" players. Ralph Waldo Emerson once defined the transcendentalists as those people who, "went ahead while everybody else stayed behind." Gradually a culture of improvement grew at Summerville Middle School. Sometimes this process was difficult because it began with getting the "right" people onto the bus. It did not matter what seat they had at first. There was time to reorganize and reallocate responsibilities, but what was most important was that a team of dedicated professionals was built to engage in disciplined reflection and action.

> **Reflection**
>
> *As the principal, how would you have gone about transforming instructional supervision?*

CONCLUSION

Instructional leadership should form the core work of school leaders. This last section of the chapter highlights the imperative for leaders to transform their school culture to strategically address ways to promote teacher professional growth in order to improve teaching and promote student learning for all students regardless of their abilities.

Why, you might ask, must we transform our schools? Why change? Schools today are more complex than schools of yesteryear. We confront a plethora of challenges—we have more students than ever identified with emotional and learning issues, and school leaders must remain responsive to a growing, varied, and diverse constituency. We need to keep pace with these internal and external vicissitudes that inevitably challenge our convictions and intestinal fortitude. Because problems are more onerous today, we need a responsive theory of leadership to guide our work in schools.

Transformational leaders work to alter school culture by nurturing a professional learning community. They serve as change agents or facilitators of change in order to actualize their vision for instructional excellence (Fullan, 2006). They work diligently and consistently to keep instructional quality as their main focus.

Transforming schools is easy if done superficially. Such change, however, is ephemeral. Unfortunately, much change, says Fullan (2003), occurs at this superficial level. In fact, he says much of the change in schools in the 1960s around innovative instructional and curricular practices was short-lived because it was implemented on the surface without a deep change in people's beliefs and behavior. Both Fullan (2003) and Starratt (1995) concur that change without addressing a change in core beliefs and values is doomed to remain temporary and superficial. "Transformational leadership," says Starratt (1995), "is concerned with large, collective values . . ." (p. 110). Leadership is predicated on the foundation of changing core beliefs and values.

Michael Fullan (1991, cited by Fullan 2003) has identified "five crucial mind and action sets that leaders in the 21st century must cultivate: a deep sense of moral purpose, knowledge of the change process, capacity to develop relationships across diverse individuals and groups, skills in fostering knowledge creation and sharing, and the ability to engage with others in coherence making amidst multiple innovations" (p. 35).

1. *Engaging people's moral purposes.* Embedded in a vision for students, in terms of their social and academic growth, should also be a detailed articulation of the school's commitment to instructional excellence for all students. A school is committed to refining the lives of children by improving the quality of the instruction they receive. Such a commitment must be further predicated on serving the needs of all students within an inclusive learning environment (Glanz, 2008) while remaining cognizant of extant research into the latest and most effective teaching pedagogies.

2. *Understand the change process.* The "implementation dip," according to Fullan, is a proverbial land mine. People, often board members, expect fast results. Fullan says, "Since change involves grappling with new beliefs and understandings, and new skills, competencies and behaviors, it is inevitable that it will not go smoothly in the early stages of implementation." Such an understanding helps people within the organization to

relax and experiment with new ideas, practices, and policies. Learning anything new is initially "awkward." Furthermore, being aware of this implementation dip actually shortens the dip, according to Fullan. Another aspect of change, for Fullan, is the realization of the necessity to overcome fear. Citing research by Black and Gregersen (2002 as cited by Fullan, 2006), Fullan explains the reason why despite a clear vision, people seem immobilized. He cites Black and Gregersen's answer:

> The clearer the new vision, the easier it is for people to see all the specific ways in which they will be incompetent and look stupid. Many prefer to be competent at the [old] wrong thing than incompetent at the [new] right thing. (p. 69)

3. *Cultures for learning.* This third mind-set of change, according to Fullan, encourages the establishment of a conducive environment "so that people can learn from each other and become collectively committed to improvement." That is why involving teachers in decision making about curriculum and instruction is so critical. Mechanisms and structures within a school need to be developed to allow for and facilitate communication among teachers and administrators about instruction.

4. *Cultures of evaluation.* Coupled with these emphases on instructional improvement is a focus on assessment. Gathering evidence of student learning continuously in aggregated and disaggregated ways, and developing action plans based on an analysis of the data from parent, teacher, and student satisfaction surveys in order to inform instructional decision making, are examples of creating a culture of evaluation or assessment in a school.

5. *Leadership for change.* Fullan asks, what is the best leadership style for effecting the changes that are necessary in schools? He explains, "It turns out that high-flying, charismatic leaders look like powerful change agents, but are actually bad for business because too much revolves around themselves." Leadership, he continues, must be distributed throughout the organization.

This case study demonstrated that work in supervision of instruction had the potential to matter greatly. It underscored the prevalence of inspectional, fault-finding supervisory practices that can negatively affect faculty morale. It highlighted the notion that faculty needed to play a more active role in leading their own professional development.

What lessons can we learn from this case? In closing, here are a few lessons:

- Resistance to change is common and should be expected.
- Success is a multilayered, gradual process not always assured, but improvements—even though incremental—do occur.
- Implement new changes slowly (even one at a time) and provide participants enough time to fully understand expectations and time to build requisite skills to ensure success of strategy.

Reflection

What lessons did you learn from reading this chapter? Share with a colleague how you can begin to go about transforming supervisory practices in your school.

- Changing and building a new culture of learning and improvement take time and continuous commitment. Positive instructional change in any school is inevitably fraught with challenges, including resistances and ambivalences. Renewal can occur in time. This school is still in process of developing new ways of learning and improving.

Supervision to Improve Classroom Instruction

Next Steps

Assume that any significant innovation, if it is to result in change, requires individual implementers to work out their own meaning.

—Fullan, 1991, p. 105

CHAPTER OVERVIEW

1. Supervisory Platform Guidelines
   a. Three Sample Platforms

2. Next Steps
   a. Inner Circle
   b. School
   c. District

3. Conclusion—or Beginning?

In the preceding chapters of this book, we have tried to provide you with a foundation of knowledge, theory, and practice to permit you to formulate your own supervisory platform. With this goal in mind, we have provided you with (a) an overview of the history of classroom and instructional supervision, (b) a description of the more recent approaches to supervision that aim to improve classroom instruction, (c) strategies and techniques for developing the skills needed to implement the different models and approaches, and (d) case studies that illustrate how individuals and schools have operationalized these models. We think that you now have the requisite knowledge, skills, and experience to draft your personal supervisory platform and begin to reach out to others. The goal of this final chapter is to facilitate the development of a personal plan to put improvement of instruction at the center of supervision in your professional environment. Our suggestions are designed to serve as a springboard for your own creativity, not as a recipe to follow.

NEXT STEPS

At this juncture, we encourage you to formulate your own beliefs related to supervision of classroom instruction and integrate them into your initial personal vision statements. Thus, next steps begin with "me," the clarification of your own supervisory beliefs. Once you have worked out your own meanings, you can begin to think about the next steps in your school environment. You can contemplate sharing them with your inner circle at school—teachers on your grade level, in your department, in your cabinet, and so forth. After the inner circle has worked out a joint direction for itself, this small group can think about consequences and ideas for the whole school and eventually for sharing, dissemination, and development in the school district. The planning outline might look like Table 7.1.

Table 7.1 Supervisory Development Plan: Next Steps in Putting Improvement of Classroom Instruction at the Center of Supervision

For me, personally	
For my inner circle	
For the rest of the school	
For the district in the future	

Source: The late Nancy Mohr, former principal and leadership consultant, gave us permission to adapt her planning sheet.

GUIDELINES FOR CREATING A SUPERVISORY PLATFORM

Because we have focused primarily on supervision of classroom instruction in this book, we limit our guidelines for the development of a personal supervisory platform to classroom supervision. Although we recognize that it is impossible to isolate supervision of classroom instruction from the other facets of supervision of instruction, such as staff, curriculum, and group development, for the purposes of this book, we have placed supervision of classroom instruction at the center of professional development. We include some questions and sample supervisory platforms to facilitate the process of clarifying your beliefs and ideas.

You can approach the following questions in at least two ways: (1) You can use some or all of your responses to these questions as a basis for your supervisory platform, or (2) you can write your platform first and verify that you have included some of the ideas contained in these questions.

1. How do you define supervision of classroom instruction?

2. What should be the ultimate goal of supervision of classroom instruction?

3. What assumptions, values, and beliefs underlie your goals and definition?

4. Who should make the decisions about supervision of classroom instruction for the school?

5. How do you envision the process developing?

6. What would the structure(s) of supervision of classroom instruction look like?

7. Who should be involved in the supervisory process? What should each party's role be? How would the roles differ?

8. What skills are needed for effective supervision?

9. What activities would be included in instructional supervision (e.g., staff development)?

10. How would you address the question of supervision versus evaluation?

11. What are your beliefs with respect to the role of the district in supervision of classroom instruction?

12. How would you assess the implementation of your ideas? What would be the indicators of success?

Be sure to offer a concluding statement.

CB&O

The following supervisory platform statements represent the thinking of students after one semester of developing their supervisory beliefs and practices. You can use these as a guide to inspire you in developing your own. These statements vary in length and style as well as content. Two pages may suffice to elucidate one person's ideas, whereas another may require 10. These differences illustrate the idiosyncratic and essentially personal nature of visioning. Christine Drucker, a Staten Island, New York, high school teacher at the time, wrote the first platform; Linda Herman, a Brooklyn, New York, early childhood teacher at that juncture, submitted the second one; the third platform was written by a then–Staten Island, New York, high school teacher, David Cugini.

Supervisory Platform 1 (Christine Drucker)

Educating our children is not the job solely of the teacher. It is a result of a community of people working together to provide students with the skills they need to succeed in the world. This community includes parents, students, teachers, and supervisors.

Supervisors of curriculum and instruction hold a very important job—to ensure that students are receiving the best-possible instruction they can from their teachers. Educators often discuss the role of the teacher as a mentor, inspirer, and facilitator for students. A supervisor holds that same role for the teacher—a mentor, inspirer, and a facilitator of learning.

The major role of a supervisor is to enhance the instruction of teachers. In order to perform this task, it is necessary for a supervisor to be a master teacher. This means that the supervisor must have a working knowledge of instructional techniques and curriculum. Teachers must have confidence and respect for their supervisor's knowledge in order to rely on that supervisor for assistance and advice. One way to accomplish this is for the supervisor to encourage teachers to visit the supervisor's own classroom. This is not only an opportunity to model teaching techniques, but it demonstrates the supervisor's confidence in teaching methods and classroom management.

Having knowledge of teaching and curriculum is helpful only if a supervisor has the ability to communicate. This is the key to successful supervision. The supervisor must develop relationships with the teachers where the teachers feel comfortable having discussions about their instruction. The relationship between the supervisor and teacher must be one of trust and mutual respect. Furthermore, teachers should be encouraged to communicate with each other. Creating the "open community" can lead to successful working relationships such as mentoring, team teaching, or coaching. It allows both teachers and the supervisor to be avenues of support, encouragement, and learning to their colleagues.

Most discussions between teachers and the supervisor are informal, and a comfort level should be developed between the teacher and supervisor through informal observations. The supervisor's presence should be commonplace—a consistent factor in the classrooms and hallways. This is very important in creating a comfortable atmosphere for the teacher and students during formal and informal observations.

Classroom observations are a key part of effective supervising. For observations to be effective, they must include communication. The communication process for classroom observations has three basic parts: the planning conference, the observation, and the feedback conference. During the planning conference, the supervisor and teacher confer about the purpose of the observation and they decide on a focus for the lesson. It should be the goal of the supervisor that the teacher be comfortable and knowledgeable enough about his or her teaching to decide what the observation should focus on.

It is important that observations be focused. When the supervisor and teacher decide to discuss, observe, and evaluate one piece of a lesson, that one piece can go into more depth. Furthermore, the teacher can feel more at ease when the focus is on a topic or issue that he or she has selected. The teacher can also feel secure in knowing that there is a valuable purpose to this observation.

In addition to a focus, the tool used for observation should be decided upon. The supervisor must have knowledge of a variety of observation tools that will assist both parties in focusing the observation and later evaluating it.

In order for the supervisor to be effective during the actual observation of a lesson, objectivity is essential. The tool selected by the teacher and the supervisor should act as a guide in focusing the supervisor and assist in maintaining the supervisor's objectivity. The supervisor's role in this step is to observe the behaviors, techniques, or issues discussed in the planning conference.

The supervisor should attempt to make the teacher as self-directed as possible during the feedback conference. At this point, the teacher, with the guidance of the supervisor, evaluates the lesson using the observation tool. If the teacher needs assistance in evaluating or understanding the observation tool, the supervisor assists while still trying to push the teacher toward independent reflection. This is the key to having successful observations. Once a teacher can look independently at observation tools and reflect on them, he or she can continue the process without the supervisor, either alone or with a colleague.

The teacher should feel comfortable at feedback conferences and be able to discuss any difficulties he or she may be having. The feelings of trust, support, and respect discussed earlier are imperative if any suggestions the supervisor makes to improve any difficulties are discussed. The focus of the feedback conference should be on the issues or topics that the teacher and supervisor agreed on earlier. This prevents the teacher from feeling overwhelmed and helps maintain the concept that the observation is for improving the instructional process, not picking on things that went wrong.

Part of enhancing the instruction of teachers is professional development. Not only should teachers be encouraged to attend workshops offered by outside organizations and through the school, but the supervisor must also create a variety of professional development activities. As the supervisor's classroom is open for teachers to visit, the teachers should be encouraged to do the same with each other. Teachers need to learn how to work with one another to share ideas, support, and advice. All teachers can learn from each other. Newer teachers can benefit from the seasoned teachers' experience in the classroom, and the seasoned teachers can learn from the new theories and practices that new teachers learned in college. Mentoring and coaching relationships can be created, and teams of teachers can work together on developing and expanding their instruction. Multiple possibilities of professional development should be available to the teachers. It demonstrates an appreciation of the diverse learning and communication styles of teachers—the same understanding of diversity that teachers are expected to have of their students.

Communication and community are the key elements of supervising instruction and curriculum. When a supervisor creates the sense of togetherness, the feeling that teachers and the supervisor are colleagues working to meet one mission—the successful education of students—there will be success.

Supervisory Platform 2 (Linda Herman)

I believe that the most important element of supervision is the tone that the supervisor sets in the school. When you walk into the building, you should feel the cooperation, support, care, common short-term goals, common long-term vision, lack of competition, safety, hard work, trust, and high expectations. It is in this kind of atmosphere, I believe, that teachers, supervisors, students, parents, and community leaders can do their best work to educate children.

I believe that supervision of classroom instruction is collaborating with teachers, helping them set their personal goals and classroom goals; helping teachers meet these goals; supporting and guiding teachers to be better teachers; helping teachers to see how their children are learning; and supporting teachers to help their children do even better. I also see supervision of classroom instruction as helping teachers enjoy teaching more, and realizing that they are not in this alone, that teaching is a "we" project. We can do together what we cannot do alone.

The ultimate goal of supervision of classroom instruction is that children learn and grow. We hope to help children not only do well on tests but also become lifelong learners who love books and discovery, and see learning and school as an exciting adventure.

In order for my supervision to be effective, all or most teachers in the school need to be onboard. Like me, they also will want to improve as teachers and as coworkers. They will want to grow. They will want to see their students improve. They will want to see the parents and community become more a part of children's education. They will view education as a process. Hopefully, some will realize that we are on a wonderful path—working with children, helping them learn and grow, and that we are all on this path together.

(Continued)

(Continued)

When I begin supervising in a school, I will make an appointment with each teacher—to get to know them. I will ask them about their ideas for the school. What they think has worked. What they think can work. What hasn't worked. I will ask them how I can help them. I will ask them what their goals for themselves and their students are. I will ask them how I can help them realize their goals. I would set up a schedule with each teacher, where I could be in their classrooms once a week to assist them in their teaching. I feel that supervisors need to know kids and groups. Hopefully, it will begin to open up a dialogue, and teachers will really feel comfortable coming to me for help. Teachers can realize that I am really there for them, for I truly am. If I support the teachers, they can do their jobs, which is my ultimate goal: to help the children.

For supervision of classroom instruction, I will meet with the teachers individually, talk about what they want to achieve, what they want to work on, what they want to know about their teaching. I will give them a copy of the supervision book, so they can decide what tool they want me to use when I observe them. We will set up a time for me to visit. I will use the tool they have chosen. I will then give the teacher a copy of my observation and make an appointment for discussion. We will meet and discuss what I have observed, how they felt, what they felt they would like to do differently, the same, what worked, and what didn't. I will try to keep this experience positive, so that the teacher can feel safe and truly grow. I would tell the teacher that I would like to visit again in a month or so and maybe he or she could try another tool and look at a different area. Hopefully, I would be able to visit each teacher four times a year.

What I would really love to encourage in my school is peer observation, using the different supervision tools. I would like each teacher to have a partner to work with and help each other improve. They could observe each other's class often, learning and growing from each other.

I think that effective supervisors need to be good listeners. They need to be good observers. They need to be experienced teachers. They need to be compassionate. They need to be able to create a positive, open energy in the school. They need to be supportive. They need to be able to see teachers' successes and celebrate them, even the small ones. They need to be able to pat teachers on the back. They need to be able to pick teachers up when they are having a hard time, encourage them to see the light, and move forward. They need to have a lot of energy.

I also think that supervisors need to really know the curriculum in the school. They need to know what is being taught. They need to think about different ways to teach so that they can be a resource. Supervisors need to be able to go into a class and teach. A supervisor should be able to model lessons. If teachers are going for workshops for a new curriculum, the supervisor should go also. It should be clear that this is a learning community for all.

There should be much professional development to help teachers grow. Teachers should be encouraged to go to workshops at colleges, at the district office. A supervisor can invite a guest speaker in on a topic that the faculty is working on. Teachers in the building can develop their own workshops for each other, teaching what they feel passionate about to their peers. A schoolwide educational journal can be started—maybe twice a year—where teachers can write about their thoughts about teaching, ideas they have tried, or books or articles they have read. There should be a teachers' library where there are curriculum books, professional magazines, and articles. Teachers should be given the time to watch each other teach. Teachers should be encouraged to team teach. Supervisors should model a lesson. Teachers should be given time to visit other teachers in other schools. Teachers can watch an educational movie together and then have a discussion afterward. An instructional supervisor should make sure that there is a space for dialogue, where teachers can share ideas and grow.

Supervision for growth and evaluation should be separate. Supervision for growth should feel safe, so that the teacher can try new ideas and experiment and learn and grow.

I hope that I can work with other principals in the district to brainstorm ideas about how to supervise teachers better, to help children learn better, to include parents in the process. I hope that I can be instrumental in helping schools be less competitive and more cooperative, for we are truly all in this together.

I would feel successful if children liked coming to school. I want children to do well on tests. I want an active PTA, where parents are involved in their children's education. I want teachers to feel happy working the best they can, but not stressed; to feel supported, to feel comfortable coming to me, to collaborate, to share ideas. I want a school that is always humming, always excited, always trying something new, alive. I think I would feel that I had really done a good job if in my second year, teachers walked in the first day and said how happy they were to be back in school!

Supervisory Platform 3 (David Cugini)

Education in our country is under siege. Countries around the world continue to outperform our students. American culture has changed. We no longer have two-parent homes with a parent who stays home full time as the norm, especially in urban areas. Educators and schools are being asked to bridge the gap. However, the American education system has not changed significantly to match the times. Attempts to use data to improve instruction and help students have not yielded the results educators desire. Change in the education system must come from within, starting with the educators in the building. As a supervisor of instruction, I hope to be an instrument of this change.

How do you classify a supervisor of instruction? The title encompasses a variety of responsibilities. A supervisor of classroom instruction has the duty to help teachers reflect on their practices, gives them the tools so the teacher can self-evaluate and improve, and provides support necessary to meet these ends. The ultimate goal is to have a staff that can operate without the need of a supervisor. They would have all the tools necessary to self-diagnose practices and correct and improve instruction.

I still remember my first year teaching. I needed all the nurturing and support I could get to survive. Regardless of the instruction I received in graduate classes, the first year was filled with tremendous pressure and self-doubt. Fortunately, my supervisor provided the guidance, support, and encouragement that allowed me to flourish as a teacher. Education can be the most difficult job, and regardless of your teaching experience, can cause a person to question his or her abilities. I want to provide a supportive atmosphere for my colleagues. The supervisor of instruction needs to give teachers the opportunity to perfect their teaching craft and maximize student potential.

To establish such a climate in a department, a supervisor needs to have certain qualities. First, the supervisor needs to be an effective communicator. Communication is a two-way street. Not only must a supervisor be able to get his or her ideas across to the intended audience, the supervisor must also be an excellent listener. An active listener will better understand the problems a teacher or student may have and be able to create a more effective solution. In regard to teachers, we are dealing with professionals who have a good understanding of where they want to go in situations. They should be allowed to discuss and develop their ideas with the supervisor. This means that a supervisor must be open minded and possess a collaborative attitude. Finally, teachers must feel that their supervisor supports them. If teachers feel the supervisor is more of a "snoopervisor," then the climate of trust will not exist. Trust is the foundation for effective relationships.

The "snoopervisor" is the educator more interested in evaluating the instruction that occurs in a classroom. It is easy to evaluate a lesson. However, evaluation is merely identifying what went well or what went wrong in a lesson. There is nothing beyond that point. Supervision should be a means to an end. The end is improving the quality of instruction. How can we get there? Evaluation is passing judgment. Evaluation is passive for the person being evaluated. Supervision has the person who is evaluated as an active member of the process. He or she can identify teaching weaknesses throughout the observation cycle and create solutions that are comfortable and effective for the teacher.

The observation cycle is the main focus of the supervisory process. The supervisor is the facilitator. The teacher is an equal partner in the process. Teachers will determine in the planning conference the areas of instruction they would like examined. Through a collaborative process, both the supervisor and teacher will establish an appropriate observation tool for the lesson. At the conclusion of the observation, the teacher will examine the lesson so more effective dialogue can occur at the feedback conference. My hope is other teachers will have the collaborative spirit and provide suggestions for their colleagues. Intervisitation and group sessions will help in this endeavor.

This climate of sharing may be a departure from the environment in which some teachers may be working. The supervisor must be active in establishing this collaborative process. The process will develop with the faculty having an understanding that they have an equal stake in everything that happens in the school. They will be encouraged to adopt a different attitude from what may have been in place before, where they felt terms were dictated to them. The supervisor should cultivate relationships with all the members of the department.

(Continued)

(Continued)

Informal conversation should develop relationships with all the members of the department. Informal conversation about family, interests, hobbies, and even work will pay dividends in the long run.

Staff development is also an essential part of education. Teachers need to be introduced to new technology, trends, and teaching styles. Valuable professional development will make the teachers more successful in the classroom. Discussing possible professional development sessions with the department is yet another way to keep them involved in the collaborative process. In addition to formal professional development, intervisitations and instructional rounds can be arranged. A supportive culture will foster an open-door policy where teachers can visit each other in search of ideas or constructive criticism. A common planning period for teachers to discuss issues is another step that is important for a supervisor to take.

Trying to evaluate the success of this environment will be difficult. People are often afraid to speak freely in front of a supervisor. Surveys and discussions with the faculty and students would be the data I would assemble to assess how the supervision is going. Teachers using new methods of instruction or incorporating technology would be an indicator of success. Another sign would be if teachers were approaching problems in a different way than before, using data and discussing problems and solutions with colleagues.

I believe change needs to come from within. Supervisors need to empower teachers and make them understand that they are the key to student success. Our school and students depend on their abilities to educate. Teachers need to feel appreciated and given encouragement to try new and different approaches to teaching. Once teachers and administrators see each other as partners, the overall success of the school and the students will soon follow.

Class Practice

Bring three copies of the first draft of your supervisory platform to class. In groups of three, read each other's vision statements, one at a time.

Please note that as you read others' statements, do not be critical or judgmental. Simply raise questions for discussion as there is no one "right" response. The purpose of these sharings is to stimulate discussion, reflection, and personal refinement of vision statements. Therefore, offer descriptive, not evaluative, feedback to others. Here are a few guidelines to consider as you read others' statements:

- What are the underlying assumptions?
- Are the statements in the platform internally consistent?
- Are there apparent inconsistencies? For instance, problematic is one who advocates self-reflection and then relies on directive methods in feedback recommendations. Remember, don't criticize but merely ask, "I've noticed you said such and such; how does it relate to what you've said earlier?"
- Take notes on the writer's perspective and value orientation to clarify your own positions and values.

Realize, of course, that as you share your statements with others, revisions are inevitable. Incorporate your colleagues' feedback and further reflections into your revisions.

"FOR ME, PERSONALLY": MY SUPERVISORY PLATFORM

We believe that the following ideas and suggestions for your inner circle, your school, and/or your district can be implemented in most school districts under many types of leadership and in diverse settings.

For My Inner Circle

Once you have completed your personal supervisory platform, you can reach out to colleagues in many ways. What we consider most important of all is to begin from the bottom up, that is, to find one or more colleagues who are amenable to beginning a conversation about transforming classroom supervision from a required, primarily evaluatory process to one of shared growth in teaching and learning. It is also essential that project participation be voluntary.

The following suggestions are some of the innumerable strategies that can open up the conversation. Some of these ideas are teacher initiated; several can emanate from either teachers or supervisors.

- Share case studies from this book with one or more colleagues and then brainstorm possibilities for your inner circle. Invite a colleague to observe a challenge or success in one of your classes and provide you with feedback.
- Discuss with a colleague a curriculum area or approach you would like to try, and plan to team-teach a lesson or observe each other teaching the innovation and give mutual feedback.
- Offer to present an introductory workshop on alternative ways to look at supervision of classroom instruction.
- Discuss the possibility of building a peer-coaching component into an annual personal, department, or grade-level goal.
- Look into grant possibilities to support your project.

For My School

Although we advise that you begin the conversation about classroom supervision with a small group, it is sometimes possible to make inroads at the school level as you introduce the idea to your immediate colleagues. Some of the inner circle suggestions are also applicable to the school level. Therefore, a few of the following ideas are variations on the inner circle:

- Request that this book and other articles and books about innovative supervisory practices be purchased for your school's professional library.
- Spearhead a voluntary professional book study group in which alternative supervision is a topic.
- Suggest that innovative classroom supervision be a school goal for the year.

- Ask that a subcommittee on your school's site-based planning team be formed to discuss innovative classroom supervision.
- Offer to develop a series of workshops on observation techniques, feedback approaches, and alternative supervision for a group of volunteer teachers.
- Offer to set up a visit for interested colleagues to schools where successful alternative supervisory practices are being implemented.

For the District in the Future

Michael Fullan (1993) concluded that "effective schools are ones that are plugged into their environments. . . . A systematic, symbiotic relationship is required between schools and local agencies. . . . Leadership in successful systems *conceptualizes* the problem as continually negotiating school and district codevelopment" (p. 16). We endorse the idea that for reform to be successful, the district and school must support each other. If alternative supervisory methods are to succeed, the district will need to support them philosophically and financially.

Therefore, even as you begin to explore alternative supervisory methods with your inner group, it is important, wherever possible, to explore connecting with the district office. The district can facilitate the process at the site level from the outset. We recommend that you consider the following suggestions, but *only* after taking into consideration (1) that the individual, inner group, or school committee needs to consult with building supervisors before making contact with district-level employees and (2) that the careful application of problem-solving and decision-making skills is essential to determine if, when, and how to proceed.

- Offer to give an introductory workshop or a series of workshops on innovative supervisory practices.
- Request staff development funds so that teachers can be released for intervisitation or staff development.
- Apply for staff development funds or a grant to facilitate developing a pilot program.
- After completing a pilot program, request permission to ask other district faculty to visit the implementation of your project.
- Request permission to offer a presentation to other interested schools.
- Ask to set up a district schedule of intervisitation to other schools and districts involved in innovative supervisory practices.
- Procure funding to attend conferences on innovative practices.
- Apply to be a presenter at a conference as a representative of your school and district.
- Explore the feasibility of setting up a district-based committee on innovative supervisory practices.
- Discuss the possibility of including innovative supervisory practices as a district goal.
- Request district support in apprising you of grant possibilities and in writing proposals.

CONCLUSION—OR JUST A BEGINNING?

A major premise of this volume has been that supervisors can become a potent vehicle for the improvement of classroom instruction. We have attempted to highlight the tools, techniques, and strategies that we think are crucial in promoting instructional excellence. Yet the challenge remains in your hands. We affirm what Harold Spears (1953) articulated more than a half century ago: "Supervision is and always will be the key to the high instructional standards of America's public schools" (p. 462). To ensure that supervision will continue as such, we have presented our modest proposal for effective supervision. We hope that you use our suggestions as a springboard for the improvement of teaching and learning in your professional environment. Please contact us (Susan Sullivan at Susan.Sullivan@csi.cuny.edu or Jeffrey Glanz at glanz@yu.edu) to share your experiences, comments, and suggestions.

Resource A

Microlab Guidelines

Microlab is a term for a planned and timed small-group exercise that addresses a specific sequence of questions and promotes active listening skills in the process. Its structure is about equalizing communication and withholding judgment. It affirms people's ideas and helps build community.[1]

Aim

The aim is to help participants learn more about themselves and others and deepen the quality of collegial sharing using a timed small-group exercise.

Setup

All groups should consist of three to five people and be about the same size. It helps if people can pull chairs into a tight, private group. The following techniques can be used to divide participants:

- Use cards with numbers on them such as three 1s, 2s, and so on. If the numbers come out uneven, avoid groups of five. Make two groups of four instead.
- Count off by three, four, or five.
- Group by level or category.

Time

It takes 15 to 40 minutes to complete a microlab—less time for groups of three addressing two to three questions, more time for groups of four to five addressing four questions. Allow time for the whole group to debrief at the end.

Directions for Facilitator

It is suggested that the group facilitator explain the process to the group members as follows:

I'll be directing what we're going to be sharing. It's not an open discussion. It's about listening and sharing nonjudgmentally. I will pose one question at a time. Each person gets approximately one minute to answer it in turn. No one else is to talk or ask questions when it's someone else's turn. The goal is active listening. I will use a timer and tell the group when they should be halfway around. I also will tell you when the time is up for that question and what the next question is. If a person gets shortchanged on time for some reason, he or she can go first in the next round. It's about being open and honest and also about respecting confidentiality. What someone says in your group is not to be repeated by anybody else. Can you agree to that?

Guidelines

- Speak from your own experience. Say *I* when speaking about yourself.
- Stay on the suggested topic.
- Listen and discover rather than give advice.
- Avoid being judgmental.
- Respect shared confidences.
- It's OK to pass.

Debrief at the End

The whole group should discuss: What do we now know about each other's ideas or experiences? Commonalities? Differences? What was helpful or positive about the process? What was difficult? Is it something to revisit in our work? How could you use the process in your work?

Practice

Set up a practice microlab using the following questions from page 7:

Who or what in your personal or professional background influenced your present supervisory beliefs?

What are some positive supervisory experiences you have encountered?

What are some negative supervisory experiences you recall?

Why did you feel that way?

What does supervision look like in your school?

Note

1. We thank Emily White of Bank Street College of Education and Linda Lantieri of Educators for Social Responsibility for allowing us to adapt their guidelines.

Resource B

Fishbowl Guidelines

The fishbowl can be used either to discuss ideas generated in small groups in a large-group setting or to provide feedback to a small group that is modeling a role play, simulation, or another group process.

Aims

The aim of the fishbowl as follow-up to small-group discussions is to provide a forum for reporting on, sharing, and discussing the ideas generated in small groups. The fishbowl also allows a new process to be modeled with the goal of the volunteers learning the process, getting feedback, and helping the observers learn from the model's experience.

Setup

Discussion fishbowl. Place one chair per small group in a circle in the middle of the room. Provide an additional chair. Each small group chooses a representative for the circle to report on the group's discussion. The rest of the class observes without participating in the debriefing. If a class observer feels strongly about making a particular point, that person can sit temporarily in the additional chair in the circle to express that point. The observer then returns to his or her seat to free the empty chair.

Model fishbowl. Students volunteer to model a particular role play, simulation, or process. The players and an observer sit in the middle of the room surrounded by the rest of the class. Videotaping of the model is highly recommended. The volunteers model the process following the Guidelines for Reflective Practice. Once the observer in the small group provides feedback, class members can make additional observations. If a number of students want to comment, it is preferable to go around the outside circle in order, allowing the students to pass if they wish.

Time

The discussion fishbowl should be given a precise time limit; 10 or 15 minutes should be sufficient. The model fishbowl also should not take more than 10 or 15 minutes and should be abbreviated when necessary. Additional observations from the outer circle in the model fishbowl exercise should be limited by going in order and allowing only one comment per person.

Practice

Set up a practice fishbowl using the following scenario: An experienced teacher discusses a classroom challenge with a supervisor or teacher leader using the self-directed approach. A third person serves as reflector, and the rest of the class/group serve as observers and general reflectors.

Resource C

Technology in the Classroom

TIPS THAT SPAN THE TRADITIONAL TO THE VIRTUAL CLASSROOM

Feedback from instructors who have used the text in virtual or distance education environments confirms that careful planning can result in an almost oxymoronic success story: a hands-on virtual classroom. Most of these ideas can be adapted to enrich the traditional college classroom. School and teacher leaders can also use them for training in any of the alternatives to traditional observations. The suggestions are organized according to their versatility in different types of college classrooms or schools.

1. E-mail, discussion boards, blogs, wikis, asynchronized and synchronized programs. The materials in the book and the assignments are an effective source for myriad online activities. Discussion boards and blogs are a perfect means for students to obtain rapid assistance and feedback on site assignments. From the first school assignment on listening skills to the final reflective supervision cycle, students can query (through e-mail, texting, discussion boards, blogs, and wikis) their colleagues and their instructors on how to approach a situation, how to handle the next steps, and how to discuss challenges and successes that took place. Microlabs can be organized online asynchronously on a discussion board or blog or through synchronized interactive programs.

2. Videos and, to a lesser extent, audiocassettes can substitute for classroom feedback from instructors in the distance or virtual classroom. Viewing of the role plays on the website can facilitate role playing and the practice of observation tools in the college classroom. Virtual classroom students can watch the role plays of the different approaches on the website, and then re-create the role plays with willing colleagues, ideally videotaping them for subsequent reflection. Effective examples of role plays can be shared on the Internet to allow students to observe as needed before class practices or recording their own site practices.

3. A highly developed technological environment can allow an actual classroom to be viewed in a smart college classroom or streamed online for a virtual course. The joint observation provides a common base for analysis and discussion.

4. If students are required to do paper or electronic portfolios, videotaping site practice conferences and assignments creates ideal portfolio artifacts. The video of the conference can be included in the paper portfolio or viewed live in the electronic portfolio.

5. Online professional development for peer coaching, mentoring, and other alternatives to traditional observations can be organized for a school district at individual school sites to avoid teacher travel during or after school.

6. The companion website contains resources that are useful for a traditional classroom setting as well as for an online course:
   - The DVD that models the different feedback approaches and contains taped classes for observation practice.
   - It contains a copy of the observation practice sheets.
   - A list of relevant websites is included.
   - Articles that support the theory and practice recommended in the text are included.

Resource D

Observation Practice Sheets

Table 3.2 Teacher Verbal Behaviors

Class:

Date:

Time began:

Time ended:

Min.	Information Giving	Questioning	Teacher Answering Own Questions	Praising	Direction Giving	Correcting	Reprimanding
1							
2							
3							
4							
5							
6							
7							
8							
9							
10							
11							
12							
13							
14							
15							
16							

Source: Glickman, Carl D.; Gordon, Stephen P.; Ross-Gordon, Jovita M., *SuperVision and Instructional Leadership: A Developmental Approach*, 8th Edition, © 2010. Reprinted by permission of Pearson Education, Inc., Upper Saddle River, NJ.

Table 3.3 Student Responses to Verbal Behaviors

Date:

Time began:

Time ended:

Students	Answered Questions	Praised	Corrected	Reprimanded	Comments

Table 3.4   Teacher Questions Using Bloom's Taxonomy

Class:

Date:

Time began:

Time ended:

Number of questions asked:

Question Category	Tally 5 min.	Tally 10 min.	Tally 15 min.	Total	Percentage	Comments
Creating						
Evaluating						
Analyzing						
Applying						
Understanding						
Remembering						

Source: Glickman, Carl D.; Gordon, Stephen P.; Ross-Gordon, Jovita M., *SuperVision and Instructional Leadership: A Developmental Approach*, 8th Edition, © 2010. Reprinted by permission of Pearson Education, Inc., Upper Saddle River, NJ.

Table 3.5   Student Responses to Questions Indicating Bloom's Taxonomy

Class:

Date:

Time began:

Time ended:

Student	1	2	3	4	5	6	Observations

Key:

✔ = correct

X = incorrect

1 = remembering

2 = understanding

3 = applying

4 = analyzing

5 = evaluating

6 = creating

Table 3.6   Teacher Questions Using Webb's Depth of Knowledge

Class:

Date:

Time began:

Time ended:

Question Category	Tally 5 min.	Tally 10 min.	Tally 15 min.	Total	Percentage	Comments
Extended Thinking						
Strategic Thinking						
Basic Applications of Skill/ Concept						
Recall						

Table 3.7   Student Responses to Questions Indicating Webb's Depth of Knowledge

Time began:

Time ended:

Class:

Date:

Student	1	2	3	4	Observations

Key: ✓ = correct; X = incorrect; 1 = recall; 2 = application of skill/concept; 3 = strategic thinking; 4 = extended thinking

Table 3.8   Student On-Task and Off-Task Behaviors

Class:

Date:

Time when sweep began:

Time ended:

Student	9:00	9:05	9:10	9:15	9:20	9:25	9:30	9:35	Observations

Key: A = at task; TK = talking (social); P = playing; O = out of seat; OT = off task

Source: Glickman, Carl D.; Gordon, Stephen P.; Ross-Gordon, Jovita M., *SuperVision and Instructional Leadership: A Developmental Approach*, 8th Edition, © 2010. Reprinted by permission of Pearson Education, Inc., Upper Saddle River, NJ.

Figure 3.3 Diagram of Verbal Interactions

Class:

Date:

Time:

Circles = students   T = teacher

Source: Glickman, Carl D.; Gordon, Stephen P.; Ross-Gordon, Jovita M., *SuperVision and Instructional Leadership: A Developmental Approach*, 8th Edition, © 2010. Reprinted by permission of Pearson Education, Inc., Upper Saddle River, NJ.

Table 3.9 Gardner's Multiple Intelligences

Class:

Date:

Time:

Elements	Response Yes	No	N/A	Observations
Logical/mathematical	❑	❑	❑	
Bodily/kinesthetic	❑	❑	❑	
Visual	❑	❑	❑	
Musical	❑	❑	❑	
Interpersonal	❑	❑	❑	
Intrapersonal	❑	❑	❑	
Linguistic	❑	❑	❑	
Naturalistic	❑	❑	❑	
Emotional	❑	❑	❑	

Source: Glickman, Carl D.; Gordon, Stephen P.; Ross-Gordon, Jovita M., *SuperVision and Instructional Leadership: A Developmental Approach*, 8th Edition, © 2010. Reprinted by permission of Pearson Education, Inc., Upper Saddle River, NJ.

Table 3.10 Student Use of Gardner's Multiple Intelligences

Class:

Date:

Time:

Student	1	2	3	4	5	6	7	8	9	Observations

Key: 1. Logical/mathematical; 2. Bodily/kinesthetic; 3.Visual; 4. Musical; 5. Interpersonal; 6. Intrapersonal; 7. Linguistic; 8. Naturalistic; 9. Emotional

Table 3.11   Hunter's Steps in Lesson Planning

Class:

Date:

Time:

Elements	Response Yes	No	N/A	Comments
Anticipatory set	❑	❑	❑	
Objective and purpose	❑	❑	❑	
Input	❑	❑	❑	
Modeling	❑	❑	❑	
Checking for understanding	❑	❑	❑	
Guided practice	❑	❑	❑	
Independent practice	❑	❑	❑	

Source: Glickman, Carl D.; Gordon, Stephen P.; Ross-Gordon, Jovita M., *SuperVision and Instructional Leadership: A Developmental Approach*, 8th Edition, © 2010. Reprinted by permission of Pearson Education, Inc., Upper Saddle River, NJ.

Table 3.12 Group Work Criteria

Class:

Date:

Time:

Elements	Response Yes	No	N/A	Comments
Students understand the task goals (academic and social)	❑	❑	❑	
The task matches the goals (leads students to what they should know, understand, and be able to do).	❑	❑	❑	
Students understand what is expected of individuals to make the group work function well (social skills taught).	❑	❑	❑	
Face-to-face interaction	❑	❑	❑	
The task requires an important contribution from each group member based on the student's skills and interests.	❑	❑	❑	
Individuals are accountable for their own understanding of all facets of the task.	❑	❑	❑	
There is a "way out" for students who are not succeeding with the group.	❑	❑	❑	
There is opportunity for teacher or peer coaching and in-process quality checks.	❑	❑	❑	
Time lines are brisk but not rigid.	❑	❑	❑	
Group processing	❑	❑	❑	
Students understand what to do next after they complete their work at a high level of quality.	❑	❑	❑	

Source: C. A. Tomlinson, *How to Differentiate Instruction in Mixed-Ability Classrooms* (2nd ed.). Copyright © 2001 by ASCD. Adapted by permission.

RESOURCE D **205**

Table 3.13   Group Performance: Assessment of Individual Participation

Student:

Class:

Date:

Time:

	Regularly	*Sometimes*	*Rarely*	*Comments*
A. Contribution to group goals				
1. Participates in the group's activities				
2. Does his or her share of work				
B. Staying on the topic				
3. Pays attention; listens				
4. Makes comments to help group get back on topic				
5. Stays on topic				
C. Offering useful ideas or information				
6. Gives helpful ideas & suggestions				
7. Offers helpful feedback & comments				
8. Influences group decisions & plans				
D. Consideration of others				
9. Makes positive, encouraging remarks about group members & their ideas				
10. Shows & expresses sensitivity to the feelings of others				
E. Involving, working, & sharing with others				
11. Tries to get the group working together to reach group agreements				
12. Considers the ideas of others; exchanges, rethinks, defends ideas				
F. Communicating				
13. Speaks clearly; easy to hear & understand				
14. Expresses ideas clearly & effectively				

Source: Modified from the Connecticut State Department of Education; sponsored by the National Science Foundation.

Figure 3.6   Feedback

Class:

Date:

Time:

Key: Pr = prompted; Pb = probed; E = encouraged; O = positively reinforced; D = discouraged pupil

Source: Glickman, Carl D.; Gordon, Stephen P.; Ross-Gordon, Jovita M., *SuperVision and Instructional Leadership: A Developmental Approach*, 8th Edition, © 2010. Reprinted by permission of Pearson Education, Inc., Upper Saddle River, NJ.

Table 3.14 Teacher–Pupil Interaction

Student:

Teacher:

Date:

Time:

Time	Student Action	Teacher Action

Table 3.15   Indicators of Culturally Diverse Learners

Class:

Date:

Time:

Teacher Indicator	Response			Comments
	Yes	No	N/A	
Displays understanding of diverse cultures	❑	❑	❑	
Displays personal regard for students of diverse cultures	❑	❑	❑	
Uses instructional materials free of cultural bias	❑	❑	❑	
Uses examples and materials that represent different cultures	❑	❑	❑	
Promotes examination of concepts and issues from different cultural perspectives	❑	❑	❑	
Intervenes to address acts of student intolerance	❑	❑	❑	
Uses "teachable moments" to address cultural issues	❑	❑	❑	
Reinforces student acts of respect for diverse cultures	❑	❑	❑	

Source: Glickman, Carl D.; Gordon, Stephen P.; Ross-Gordon, Jovita M., *SuperVision and Instructional Leadership: A Developmental Approach*, 8th Edition, © 2010. Reprinted by permission of Pearson Education, Inc., Upper Saddle River, NJ.

Table 3.16   Strategies for Diverse Learners

Class:

Date:

Time:

Teacher Indicator	Response			Examples
	Yes	No	N/A	
Proximity to students	❏	❏	❏	
Different ways of encouraging students	❏	❏	❏	
Positive reinforcement techniques	❏	❏	❏	
Modifications for individual children or types of learners	❏	❏	❏	
Use of children's strengths	❏	❏	❏	
Multiple ways in which lesson is unfolding	❏	❏	❏	
Integration of grouping according to needs and skills	❏	❏	❏	
Scaffolding of instruction	❏	❏	❏	

Table 3.17 Accommodations and Modifications for English-Language Learners

Accommodation Modification	Was This Element Present?			What Is the Evidence?
	Yes	No	N/A	
Teacher talk is modified: slower speech, careful choice of words, idioms, expressions	❑	❑	❑	
Teacher allows wait time and monitors teacher input vs. student output	❑	❑	❑	
Definitions and language are embedded in content/context	❑	❑	❑	
Real-world artifacts present that support comprehension	❑	❑	❑	
Elicits and draws on students' backgrounds to build prior knowledge	❑	❑	❑	
Teacher uses nonverbal cues to support comprehension	❑	❑	❑	

Table 3.18 The Differentiated Classroom

Class:

Date:

Time:

Classroom Characteristics	Presence of Element			Comments/Description
	Yes	No	N/A	
1. Range of activities • whole-class instruction • small-group activities (pairs, triads, quads) • individualized activities (e.g., learning centers, independent study) • student–teacher conferences	❑ ❑ ❑ ❑	❑ ❑ ❑ ❑	❑ ❑ ❑ ❑	
2. Students express themselves in diverse ways • artistically • musically • technologically • scientifically • athletically • through drama/speeches • traditional compositions • building models • other	❑ ❑ ❑ ❑ ❑ ❑ ❑ ❑ ❑	❑ ❑ ❑ ❑ ❑ ❑ ❑ ❑ ❑	❑ ❑ ❑ ❑ ❑ ❑ ❑ ❑ ❑	
3. Students construct meaning on their own; take responsibility for their own learning; plan activities on their own	❑	❑	❑	
4. Learning activities are provided for students who complete work before others	❑	❑	❑	
5. Peer tutoring to reinforce more advanced learners and support less advanced	❑	❑	❑	
6. Different types of assessment are ongoing and integrated	❑	❑	❑	

Table 3.19 Students' Construction of Meaning on Their Own

Class:

Date:

Time:

Teacher Indicator	Response			Examples
	Yes	*No*	*N/A*	
Teacher preassesses student knowledge, skills, and interests	❏	❏	❏	

Student activities:
  a. Centers
    • Provide clear guidelines
    • Promote self-construction of meaning
	
	❏
	❏
		
		❏
		❏
			
			❏
			❏	

b. Independent activities
    • Provide clear guidelines
    • Promote self-construction of meaning
	
	❏
	❏
		
		❏
		❏
			
			❏
			❏	

c. Anchor activities
    • Provide clear guidelines
    • Promote self-construction of meaning
	
	❏
	❏
		
		❏
		❏
			
			❏
			❏	

Groups vary with assignment—some homogeneous, some heterogeneous Roles assigned according to learner needs	❏	❏	❏	
Students self-assess & share feedback wherever possible	❏	❏	❏	

Tiered activities:
  • match students' current understanding
  • challenge with higher-level thinking
	
	❏
	
	❏
		
		❏
		
		❏
			
			❏
			
			❏	

Students choose from a variety of activities and assignments wherever possible	❏	❏	❏	

Source: Developed in collaboration with leaders from P.S. 145, Brooklyn, New York.

Table 3.20 Learning Centers

Class:

Date:

Time began:

Time ended:

Learning Center Focus	*Always Present*	*Somewhat Present*	*Not Present*	*Not Applicable*	*Comments*
Learning centers are established and being used for every core curriculum subject.	❑	❑	❑	❑	
• Math	❑	❑	❑	❑	

• Literacy:
  o Reading
  o Writing
	❑
	❑
		❑
		❑
			❑
			❑
				❑
				❑	

• Science	❑	❑	❑	❑	
• Social Studies	❑	❑	❑	❑	
• Other	❑	❑	❑	❑	
Center work is interdisciplinary	❑	❑	❑	❑	
Tasks are standards based	❑	❑	❑	❑	
Tasks are skill-driven	❑	❑	❑	❑	
Support independence by accessing prior knowledge of: • Strategies • Content • Other	❑	❑	❑	❑	
Tasks are matched to: • Readiness • Interests • Learning styles	❑	❑	❑	❑	

Provides system(s) for students' self-assessment and/or peer assessment:					
• Actual work at center or	❏	❏	❏	❏	
• Usage chart or	❏	❏	❏	❏	
• System for tracking students' product-choice and /or completion of product	❏	❏	❏	❏	
• Provides system(s) for students to record their own progress at centers.	❏	❏	❏	❏	
Development of technology skills is incorporated into tasks	❏	❏	❏	❏	
Overall center rituals and routines are clearly defined and on display in the room:					
• Guidelines for student behavior when doing center work	❏	❏	❏	❏	
• Guidelines for materials management, including storage of final products	❏	❏	❏	❏	

Source: Developed in collaboration with school leaders from P.S. 145, Brooklyn, New York.

Table 3.21   Co-teaching: Push-in Model (initial)

Class:

Date:

Time:

Observations	Frequently	Sometimes	Rarely	Notes
Both teachers are involved in the lesson (i.e., one teaches, one supports)				
Both teachers are instructing small groups; or both are conferring with students				
There is a note-taking system; both teachers are taking notes on students				
There is enough space/tables for each teacher to conduct a small group				
Both teachers support the classroom rules				
Both teachers are using the classroom consequences				
The students seem to view both teachers as classroom teachers				
The ESL-certified teacher* is servicing students in small groups				
There is early evidence of two teachers in the room (charts, note taking, visuals in different handwriting)				
Other ideas to help facilitate co-teaching, possible next steps and connections to support further co-teaching				

*Could be special education, speech, etc.

Source: Adapted with permission from Maria della Ragione, New York City network leader.

Table 3.22   Strategies for Students With Speech and Language Impairments

Class:

Date:

Time:

Teacher/Therapist Indicator	Observed				Comments/Description
	Often	Sometimes	Rarely	N/A	
Is scaffolding of previous skills present?	❑	❑	❑	❑	
Does lesson include differentiation for the different learning styles (visual, auditory, tactile, kinesthetic)?	❑	❑	❑	❑	
Are skills/strategies modeled for the students?	❑	❑	❑	❑	
Is the appropriate level of prompting used?	❑	❑	❑	❑	
Are questions differentiated for each student's needs?	❑	❑	❑	❑	
Is the appropriate wait time given to answer questions?	❑	❑	❑	❑	
Is vocabulary reviewed prior to the lesson?	❑	❑	❑	❑	
Does teacher/therapist explain unknown vocabulary to the student during the lesson?	❑	❑	❑	❑	
Are materials appropriate for the students?	❑	❑	❑	❑	
Does teacher/therapist address how session objectives are applied (generalized) to classroom activities?	❑	❑	❑	❑	

Source: This tool was adapted from one that Melissa Wildes, a speech therapist in Brooklyn, New York, and a leadership candidate, created.

Table 3.23   Guided Reading

Class:

Date:

Time:

Guided Reading Teacher Indicator	Yes	No	N/A	Comments/Examples
Management				
Was the transition from the mini-lesson to group work implemented in an orderly fashion?	❑	❑	❑	
Were the other children on task while the teacher was in small-group instruction?	❑	❑	❑	
Was the time allotted for the guided reading group appropriate?	❑	❑	❑	
Instruction				
Was the text for guided reading introduced in a manner that provided knowledge? Was there support so that students could read independently and successfully?	❑	❑	❑	
Were the children interested in and did they grasp the concepts being taught?	❑	❑	❑	
Was the text appropriate for the group with respect to the level, content, and interest?				
Were support, challenges, and opportunities for problem solving provided?	❑	❑	❑	
Did the students read independently?	❑	❑	❑	
Did assessment take place? What types?	❑	❑	❑	
Did the teacher allow students to be responsible for what they already know?	❑	❑	❑	
Did questions include the full range of Bloom's Taxonomy?	❑	❑	❑	
Did the teacher help students strengthen their strategies?	❑	❑	❑	

Source: This instrument was adapted from one that Suzanne Dimitri, a Brooklyn, New York, literacy coach, created. It is used with her permission.

Table 3.24 Read-Aloud/Story Time

Class: Date: Time:

Title of book: Author:

Type of book:

New words:

Other comments:

Teacher Behaviors	Yes	No	N/A	Comments/Examples
Introduces book by showing cover and reading title. Encourages students to share thoughts about book based on these features.	❏	❏	❏	
Reads name(s) of author and illustrator. Asks students to point to title, author, illustrator, and encourages discussion about these features.	❏	❏	❏	
Introduces at least three words that will be in story by showing cards with words and pictures representing them.	❏	❏	❏	
Attempts to capture/maintain students' interest. Uses facial expression and changes in tone, pitch, and so on to represent different characters and emphasize words or facts.	❏	❏	❏	
Involves children throughout the story by encouraging comments and questions.	❏	❏	❏	
Asks open-ended questions, such as What if? What would you do if? and so on, and provides wait time. When voluntary responses are limited, initiates discussion of facts, plot and/or characters.	❏	❏	❏	
Involves children in extension activities by creating charts or other visuals, for example, T charts, story maps, word/character webs.	❏	❏	❏	
Invites children to retell story in their own words (through pretending to read the book to the class, using puppets, etc.).	❏	❏	❏	

Table 3.25 Teacher Language During Center-Based Learning in Pre-Kindergarten Classrooms

Site/Class:

Date:

Beginning Time:

Ending Time:

Class:

Teacher Language	Tally	Examples
Talk about logical relationships while children play with materials that stimulate reasoning, i.e., sorting or sequencing materials		
Encourage children to explain their reasoning when solving problems, i.e., why they sorted objects into different groups		
Add information or new vocabulary to expand on ideas presented by the children (not in the form of a question)		
Ask questions to encourage students to give longer and more complex answers, i.e., "what," "where," "why," or "how"		
Introduce concepts in response to children's interests or needs to solve problems, i.e., how to balance a tall block building		

Source: Adapted by Carol Berg, an early childhood instructional coordinator, from Harms, T., Clifford, R. M., & Cryer, D. (2005). *Early Childhood Environment Rating Scale-Revised.* New York, NY: Teachers College Press.

Table 3.26   Teacher Encouragement of Students' Problem-Solving Skills and Reasoning (Mathematics Common Core Standards)

Class:

Focus:

Date:

Time:

Teacher Encourages Students:	Frequently	Sometimes	Rarely	Examples
To analyze givens, constraints, relationships, and goals.				
To use mathematical models, such as simple addition equations, formulas, and flowcharts, to solve problems arising in everyday life.				
To use appropriate tools, such as ruler, calculator, or website.				
To attend to precision by: • using correct units of measure, • calculating accurately, and • using mathematical tools correctly.				
To find patterns and use them in solving problems, including looking for shortcuts to solve problems.				

Table 3.27   Teacher Encouragement of Mathematical Communication During Problem Solving
(Mathematics Common Core Standards)

Class:

Focus:

Date:

Time:

Teacher encourages students:	Frequently	Sometimes	Rarely	Examples
To explain the meaning of the representation(s) they used to begin to solve a problem. (These representations may include numbers, words, pictures, concrete objects, graphs, etc.)				
To explain: <ul><li>what they are doing to solve the problem</li><li>why they are doing it.</li></ul>				
To make logical arguments while explaining their reasoning.				
To explain why the answer they have found is reasonable.				
To try to make sense of others' mathematical thinking.				
To ask useful questions to clarify or improve others' reasoning.				

Note: We thank Judy Walsh, an instructor of math methods at the College of Staten Island, City University of New York, and a former supervisor and teacher of mathematics, for her lead role in developing the math tools.

Table 3.28   Teacher Behaviors Keyed to Accountable Talk

Class:

Date:

Time:

Teacher Indicators	Response Yes	No	N/A	Observations
Engages students in talk by:				
• Providing opportunities for students to speak about content knowledge, concepts, and issues	❑	❑	❑	
• Using wait time/allowing silence to occur	❑	❑	❑	
• Listening carefully	❑	❑	❑	
• Providing opportunities for reflection on classroom talk	❑	❑	❑	
Assists students to listen carefully to each other by:				
• Creating seating arrangements that promote discussion	❑	❑	❑	
• Providing clear expectations for how talk should occur	❑	❑	❑	
• Requiring courtesy and respect	❑	❑	❑	
• Reviewing major ideas and understandings from talk	❑	❑	❑	
Assists students to elaborate and build on others' ideas by:				
• Modeling reading processes of predicting, looking for key words, engaging prior knowledge, and so on	❑	❑	❑	
• Facilitating rather than dominating the talk	❑	❑	❑	
• Listening carefully	❑	❑	❑	
• Asking questions about discussion ideas and issues	❑	❑	❑	
Assists in clarifying or expanding a proposition by:				
• Modeling methods of restating arguments and ideas and asking if they are expressed correctly	❑	❑	❑	
• Modeling and providing practice at responding appropriately to criticism	❑	❑	❑	
• Modeling expressing own puzzlement or confusion	❑	❑	❑	

Table 3.29   Student Behaviors Keyed to Accountable Talk

Class:

Date:

Time:

Student Indicators	Response			Observations
	Yes	No	N/A	
Students are engaged in talk when they:				
• Speak appropriately in a variety of classroom situations	❑	❑	❑	
• Allow others to speak without interruption	❑	❑	❑	
• Speak directly to other students	❑	❑	❑	
Students are listening attentively to one another when they:				
• Make eye contact with speaker	❑	❑	❑	
• Refer to a previous speaker	❑	❑	❑	
• Connect comments to previous ideas	❑	❑	❑	
Students elaborate and build on others' ideas when they:				
• Make comments related to the focus of the discussion	❑	❑	❑	
• Introduce new, related issues	❑	❑	❑	
• Listen carefully	❑	❑	❑	
• Talk about issues rather than participants	❑	❑	❑	
Students work toward clarifying or expanding a proposition when they:				
• Model methods of restating arguments and ideas and ask if they are expressed correctly	❑	❑	❑	
• Model and provide practice at responding appropriately to criticism	❑	❑	❑	
• Model expressing own puzzlement or confusion	❑	❑	❑	

Table 3.30   Nonverbal Techniques

Class:

Date:

Time:

Nonverbal Technique	Frequency	Anecdotal Observations/Student Responses
Proxemics • Standing near student(s) • Moving toward student(s) • Touching student(s) • Moving about room		

Kinesics
 a. Affirmation
   • Eye contact
   • Touching
   • Smiling
   • Nodding
   • Open arm movements		

b. Disapproval
   • Frowning
   • Stern look
   • Finger to lips
   • Pointing
   • Arms crossed
   • Hands on hips		

Prosody • Varies voice tone • Varies pitch • Varies rhythm		
Immediacy • Responds with warmth		

Source: Glickman, Carl D.; Gordon, Stephen P.; Ross-Gordon, Jovita M., *Supervision of Instruction: A Developmental Approach*, 4th Edition, © 1998. Reprinted by permission of Pearson Education, Inc., Upper Saddle River, NJ.

Table 3.31 Guided Reading

Class:

Date:

Time:

Selects appropriate text for small-group instruction	Helps children to think, talk, and question through the story
Introduces story to the group as well as vocabulary concepts and text features	Allows small groups to read independently with minimum teacher support
Provides or reinforces reading strategies and provides students with the opportunity to use the strategy	
Records reflections on the students' reading behaviors during and after reading	Engages students in a brief discussion after reading the story

References

Acheson, K. A., & Gall, M. D. (1997). *Techniques in the clinical supervision teachers.* New York, NY: Longman.

AchieveGlobal, Inc. (1999). *Frontline leadership series.* San Jose, CA: Zenger-Miller.

Alfonso, R. J., & Firth, G. R. (1990). Supervision: Needed research. *Journal of Curriculum and Supervision, 5,* 181–188.

Alfonso, R. J., Firth, G. R., & Neville, R. F. (1975). *Instructional supervision.* Boston, MA: Allyn & Bacon.

Ambrose, D., & Cohen, L. M. (1997). The post-industrial era: Finding giftedness in all children. *Focus on Education, 41,* 20–24.

Anderson, R. H. (1993). Clinical supervision: Its history and current context. In R. H. Anderson & K. J. Snyder (Eds.), *Clinical supervision: Coaching for higher performance* (pp. 5–18). Lancaster, PA: Technomic.

Anonymous. (1929). The snoopervisor, the whoopervisor, and the supervisor. *Playground and Recreation, 23,* 558.

Argyris, C., & Schon, D. A. (1974). *Theory in practice: Increasing professional effectiveness.* San Francisco, CA: Jossey-Bass.

Association for Supervision and Curriculum Development. (1995). *Action research: Inquiry, reflection, and decision-making* [Video series]. Alexandria, VA: Author.

Balliet, T. M. (1894). What can be done to increase the efficiency of teachers in actual service? *National Educational Association Proceedings, 32,* 365–379.

Barr, A. S. (1925). Scientific analyses of teaching procedures. *The Journal of Educational Method, 4,* 361–366.

Barr, A. S. (1931). *An introduction to the scientific study of classroom supervision.* New York, NY: Appleton.

Benedetti, T. (1997). Tips from the classroom. *TESOL Journal, 7*(1), 41–47.

Blase, J., & Blase, J. (1986). *Handbook of instructional leadership: How really good principals promote teaching and learning.* Thousand Oaks, CA: Corwin.

Blase, J., & Blase, J. (2004). *Handbook of instructional leadership: How successful principals promote teaching and learning.* Thousand Oaks, CA: Corwin.

Bobbitt, F. (1913). Some general principles of management applied to the problems of city-school systems. In *The twelfth yearbook of the National Society for the Study of Education,* Part I, *The supervision of city schools* (pp. 7–96). Chicago, IL: University of Chicago Press.

Boehm, A. E., & Weinberg, R. A. (1997). *The classroom observer: Developing observation skills in early childhood settings.* New York, NY: Teachers College Press.

Bolin, F. S. (1987). On defining supervision. *Journal of Curriculum and Supervision, 2,* 368–380,

Bolin, F. S., & Panaritis, P. (1992). Searching for a common purpose: A perspective on the history of supervision. In C. D. Glickman (Ed.), *Supervision in transition* (pp. 30–43). Alexandria, VA: Association for Supervision and Curriculum Development.

Bolton, R. (1979). *People skills.* New York, NY: Simon & Schuster.

Borich, G. D. (2002). *Observation skills for effective teaching.* Columbus, OH: Merrill.

Bowers, C. A., & Flinders, D. J. (1991). *Culturally responsive teaching and supervision: A handbook for staff development.* New York, NY: Teachers College Press.

Bridges, E. (1992). *Problem-based learning for administrators.* Eugene, OR: ERIC Clearinghouse on Educational Management, University of Oregon.

Bullough, W. A. (1974). *Cities and schools in the gilded age.* New York, NY: Kennikat Press.

Burke, P. J., & Krey, R. D. (2005). *Supervision: A guide to instructional leadership* (2nd ed.). Springfield, IL: Charles E. Thomas.

Burton, W. H. (1930). Probable next steps in the progress of supervision. *Educational Method, 9,* 401–405.

Burton, W. H., & Brueckner, L. J. (1955). *Supervision: A social process.* New York, NY: Appleton-Century-Crofts.

Button, H. W. (1961). *A history of supervision in the public schools, 1870–1950.* Unpublished doctoral dissertation, Washington University, St. Louis, MO.

Calabrese, D., & Zepeda, S. (1997). *The reflective supervisor.* Larchmont, NY: Eye on Education.

Carnegie Forum on Education and the Economy. (1986). *A nation prepared: Teachers for the 21st century.* New York, NY: Carnegie Corporation.

Carroll, D., Featherstone, H., Featherstone, J., Feiman-Nemser, S., & Roosevelt, D. (2007). *Transforming teacher education: Reflections from the field.* Cambridge, MA: Harvard Education Press.

Cerbin, W., & Kopp, B. (2006). Lesson study as a model for building pedagogical knowledge and improving teaching. *International Journal of Teaching and Learning in Higher Education, 18*(3), 250–257.

Champagne, D. W., & Hogan, R. C. (2006). *Interpersonal and consultant supervision skills: A clinical model* (4th ed.). Normal, IL: Business Writing Center.

Chancellor, W. E. (1904). *Our schools: Their administration and supervision.* Boston, MA: D. C. Heath.

City, E., Elmore, R., Fiarman, S., & Teitel, L. (2009). *Instructional rounds in education: A network approach to improving teaching and learning.* Boston, MA: Harvard Education Press.

Cogan, M. L. (1973). *Clinical supervision.* Boston, MA: Houghton Mifflin.

Collins, J. (2001). *Good to great: Why some companies make the leap . . . and others don't.* New York, NY: Harper Business.

Costa, A., & Garmston, R. (1997). *Cognitive coaching: A foundation for renaissance schools.* Norwood, MA: Christopher Gordon.

Cronin, J. M. (1973). *The control of urban schools.* New York, NY: Free Press.

Danielson, C. (1996). *Enhancing professional practice: A framework for teaching.* Alexandria, VA: Association for Supervision and Curriculum Development.

Danielson, C. & McGreal, T. (2000). *Teacher evaluation to enhance professional practice.* Princeton, NJ: Educational Testing Service.

Darling-Hammond, L., & Goodwin, A. L. (1993). Progress toward professionalism in teaching. In G. Cawelti (Ed.), *Challenges and achievements of American education* (pp. 19–52). Alexandria, VA: Association for Supervision and Curriculum Development.

Dewey, J. (1929). *The sources of a science of education.* New York, NY: Liveright.

Dunlap, D. M., & Goldman, P. (1991). Rethinking power in schools. *Educational Administration Quarterly, 27,* 5–29.

Educational Testing Service. (1992). *The second international assessment of educational progress.* Princeton, NJ: Author.

Eisner, E. W. (1994). *The educational imagination* (3rd ed.). New York, NY: Macmillan.

Elliott, J. (1991). *Action research for educational change.* Bristol, PA: Falmer.

Farrell, T. S. C. (2003). Reflective practice in action. Thousand Oaks, CA: Corwin.

Firth, G. R., & Eiken, K. P. (1982). Impact of the schools' bureaucratic structure on supervision. In T. J. Sergiovanni (Ed.), *Supervision of teaching* (pp. 153–169). Washington, DC: Association for Supervision and Curriculum Development.

Firth, G. R., & Pajak, E. F. (1998). *Handbook of research on school supervision.* New York, NY: Macmillan.

Fitzpatrick, F. A. (1893). How to improve the work of inefficient teachers. *National Educational Association Proceedings, 31,* 71–78.

Fosnot, C. T. (1993). *In search of understanding: The case for constructivist classrooms.* Alexandria, VA: Association for Supervision and Curriculum Development.

Fullan, M. (1991). *The new meaning of educational change.* New York, NY: Teachers College Press.

Fullan, M. (1993). Coordinating school and district development in restructuring. In J. Murphy & P. Hallinger (Eds.), *Restructuring schooling: Learning from ongoing efforts* (pp. 143–164). Newbury Park, CA: Corwin.

Fullan, M. (1999). *Change forces: The sequel.* London, England: FalmerPress.

Fullan, M. (2003). *Change forces with a vengeance.* London, England: Routledge & Falmer Press

Fullan, M. (2006). *Turnaround leadership.* San Francisco, CA: Jossey-Bass.

Garman, N. B. (1997). Is clinical supervision a viable model for use in the public schools? No. In J. Glanz & R. F. Neville (Eds.), *Educational supervision: Perspectives, issues, and controversies.* Norwood, MA: Christopher Gordon.

Glanz, J. (1991). *Bureaucracy and professionalism: The evolution of public school supervision.* Rutherford, NJ: Fairleigh Dickinson University Press.

Glanz, J. (1992). Curriculum development and supervision: Antecedents for collaboration and future possibilities. *Journal of Curriculum and Supervision, 7,* 226–244.

Glanz, J. (1998). Histories, antecedents, and legacies: Constructing a history of school supervision. In G. R. Firth & E. F. Pajak (Eds.), *Handbook of research on school supervision* (pp. 39–79). New York, NY: Macmillan.

Glanz, J. (2002). *Finding your leadership style: A guide for educators.* Alexandria, VA: Association for Supervision and Curriculum Development.

Glanz, J. (2003). *Action research: An educational leader's guide to school improvement* (2nd ed.). Norwood, MA: Christopher Gordon.

Glanz, J. (2008). *The ethics of exclusion: Pedagogical, curricular, leadership, and moral imperatives for inclusive practice in Jewish schools* [Monograph]. New York, NY: The Azrieli Graduate School for Jewish Education and Administration at Yeshiva University.

Glickman, C. D. (1981). *Developmental supervision.* Washington, DC: Association for Supervision and Curriculum Development.

Glickman, C. D. (Ed.). (1992). *Supervision in transition.* Alexandria, VA: Association for Supervision and Curriculum Development.

Glickman, C. D., Gordon, S. P., & Ross-Gordon, J. M. (1998). *Supervision of instruction: A developmental approach* (4th ed.). Boston, MA: Allyn & Bacon.

Glickman, C. D., Gordon, S. P., & Ross-Gordon, J. M. (2010). *SuperVision and instructional leadership: A developmental approach* (8th ed.). Boston, MA: Allyn & Bacon.

Goldhammer, R. (1969). *Clinical supervision: Special methods for the supervision of teachers.* New York, NY: Holt, Rinehart & Winston.

Goldhammer, R., Anderson, R. H., & Krajewski, R. J. (1993). *Clinical supervision: Special methods for the supervision of teachers* (3rd ed.). Fort Worth, TX: Harcourt Brace Jovanovich.

Goldstein, J. (2007, May). Easy to dance to: Solving the problems of teacher evaluation with peer assistance and review. *American Journal of Education, 113*, 479–508.

Good, T. L., & Brophy, J. E. (2002). *Looking in classrooms* (9th ed.). New York, NY: Longman.

Greenwood, J. M. (1888). Efficient school supervision. *National Educational Association Proceedings, 26*, 519–521.

Greenwood, J. M. (1891). Discussion of Gove's paper. *National Educational Association Proceedings, 19*, 227.

Grimmet, P. P., Rostad, O. P., & Ford, B. (1992). Linking preservice and inservice supervision through professional inquiry. In C. D. Glickman (Ed.), *Supervision in transition* (pp. 169–182). Alexandria, VA: Association for Supervision and Curriculum Development.

Grumet, M. (1979). Supervision and situation: A methodology of self-report for teacher education. *Journal of Curriculum Theorizing, 1*, 191–257.

Hammock, D. C. (1969). *The centralization of New York City's public school system, 1896: A social analysis of a decision.* Unpublished master's thesis, Columbia University.

Harms, T., Clifford, R. M., & Cryer, D. (2005). *Early Childhood Environment Rating Scale-Revised.* New York, NY: Teachers College Press.

Harris, B. M. (1969). New leadership and new responsibilities for human involvement. *Educational Leadership, 26*, 739–742.

Hazi, H. M. (1994). The teacher evaluation-supervision dilemma: A case of entanglements and irreconcilable differences. *Journal of Curriculum and Supervision, 9*, 195–216.

Hazi, H. M. (2012, April). *Expert judgement: A concept for teacher evaluation in a postmodern world.* Paper presented at the meeting of the American Educational Research Association, Vancouver, BC.

Hill, S. (1918). Defects of supervision and constructive suggestions thereon. *National Educational Association Proceedings, 56*, 347–350.

Hill, W. M. (1968). I-B-F supervision: A technique for changing teacher behavior. *The Clearing House, 43*, 180–183.

Hoetker, W. J., & Ahlbrand, W. P. (1969). The persistence of the recitation. *American Educational Research Journal, 6*, 152–176.

Holmes Group. (1986). *Tomorrow's teachers: A report of the Holmes Group.* East Lansing, MI: Author.

Hord, S. M., Roussin, J. L., & Sommers, W. A. (2009). *Guiding professional learning communities.* Thousand Oaks, CA: Corwin.

Hosic, J. F. (1920). The democratization of supervision. *School and Society, 11*, 331–336.

Hosic, J. F. (1924). The concept of the principalship-II. *Journal of Educational Method, 3*, 282–284.

Howe, R. L. (1963). *The miracle of dialogue.* New York, NY: Seabury.

Hunter, M. (1983). Script-taping: An essential supervisory tool. *Educational Leadership, 41*(3), 43.

Jackson, P. (1990). *Life in classrooms.* New York, NY: Teachers College Press.

Johnson, C. C., & Fargo, J. D. (2010). Urban school reform enabled by transformative professional development: Impact on teacher change and student learning of science. *Urban Education, 45*(1), 4–29.

Johnson, D. W., & Johnson, R. T. (1989). *Cooperation and competition: Theory and practice.* Edina, MN: Interaction.

Johnson, S. M. (1990). *Teachers at work: Achieving success in our schools.* New York, NY: Basic Books.

Johnston, C. A., & Dainton, G. (1997). *The learning combination inventory.* Pittsgrove, NJ: Let Me Learn, Inc.

Joyce, B., & Showers, B. (1980). Improving inservice training: The messages of research. *Educational Leadership, 37*(2), 379–385.

Kaestle, C. F. (1973). *The evolution of an urban school: New York City 1750–1850.* Cambridge, MA: Harvard University Press.

Kirby, P. C. (1991, April). *Shared decision making: Moving from concerns about restrooms to concerns about classrooms.* Paper presented at the meeting of the American Educational Research Association, Chicago, IL.

Kolb, D. A. (1984). *Experiential learning: Experience as the source of learning and development.* Englewood Cliffs, NJ: Prentice Hall.

Lambert, L., Walker, D., Zimmerman, D. P., Cooper, J. E., Lambert, M. D., Gardner, M. E., & Szabo, M. (2002). *The constructivist leader* (2nd ed.). New York, NY: Teachers College Press.

Lasley, T. J. (1992). Promoting teacher reflection. *Journal of Staff Development, 13*(1), 24–29.

Lazerson, M. (1971). *Origins of the urban school: Public education in Massachusetts, 1870–1915.* Cambridge, MA: Harvard University Press.

Leeper, R. R. (Ed.). (1969). *Supervision: Emerging profession.* Washington, DC: Association for Supervision and Curriculum Development.

Leithwood, K., & Jantzi, D. (1990, April). *Transformational leadership: How principals can help reform school cultures.* Paper presented at the meeting of the American Educational Research Association, Boston, MA.

Lewis, C. (2000, April). *Lesson study: The core of Japanese professional development.* Paper presented at the American Educational Research Association Meeting, New Orleans, LA.

Lieberman, A. (1995). Practices that support teacher development. *Phi Delta Kappan, 76,* 591–596.

Markowitz, S. (1976). The dilemma of authority in supervisory behavior. *Educational Leadership, 33,* 365–369.

Marshall, C. (1992). *The assistant principal: Leadership choices and challenges.* Newbury Park, CA: Corwin.

Marzano, R. J., Frontier, T., & Livingston, D. (2011). *Effective supervision: Supporting the art and science of teaching.* Alexandria, VA: Association for Supervision and Curriculum Development.

McAndrew, W. (1922). The schoolman's loins. *Educational Review, 22,* 90–99.

McBer & Company. (1994). *Inventories.* Boston, MA: Author.

McLean, J. E. (1995). *Improving education through action research: A guide for administrators and teachers.* Thousand Oaks, CA: Corwin.

Morrissey, M. S. (2000). *Professional learning communities: An ongoing exploration.* Austin, TX: Southwest Educational Development Library (SEDL).

Murata, A., & Takahashi, A. (2002, October). *Vehicle to connect theory, research, and practice: How teacher thinking changes in district-level lesson study in Japan.* Proceedings of the twenty-fourth annual meeting of the North American Chapter of the International Group for the Psychology of Mathematics Education (1879–1888). Athens, GA. [ERIC No. ED 471 780]

Murphy, J., & Hallinger, P. (1993). *Restructuring schooling: Learning from ongoing efforts.* Newbury Park, CA: Corwin.

Myers, I. B., & McCaulley, M. H. (1985). *Manual: A guide to the development and use of the Myers-Briggs Type Indicator.* Palo Alto, CA: Consulting Psychologists Press.

National Commission on Excellence in Education. (1983). *A nation at risk: The imperative for educational reform.* Washington, DC: U.S. Department of Education.

Newlon, J. H. (1923). Attitude of the teacher toward supervision. *National Educational Association Proceedings, 61,* 546–549.

Nolan, J., Jr., & Hoover, L. A. (2011). *Teacher supervision and evaluation: Theory into practice* (3rd ed.). New York, NY: Wiley.

Northern Valley Regional High School District. (1996). *Differentiated supervision.* Darnerest, NJ: Author.

Null, G. (1996). *Who are you, really? Understanding your life's energy.* New York, NY: Carroll & Graf.

Osterman, K. F. (1994). Feedback in school settings: No news is bad news. *Journal of Management Science, 6*(4), 28–44.

Osterman, K. F., & Kottkamp, R. B. (2004). *Reflective practice for educators: Professional development to improve student learning.* Thousand Oaks, CA: Corwin.

Pajak, E. (1989). *The central office supervisor of curriculum and instruction: Setting the stage for success.* Needham, MA: Allyn & Bacon.

Pajak, E. (1993). *Approaches to clinical supervision: Alternatives for improving instruction.* Norwood, MA: Christopher Gordon.

Pajak, E. (2000). *Approaches to clinical supervision: Alternatives for improving instruction* (2nd ed.). Norwood, MA: Christopher Gordon.

Pajak, E. (2008). *Supervising instruction: Differentiating for teacher success* (3rd ed.). Norwood, MA: Christopher Gordon.

Payne, W. H. (1875). *Chapters on school supervision: A practical treatise on superintendency grading; arranging courses of study; the preparation and use of blanks, records, and reports; examination for promotion, etc.* New York, NY: Van Antwerp Bragg.

Poole, W. (1994). Removing the "super" from supervision. *Journal of Curriculum and Supervision, 9,* 284–309.

Ravitch, D. (1995). *National standards in American education: A citizen's guide.* Washington, DC: The Brookings Institution.

Reiman, A. J., & Thies-Sprinthall, L. (1998). *Mentoring and supervision for teacher development.* New York, NY: Longman.

Reitzug, U. C. (1997). Images of principal instructional leadership: From supervision to collaborative inquiry. *Journal of Curriculum and Supervision, 12,* 324–343.

Reports of the Record Commissions of the City of Boston. (1709). New York, NY: Teachers College Archives.

Rousmaniere, K. (1992). *City teachers: Teaching in New York City schools in the 1920s.* Unpublished doctoral dissertation, Columbia University.

Schon, D. A. (1987). *Educating the reflective practitioner: Toward a new design for thinking and learning in the professional.* San Francisco, CA: Jossey-Bass.

Schon, D. A. (1988). Coaching reflective teaching. In P. P. Grimmett & G. F. Erickson (Eds.), *Reflection in teacher education* (pp. 19–30). New York, NY: Teachers College Press.

Seguel, M. L. (1966). *The curriculum field: Its formative years.* New York, NY: Teachers College Press.

Sergiovanni, T. J. (1992). Moral authority and the regeneration of supervision. In C. D. Glickman (Ed.), *Supervision in transition* (pp. 30–43). Alexandria, VA: Association for Supervision and Curriculum Development.

Showers, B., & Joyce, B. (1996). The evolution of peer coaching. *Educational Leadership, 53*(6), 12–16.

Silberman, C. E. (1970). *Crisis in the classroom.* New York, NY: Random House.

Silins, H. C., Mulford, W. R., & Zarins, S. (2002). Organizational learning and school change. *Educational Administration Quarterly, 38*(2), 613–642.

Smyth, J. (1991). Instructional supervision and the redefinition of who does it in schools. *Journal of Curriculum and Supervision, 7,* 90–99.

Spaulding, F. E. (1955). The application of the principles of scientific management. *National Educational Association Proceedings, 51,* 259–279.

Spears, H. (1953). *Improving the supervision of instruction.* Englewood Cliffs, NJ: Prentice Hall.

Starratt, R. J. (1995). *Leaders with vision: The quest for school renewal.* Thousand Oaks, CA: Corwin.

Stepanek, J., Appel, G., Leong, M., Turner Mangan, M., & Mitchell, M. (2007). *Leading lesson study: A practical guide for teachers and facilitators.* Thousand Oaks, CA: Corwin.

Stigler, J. W., & Hiebert, J. (1999). *The teaching gap: Best ideas from the world's teachers for improving education in the classroom.* New York, NY: Free Press.

Stringer, E. T. (1999). *Action research: A handbook for practitioners* (2nd ed.). Thousand Oaks, CA: Sage.

Sullivan, S., & Glanz, J. (2006). *Building effective learning communities: Strategies for leadership, learning, and collaboration.* Thousand Oaks, CA: Corwin.

Tanner, D., & Tanner, L. N. (1987). *Supervision in education: Problems and practices.* New York, NY: Macmillan.

Taylor, F. W. (1911). *The principles of scientific management.* New York, NY: Harper & Brothers.

Tomlinson, C.A. (2001). *How to differentiate instruction in mixed-ability classrooms* (2nd ed.). Alexandria, VA: Association for Supervision and Curriculum Development.

Torff, B., & Warburton, E. (2005). Assessment of teachers' beliefs about classroom use of critical-thinking activities. *Educational and Psychological Measurement, 65,* 155–179.

Tsui, A. B. M. (1995). Exploring collaborative supervision in inservice teacher education. *Journal of Curriculum and Supervision, 10,* 346–371.

Tyack, D. B. (1974). *The one best system: A history of American education.* Cambridge, MA: Harvard University Press.

Tyack, D. B., & Hansot, E. (1982). *Managers of virtue: Public school leadership in America, 1820–1980.* New York, NY: Basic Books.

Ubben, G. C., Hughes, L. W., & Norris, C. J. (2004). *The principal: Creative leadership for excellence in schools* (5th ed.). Boston, MA: Pearson Allyn & Bacon.

Weller, R. (1971). *Verbal communication in instructional supervision.* New York, NY: Teachers College Press.

Wheatley, M. J. (2002). *Turning to one another.* San Francisco, CA: Berrett-Koehler Publishers.

Wilhelms, F. T. (1969). Leadership: The continuing quest. In R. R. Leeper (Ed.), *Supervision: Emerging profession.* Washington, DC: Association for Supervision and Curriculum Development.

Willerman, M., McNeely, S. L., & Koffman Cooper, E. (1991). *Teachers helping teachers: Peer observation and assistance.* New York, NY: Praeger.

Zepeda, S. J. (2012). *Instructional supervision: Applying tools and concepts* (3rd ed.). Larchmont, NY: Eye on Education.

Zepeda, S. J., & Ponticell, J. A. (1998). At cross purposes: What do teachers need, want, and get from supervision? *Journal of Curriculum and Supervision, 14*(1), 68–87.

Index

CORWIN

A SAGE Company

The Corwin logo—a raven striding across an open book—represents the union of courage and learning. Corwin is committed to improving education for all learners by publishing books and other professional development resources for those serving the field of PreK–12 education. By providing practical, hands-on materials, Corwin continues to carry out the promise of its motto: **"Helping Educators Do Their Work Better."**

Communication Techniques

Listening	Nonverbal Clues	Reflecting and Clarifying
"Uh-huh."	Affirmative nods and smiles	"You're angry because . . ."
"OK."	Open body language, e.g., arms open	"You feel . . . because . . ."
"I'm following you."	Appropriate distance from speaker—not too close or too far	"You seem quite upset."
"For instance,"	Eye contact	"So, you would like . . ."
"And?"	Nondistracting environment	"I understand that you see the problem as . . ."
"Mmm."	Face speaker and lean forward	"I'm not sure, but I think you mean . . ."
"I understand."	Barrier-free space, e.g., desk not used as blocker	"I think you're saying . . ."
"This is great information for me."		
"Really?"		
"Then?"		
"So?"		
"Tell me more."		
"Go on."		
"I see."		
"Right."		

Barriers to Communication

Barrier Type	Examples
1. Judging	1. Judging
• Criticizing	• "You are lazy; your lesson plan is poor."
• Name calling and labeling	• "You are inexperienced, an intellectual."
• Diagnosing—analyzing motives instead of listening	• "You're taking out your anger on her." • "I know what you need."
• Praising evaluatively	• "You're terrific!"
2. Solutions	2. Solutions
• Ordering	• "You must . . ." "You have to . . ." "You will . . ."
• Threatening	• "If you don't . . ." "You had better or else."
• Moralizing or preaching	• "It is your duty/responsibility; you should."
• Inappropriate questioning or prying	• "Why?" "What?" "How?" "When?"
• Advising	• "What I would do is . . ." "It would be best for you."
• Lecturing	• "Here is why you are wrong . . ." "Do you realize . . ."
3. Avoiding the other's concerns	3. Avoiding the other's concerns
• Diverting	• "Speaking of . . ." "Apropos . . ." "You know what happened to . . ."
• Reassuring	• "It's not so bad . . ." "You're lucky . . ." "You'll feel better."
• Withdrawing	• "I'm very busy . . ." "I can't talk right now . . ." "I'll get back to you . . ."
• Sarcasm	• "I really feel sorry for you."

KEY STEPS—SELF-DIRECTED APPROACH

1. Listen carefully to the teacher's initial statement.
2. Reflect on your understanding of the problem.
3. Constantly clarify and reflect until the real problem is identified.
4. Have the teacher problem solve and explore the consequences of various actions.
5. The teacher commits to a decision and firms up a plan.
6. The supervisor restates the teacher's plan and sets a follow-up meeting.

KEY STEPS—PLANNING CONFERENCE

1. Decide the focus of the observation (choose a general approach: directive informational, collaborative, or self-directed).
2. Determine the method and form of observation. Problem solve or plan professional development where appropriate.
3. Set up the time of the observation and the feedback conference.

KEY STEPS—COLLABORATIVE REFLECTION

1. What was valuable in the process we just completed?
2. What was of little value?
3. What changes would you suggest for the next cycle?

KEY STEPS—DIRECTIVE INFORMATIONAL APPROACH

1. Identify the problem or goal and solicit clarifying information.
2. Offer solutions. Ask for the teacher's input into the alternatives offered and request additional ideas.
3. Summarize chosen alternatives, ask for confirmation, and request that the teacher restate final choices.
4. Set a follow-up plan and meeting.

KEY STEPS—COLLABORATIVE APPROACH

1. Identify the problem from the teacher's perspective, soliciting as much clarifying information as possible.
2. Reflect on what you've heard for accuracy.
3. Begin collaborative brainstorming, asking the teacher for his or her ideas first.
4. Problem solve through a sharing and discussion of options.
5. Agree on a plan and follow-up meeting.